THE HEART OF AN ADVOCATE

VILMA LUZ CABÁN

GREEN HEART
LIVING
—PRESS—

ISBN Paperback: 978-1-954493-55-1

Cover art: Hiram Melendez

Published by Green Heart Living Press

Dedication

To Christopher,
My beloved son...la luz de mi vida.

CONTENTS

FOREWORD

In 2021 Puerto Rico declared a state of emergency in regard to gender-based violence. The government was pressed by activists to do something about a wave of killings targeting women. While partially due to tensions from rising economic distress and climate disasters, the crisis had been brewing for years. At least 60 femicides were reported in 2020, and more than 5,500 women were victims of domestic violence in 2021. A decade earlier the American Civil Liberties Union revealed that the island had the highest per capita rate *in the world* of women killed by their partners. As the governor stated to the media, "Victims have suffered the consequences of systematic machismo, inequity, discrimination, lack of education, lack of guidance and above all lack of action." This belated statement came from an executive whose party has not been conspicuous for defending the rights of women.

The problem is not restricted to the Caribbean island. One would not be mistaken in supposing that New York City is also gravely afflicted. Recently the city legislated an increase in protective services for women. As one City Councilwoman declared, "Domestic violence is an epidemic for Black and Brown women across New York City, and especially in the Bronx."

The book you hold in your hands will take you through the life of a brave woman who experienced domestic conflict from an early age. Vilma Cabán immerses us in her daily life, full of a mother's love but vulnerable to a step-father's brutality. She tells of the changing roles that such a child assumes over time: as the interpreter between parent and outside authority figures, often as a teller of lies; as the keeper of secrets to safeguard her mother, where one indiscretion or misstep can have a bloody consequence at the hands of a drunk, out-of-control father; as a co-conspirator with *Mami* in various schemes to avoid domination. An early turning point comes when the teenage Vilma seizes her independence in an act of escape. Free in one sense, she feels guilty about leaving her mother behind.

What begins as a coming-of-age story in an immigrant household evolves into a grand journey toward understanding and meaning, as we follow Vilma's later years. Along the way, we learn much about the condition of women in the Global South. It's not a pretty picture. We learn through the hands-on experience of a practitioner, educator, and advocate. Though she travels thousands of miles from her Bronx beginnings, she repeatedly witnesses the dilemmas that women everywhere confront. She is never too far removed from the realities of abused women, the realities she herself was subjected to. She is determined to create a life out of this challenging reality. She is determined to achieve her humanity.

Vilma's story speaks to me in part for the similarities in our upbringing: our Puerto Ricanness, our Bronx roots, and our struggle for a decent living. We are separated by decades but her narrative describes a daily existence that resonates with mine. We differ in one important respect, however. Vilma's family was plagued by disunity at the core, driven by domestic abuse. Some will say that this sickness is but a symptom of society's warped priorities, that until we eliminate poverty all the ills we face will persist. This is true to a degree. But in the meantime, how does a mother get through the day? How does she raise her children? This story relates one family's trajectory through that fire, from the perspective of the eldest child in that household. It is a poignant and impactful account.

Vilma–whom I know for years as a dear family friend–and I are different. But don't get me wrong. My early life was far from one of privilege. My family was marked by its own difficulty since my parents were both born profoundly deaf. I understand Vilma's yearning to tell her story, for I too spent years grappling with the need to write a family history; in my case as the only child in a deaf household. But the contrast between the two memoirs could not be greater. It is one thing to contend with disability at the core. It is another to contend with a sickness that shreds the bonds of love. My parents loved the young boy in their midst and, with all their limitations, devoted themselves to him. Pop never hit me once. He was a simple man with a big heart. Mom was a simple *jíbara* bewildered by the often-cruel hearing world. The violence she sent my way was to wring my ears when I drove her crazy, but that was it. Both Mom and Pop put me on a pedestal from day one. (Not that this dynamic was an unequivocal blessing for me. But that's another story.) Reading Vilma's narrative heightened the sense of difference and reminded me that love can conquer all.

Vilma's story also speaks to me because of the professional work I have pursued over the years. As a professor, researcher, and advocate I have focused largely on the condition of poor and working-class families in racialized communities. I have studied the power structures that facilitate persistent inequality and the ideologies that rationalize social deprivation. I have examined proposed policies and programs that address these conditions. This memoir touches on many of the topics covered in my own search for understanding. Vilma doesn't offer a magic answer to what seems an overwhelming dilemma but in the end, she takes the bold step of walking the talk, of putting her own skin in the game. She crafts a concrete programmatic solution to domestic violence, one rooted in her personal history. She leaves the reader rooting for her and hopeful that she will succeed.

I think Vilma is speaking directly to her Latina sisters who have had to deal with domestic abuse. These women will connect powerfully with the personal history rendered here. But there are other audiences who will benefit from this remarkable account: practitioners and advocates in the field of gender-based violence who will learn of the specific experiences of Hispanic women, one of the fastest-growing populations. As someone who knows the joys of being a father, I so hope this story will reach many male readers. For the men, who after all hold up the other half of the world, this book just might help develop a sense of empathy with their *hermanas* and guide them to make sensible choices in this life.

Andrés Torres
Author, *Signing in Puerto Rican*

INTRODUCTION

It is the questioning mind and the thirsty soul that can drive us to seek clarity in the most difficult of circumstances. Questions helped reveal how I lived my way through the answers and held on to my essence. At times, I clung to my sanity. With the right conditions, I was fortunate to pen my truth. A truth that I hope can inspire and comfort other women who have lived through similar circumstances of deception, disappointment, rejection, and trauma. All of these circumstances have shaped the being that is writing to you now. However, this narrative is simply *not* just about me. It captures a community portrait of good-willed souls that helped this first-generation Puerto Rican woman rise out of poverty, abuse, and life's most traumatic situations. A dear friend reminded me that a broken crayon can still color. So here I am coloring my life's portrait. With the utmost level of gratitude, I humbly seek to pay it forward and present to you the landscape of my journey as a person trying to make a difference.

This memoir is a compilation of five critical stages of my life. I unveil numerous life-changing moments, traumas, disappointments, and losses which wove the heart of this advocate. I share some tough memories from my tender but not-so-innocent childhood days, teen years, college adventures, professional pathways, and humanitarian quests. At the end of each memory, I excavate a multidimensional gem that was refined under life's pressure. This gem holds the lesson that prepared me to be the woman that I am today, a woman seeking to remain a resilient champion fighting for the protection and well-being of women and children.

For this first-generation Nuyorican woman, writing my memoir was an arduous cerebral nosedive that was informed by a host of painfully repressed memories. It meant having to revisit heartbreaking recollections that tore open scars. From time to time, it felt extremely counterintuitive. Doubt would visit me and whisper over my shoulder telling me to stop. *Why did I begin this memoir after being able to successfully untangle myself from trauma-bonded relationships? Why was I going back?* I struggled to formulate the hidden narrative of these difficult memories fraught with poverty, food insecurity, racial discrimination, socio-political inequities, domestic abuse, alcoholism, and the threat of sexual violence at different times of my life.

At times, a calcified heart made it difficult to reflect, but with much prayer, patience, and professional counseling, the happier moments sprang forth. There were elusive revelations deep inside my wounded soul. With a little coaxing, they rose above the surface. Revelations that made me speak out loud were released out into the universe and magically the spoken word became the written word. It required that I have patience with everything that was unresolved in my mind, body, and soul.

With the grace, grit, and tenacity of a street fighter, I pushed through to bring forth my personal story. Self-reflective questions guided me in loosely stringing together the memories and words of this memoir. *Why did he hit Mami? How can I get away from here? Will he really kill my bird? Why is he staring at me? What can I do to save my brother? How do I escape this African chief's compound? Did this woman know what he would do to me? Why is there a dead dog outside the gate? Is that a warning?* These were some of the questions that swirled around in the whirlpool of my memories.

In hindsight, those questions all pointed to the identity that crystallized as a young adult to this present moment. I always loved to help others and it wasn't until I got older that someone I cared about gave me a tender label. She said, "Vilma, you are a loving advocate." That is when it clicked, and I began to wrap my memories around this gem of a notion. *What is an advocate? How does the world view an advocate? How does one describe an advocate?*

Professionally defined, an advocate is a person who publicly supports or recommends a particular cause or policy. This definition seemed bureaucratic and so devoid of passion. Where was the passion and drive to help others? I always felt passionate about helping others. However, could I really be considered an advocate? I sought to uncover the multifaceted definition of this word. I believed there were many sides of an individual that formed an advocate. It wasn't enough to understand the mind of an advocate. What was the beating and bleeding heart of an advocate? What were the actions of an advocate that brought forth public support or informed policy? How did an advocate move hearts toward a particular cause? Many people may perceive an advocate as more of a legal role such as a lawyer. The term advocate is usually associated with the law. In my eyes, I believed an advocate was a person who possessed many traits that equipped the individual to be very effective in promoting change for those in need and for the greater good.

The prefix "ad" in the word advocacy comes from the Latin root which means moving in the direction toward. The Latin root "voc" means to speak and call out. My memoir captures how I did just that, moving forward toward my destiny and purpose and speaking out on behalf of others as an ad-voc-ate. As such, in this archaeological dig through my memories, I found different life markers where I demonstrated the characteristics of an advocate, and how that role soul-shifted as I moved along different stages in my life.

The Spanish word for advocate is *defensora*. I love the root word "defense' inside this context. What are the key characteristics of a *defensora*? Thinking about all I have experienced, throughout different stages of my life, helped me define the multifaceted skill set of an advocate. Therefore, my memoir will describe five stages of my life. These stages played a central role in the self-actualization of *la defensora* and how it shaped the heart of this advocate.

This *defensora* is grateful for those challenging events because they all facilitated every stage of my life's odyssey. Like the broad and fine strokes of an abstract painting, these experiences shaped me. It wasn't always immediately obvious. It took time to recognize and connect this complex composition. Throughout the process of honing in and studying the intricacies of color, mood, as well as the rough and smooth textures of my life, I was able to appreciate the holistic portrait of Vilma Luz, *la hija de María*.

STAGE 1:
THE YOUNG
AWAKENING

CHAPTER ONE

THE
CONCEPTION

I am the only daughter of a Puerto Rican mother, María Concepción Core Ayala. In the mid-1960s my *pobre y inocente campesina* mother came from the mountainous region of Toa Alta, Puerto Rico to the Nuyorican world in Spanish Harlem, New York City. María the country girl moved with her two older brothers and her twin sister into a tiny apartment in a dilapidated pre-war building in the big city. Slumlords owned these old buildings and all they did was collect rent from poor immigrants, having them live with lead-painted walls in roach and rat-infested apartments that didn't consistently have hot water or heat.

María's older brothers and her twin sister Lolita had left a few years earlier. They left María behind with her youngest sister Teresa along with her alcoholic father and battered mother Juana. After receiving monthly letters with enticing details of finding jobs in the great city of Manhattan, as well as reading anecdotes of how they were living their best life together, my mother begged them to join them. At last, one of these letters came with a plane ticket and some money to fly to New York City.

At the age of 20, María was excited about reaching for the American Dream. In the hopes that she would make it there one day, prior to arriving in *Nueva York,* she learned a trade. Her cousin Yaya who lived next door to her in Toa Alta, Puerto Rico showed my mother how to sew using a sewing machine as well as sewing sequins by hand. Yaya would say, *–Prepárate para que puedas encontrar un trabajito en la ciudad.–* Yaya meant to prepare her to get a job in *la ciudad* de Bayamón and not New York City. Without knowing it, Yaya was the wind beneath my mother's wings.

In a city where so many people spoke a foreign language that María didn't understand, it was like a comforting salve for her homesick heart to hear someone speak her language. The day that she heard Julio Ceasar Cabán's voice, María felt like her heart had come home. She fell in love with a tall and handsome *Puertorriqueño* from the southern part of Puerto Rico in *La Playa de Ponce.* When he had boldly arrived in New York a few years earlier, he made a vow to himself that he was going to be someone famous.

At the time María met Julio, he worked as a salesman in a furniture store that was not too far from her job. She happened to stroll in to check out the prices of the full-size mattresses. Sadly the mattress that she shared with her sister Lolita was sinking in the middle. It was a mattress that had already been in the apartment when they moved it. When she spotted that tall, slim, and handsome Julio approach her, it took her breath away in an instant. He had quite the smooth seductive radio voice. His smile would light up a room, and he had the deepest, sexiest eyes that would compel anyone to lean in and listen. Throughout the sales pitch and the flirtatious smiles, my mother learned that this smooth guy had big dreams! By night the salesman became one of the most famous *Boricua* (Puerto Rican) voices as a *locutor* or radio personality for Radio WADO. This was the first Puerto Rican FM radio station in the city. But it didn't pay too well, so he survived by selling mattresses, furniture, and dreams to unsuspecting *mancita mujeres* (naïve women).

The rest they say is history. A sad her-story. Fast forward two years later, to a small lower east row house apartment on Avenue B and 6th

Street. María moved out of the apartment with her siblings because she was pregnant with his baby. Me! Julio didn't want to get married and he told María that he had no intention of marrying her. Each month that passed, her shame swelled up in her belly as a tiny and fragile being grew. She had rented the studio apartment hoping that he would change his mind. Maria wanted to make right the shameful wrongs they had both done before the eyes of her family. From time to time, he would come by and stay with her a few nights, then disappear for weeks. He would return with flowers and a bag of groceries wrapped with the same lame excuses and apologies. My mother felt conflicted. She always kept hope alive that they would get married.

In her final trimester, with a large belly sticking out of her thin and frail body, my mother was coping with the consequences of her decision to love Julio. This tiny dilapidated Lower East Side apartment housed her biggest hopes to be loved by this fleeting love. The studio only housed despair and unfulfilled promises along with a mattress, a chair, and a small transistor radio. My father Julio Ceasar Cabán left behind a pencil-written note scratched on a piece of brown paper bag along with a wrinkled twenty-dollar bill. He wrote that he could not make my mother María happy and that the young seven-month pregnant María had to find her happiness elsewhere. What my mother didn't know was that he had two women pregnant at the same time! They were only four months apart. His first wife in La Playa de Ponce was due in November. My mother was due in July. He needed to go back to Puerto Rico to *dale cara* or in other words show face to his wife *reclamando* (demanding) that she needed help and money for their children.

My mother didn't know any of this, she just knew that Julio was going to Puerto Rico to handle some radio business. He had done this before *y de momento rancaba a Puerto Rico*. When María, also known in the family as Conchita, read his chicken-scratched note, it was a tough blow. Julio would come back. He always did. She would be patient and wait until he returned. Her only recourse was to embrace her swollen belly and wait for her baby and the love of her life. Instead, labor pains came, and she was rushed to Bellevue Hospital. There was no one there to hold her, but she could hold onto hope. Her baby was her hope for true love. There for the first time, she saw as she described *"la luz de me vido."*

This little girl was the light of her life, so she named her hope Vilma Luz.

For the few first months of my life, I was an illegitimate daughter that was abandoned in-utero by my biological father Julio Ceasar. What my unsuspecting mother didn't know was that he was a married man living a double life with his original family in La Playa de Ponce, Puerto Rico. I resentfully refer to them as the Seminole Cabán siblings. The original Cabán children. The legitimate ones. The first victims of my biological father. My mother had no clue that before Julio Ceasar met her, he had eleven children from three other women. Six children lived in La Playa de Ponce, three children existed in Yauco outside of Ponce, and two boys ruled in New York City (in the Lower East Side). Some of them were illegitimate without his last name, and others had his last name. They were walking this Earth while their father was galavanting and being a smooth radio voice in their mothers' ears.

Julio Ceasar Cabán was not a *galán*. He certainly wasn't her prince in shining armor. There wasn't anything chivalrous about him. All he ever did for this daughter was to plant the generational seed of abandonment in her mother's womb.

My *pobrecita* mother worked hard to raise me as a single mother. In order to survive, María had to fend for herself as a seamstress sewing for long twelve-hour days in a sweatshop within the garment district. Her youngest niece Alicia flew in from Puerto Rico to take care of me when I was only a couple of weeks old. With the help of her young 17-year-old niece, who had just graduated from high school, María could breathe easier knowing that her baby girl was in the hands of family and not strangers. *Mami todavía estaba en la cuarentena.* My mother had no choice but to go back to work. She had a little mouth to feed. She had received so much rejection from her brothers who lived in Spanish Harlem. They shamed her for having a child out of wedlock. They offered no help. It was cruel and unjust.

María made up her mind to do something about this *humillación*. When I was a few months old, she brought me to see my biological father. She insisted that he give me his last name. She yelled that if he didn't do this, she would end up at his job at the radio station and create quite a scandal. After much protest, he yielded to her request and together they went to the Bureau of Vital Statistics to register me with my new last name. My mother dealt with this a little better by sharing that I could be recognized and legitimized with a father's last name. She often described it as *–Ahora mi hija está reconocida. Ahora ella tiene su apellido.–*

My mother's story as a single mother evolved into a more tragic situation. When I was two years old, she married someone that she thought she could really count on. In fact, he was family. He was her maternal first cousin José from the Ferrer-Ayala family. (Just like the famous Latino actor José Ferrer.) Well, this actor was playing his best role in seducing his new victim, my mother. José was ten years older than my mother. Her cousins shared that he had a history of drinking and being physically abusive with his first wife. It didn't matter that her cousins and even her sister-in-laws warned her. The Latino adage *los primos se exprimen* was in full effect. She was ripe for the picking and he saw his opportunity. My mother fell in love with a batterer. After they married, my stepfather moved us away from the Lower East Side to the South Bronx because it was closer to his Ferrer family near Allerton Avenue. At that young age, I didn't know the truth about my stepfather. For many years, I was raised thinking he was my biological father. I would call him *Papi*.

CHAPTER TWO

INTERVENING HEART

W hen I was five years old, I was living in a one-bedroom apartment in the South Bronx with my Mami, Papi, and younger two-year-old brother Rafy. It was a cold and windy wintery day. I was with my Mami, and my little brother as we took the train to visit my mother's former neighbor Doña Hilda who lived in the Lower East Side of Manhattan. I remember it was always a very long train ride to Astor Place on the number 6 train. My little brother was always excited about going on the train. Standing up on the train seat, he would press his cute little nose against the window to try to see inside the dark subway tunnels. Rafy would jump up and down on the seat making train noises, as he would cling on to his large toy police car.

Doña Hilda still lived in the building that I grew up in for the first two years of my life. It was on 6th Street and Avenue B near Tompkins Square Park. This area is known as Alphabet City close to the East Village. Mami would say that the neighborhood was always full of hippies. I didn't know what a hippy was. Was it like a hippo? –¿Qué sabía yo?– I remember the buildings were tiny compared to our apartment building in the Bronx.

After moving from the neighborhood, Mami remained in touch with Doña Hilda because she played such an instrumental role in my upbringing. Mami was eternally grateful that when I was a newborn infant, Doña Hilda would take care of me while my mother worked twelve hours sewing bras. My mother's younger cousin who originally came from Puerto Rico with the intention to take care of me became homesick. Alicia decided to go back to Puerto Rico. This left my mother in a difficult position. One day after coming from the grocery store, she saw Doña Hilda in the lobby. Mami asked her if she knew anyone who would take care of her children. She explained her circumstances and Doña Hilda felt so sorry for my mother. Mami made very little money. Many times she couldn't afford to pay Doña Hilda. Thankfully, this older woman was very generous with my mother. She would tell Mami not to worry about bringing any food or milk for me. Doña Hilda took care of me. Mami just would have to worry about giving her a few dollars whenever she could. Doña Hilda became like a mother figure to my dear mother. I am sure they spent many days speaking over *un cafecito* as my poor mother struggled to make ends meet.

Five years later, I found myself walking through the streets of the Lower East Side of Manhattan, holding my little brother's hand. I can still remember his olive green coat with the large furry hood that was wrapped around his little face. The high zippered hood made him look like a little Eskimo. Mami always tried to have a firm grip holding his tiny hand. As always, he would try to get away from her Kung Fu grip and run ahead of my mother. A toddler seeking to run free. Always running towards the densely populated three-lane avenue full of cars racing down the avenue to beat the next traffic light. That day as we were walking to Doña Hilda's apartment, I was the one holding onto my little brother's hand (as a precautionary measure so he wouldn't run into the street). I remember feeling like there was something wrong with my Mami. So to help out, I was holding on tightly to Rafy's little hand with the chubby little fingers.

While visiting Doña Hilda, I remember feeling scared. There was something that seemed so off about Mami. It didn't feel like one of the normal visits. I remember seeing her cry a lot in that lady's house. As both women spoke with low whispers in the kitchen, I played on the floor with my little brother as he rolled around his toy police car down the long wooden floor of the narrow hallway. The very old and worn wooden slats of the wood floors had deep grooves. We pretended that they were railroad tracks. After some time playing, I came to the realization that I didn't see my mother. I was wondering where Mami was.

I got up and started looking around for her. I heard her voice behind a tall and narrow door. It was the bathroom inside this railroad-style apartment where the hallway connected to each of the rooms in the long and narrow space. Mami was inside the water closet that was next to the kitchen. It was a small room with just a small toilet that had a large tank of water above it. This Victorian high tank was so ominous and extremely scary from the point of view of a child. You had to pull on a metal string to flush the toilet. *What if I pull on the string too hard and it falls on me? My mom was inside there too long. Did that happen to her? Did the toilet tank fall on her?* I was nervous as I stared at the narrow door. Doña Hilda was standing next to the bathtub which was inside the kitchen across from the stove. This was the convenient plumbing layout of these run-down tenements. Our apartment in the South Bronx had a bathroom with a sink, toilet, and tub in the same room. Everything about Doña Hilda's small apartment was odd. In the middle of both extreme walls was a round small kitchenette dining set. I noticed that Mami's coffee cup was still full. Was my mother sick? She always drank all of her *cafecito*.

At that moment, I remember pushing the bathroom door open and seeing Mami's red pool of blood on the bathroom floor. Mami looked at me horrified. She just stood there frozen telling me to close the door. I was so worried that I saw all of that blood on the toilet, her pants, and on the bathroom floor. I started to scream and Doña Hilda came over to us. She started to yell too saying that she was going to call the ambulance. I remember Mami looking very calm and telling her that no she was fine. She couldn't go in an ambulance. She needed to take us home. I knew she was lying. My mother was not fine. So Doña Hilda helped her clean up and gave her some pants.

As we left Doña Hilda's apartment, I felt scared that my mother might start bleeding again. I wanted to make sure she was okay. I held on to her hand, and with the other hand, I held on to my little brother's hand. Both of them were walking slowly down the steps and out of the building. Mami walked slowly in pain, and my little brother walked slowly with his short legs. The walk to the train station seemed so far away. With every painstaking step, I would glance up and look at my poor mother's face. She looked like she was in excruciating pain. Finally, as we were making our way to the train station, in the middle of the sidewalk, Mami stopped. She leaned over yelling in pain. In that instance, I glanced at my little brother's toy car and immediately I got an idea. That's it! I must look for a police car! The police will help us. I learned that on *Sesame Street* if you need help you can call 911 or tell a police officer.

All of a sudden, I pulled my hand out of Mami's hand and made a quick dash for the street. I spotted a bright blue police car. On top of the vehicle, it had emergency lights and a big white siren in between the lights. It was coming down the street very close to the sidewalk. I don't know what got into me. I immediately ran off, stepping off of the sidewalk onto the street, while passing cars honked at this crazy little girl. But they did not dissuade me. I kept running straight toward the police car. My eyes locked onto the face of the police officers inside the police car. Locking eyes with my potential hero behind the steering wheel. I started waving and yelling. "HELP!" What I failed to remember was that I was still holding onto my little brother's hand. He was running with me as I desperately tried to stop the police car. When I glanced down to look at his little face, he was a happy little boy. He was getting closer to a real-life police car! In the middle of the street, honking cars breezed by our little bodies. The sensation of the air that swirled past us filled me with more courage to act. As we heard blaring horns, I was not phased, and neither was my brother. I had made Rafy's day. He was going to be my superhero sidekick. The Robin to my Batman. The two policemen in the car looked at me with their startled and terrified eyes wide open. They immediately stopped the police car. I remember yelling "Help my Mami. She has blood!"

When I looked back at my mother, she was still leaning over. She was not aware that we were in the middle of the street. I remember my mom crying and not understanding what the police were saying to her. I screamed. "Help, help my Mami! She is bleeding!" She opened her coat, and there was a huge bloodstain going down the leg pants. I started to feel a bit dizzy, but I tried to remain strong. The sensation of feeling dizzy is something I can still associate with this day. Whenever I get dizzy, it immediately brings me back to this helpless moment as a child.

In time an ambulance appeared in front of us, and my little brother was crying because Mami was on a bed with wheels going inside the tall big box with a door called an ambulance. It was the strangest scene for my young eyes. The policeman picked my brother up, and I followed him as he walked over to the police car. The kind policeman led my little brother and me into the backseat of the squad car. He asked. "Do you want to go for a ride in my police car?" I was numb. I was quiet. They put on the siren and the emergency lights as they followed the ambulance to the hospital. I saw reflections of the red lights on the passing windows of the cars and the storefronts as we drove following the scary vehicle that took my mother. Why couldn't we go with her? Who are these men dressed as police officers in the front seat? The back of their heads terrified me. Every once in a while, one of them would turn back and smile at me telling me everything was going to be ok. This reassurance helped me a bit. During the whole ride, my brother stood up, just like he did on the subway train, and looked out of the rear window. He jumped with glee. Oblivious to what was happening, but delighted that he was in a police car. That is a memory that comes to mind whenever I look at a toy police car. It triggers that terrifying moment. It always takes my breath away. I regroup and try to breathe through the pain of that memory.

At Bellevue Hospital, I remember my mother's screams behind a looming white curtain. Those screams were eerily familiar. Come to think of it, I heard my mom scream a lot. Those screams in the Bellevue

Hospital emergency room were blood-curdling. To this day, I don't know why they allowed my brother and I to hear that. It was so disturbing to be in the hospital. After some time, a few family members arrived. They were from my stepfather's side. We only saw this side of the family on the holidays. They felt like strangers. These family members weren't as loving as my mom's sisters or brothers. They were the sister-in-laws. They came to get us so they could take care of us. I didn't want to leave the hospital. I remember having a loud tantrum. They teased me and said I was acting like my little baby brother Rafy. I had to be a big girl. I remember screaming. "I don't want to be a big girl!!!!"

I remember eavesdropping as the adults spoke in Tía Nanin's kitchen. They said my mom was going crazy. *–Conchita tenía una infección mala de sangre.–* My mother had a bad blood infection. The family members called her Conchita. I always loved that name. But I didn't like the way they spoke of her when they thought I wasn't watching them. This situation was shrouded in secrecy. That evening Papi didn't come to get us. He had to go to work at the bookbinding factory all the way in Elizabeth, New Jersey, so I stayed there for a few days with my aunt. It felt like I was in jail. I didn't like it. I cried so much. What I didn't understand at the time was that the reason why my mom was admitted was that my mom had a miscarriage because my alcoholic stepfather had punched her in the stomach. It was a family secret, and I was not allowed to talk about it or ask questions.

Today I understand it. At that young age, I remember them arguing a lot and feeling terrified. I was too young to make the connection between the fights and the miscarriage. When he would hit her, I would hide behind the sofa with my little brother. I would wait until it was quiet again and check on my mother. She would quietly sob and just hold me. I can remember the taste of Mami's tears, as I would kiss her on her cheek. Her salty tears mixed with my salty tears.

At this time in my life, I learned to plead on behalf of my mother. There I was...running into the street like Wonder Woman stopping a police car for my mommy.

CHAPTER THREE

SPEAK UP
LITTLE GIRL

T wo years later when I was in second grade, my mother was getting ready to give birth to my youngest little brother Freddy. It was the middle of March, and she pulled me out of school to start packing my luggage. When she told me that I was going to Puerto Rico, I was so happy because eight months earlier, during the summer of 1975, I visited Abuelita with my mother and my little brother Rafy. I loved it there! I didn't care that I was going to miss school. I didn't like my mean second-grade teacher Mrs. Marks. When she looked at me with her serious hard stare, I felt like she was an ice queen. Puerto Rico here I come. Please melt that ugly mean teacher's face off!

I remember my mother's big belly. Everyone who would talk to her would touch it. I couldn't believe that a new brother just like my little brother Rafy would come out of there. I was too young to remember when my little brother Rafy was born. I was just a toddler. But now as a second grader, I was more self-aware and making stronger associations and connections about life. I would ask her tons of questions about when the baby was coming. I would ask her what names she was thinking about for my brother. I was surprised when she said that she was going to call him Jose Alfredo (Freddy would be his nickname).

Then to placate me and make the questions stop, Mami would say that *el bebé* was coming soon. She assured me that when the time came, she was going to the hospital. I remember feeling so scared that my mom was going to the hospital to have a baby. I wondered if Mami was going to scream the way she did that day in Bellevue. I would have nightmares, night terrors, and night sweats waking up screaming and realizing that I had urinated on myself. Those night bedwetting accidents would make my mother very upset. After a few slaps on my bottom for peeing on the bed, I would cry. I didn't want my Mami to die. Was she going in an ambulance again?

Right before my little brother Freddy was born, my mother took me to the airport. She walked me up to the plane at the gate. My mother didn't get on the plane with me. I was so confused. At seven years old, I was on an airplane alone to San Juan, Puerto Rico. It was another moment when I felt lonely and scared. The American Airlines flight attendant tried to make me feel better by giving me an American Airlines pin that had airplane wings. The food that they gave me tasted horrible. It wasn't my mother's *arroz con pollo*. I couldn't stop crying the whole flight. When the plane landed, and the passengers were getting off, I held the flight attendant's hand with a firm grip. My mother didn't tell me who was getting me. In retrospect, I honestly don't think she knew. That was the way my family functioned. They didn't have normal conversations, nor did they include the children in their adult plans. What a mess!

I remember seeing a familiar face when we landed. It was my Aunt Tía Carmelina smiling and greeting me just as we got off the plane. In that instant, I had a flashback of the summer before when we had gone to Puerto Rico. I stayed there the whole summer with my mom and my little brother. It was paradise compared to our little apartment on Stratford Avenue. I loved climbing the *Kenepa* tree on Tía Carmelina's property in Naranjito and gathering eggs from Abuelita's chicken coop in Toa Alta. The moment that I walked off the plane and saw her beautiful smile, I ran to Tía Carmelina and cried. It was a long ride from the airport to my Abuelita's house. There were so many sharp turns and so many hills. I got car sick and threw up in the back of her car. She didn't look happy about that. When we arrived at my dear grandmother's house, I felt so much better. Over time my visit to Puerto Rico was like a dream. Even though I missed my mother and my little brother, I felt very safe and free. I didn't miss *Papi*.

My favorite part of the day in Puerto Rico was in the morning. I loved the smell of the coffee as I opened my eyes and I saw the white mosquito net around my bed. I felt like a princess having my bed covered up with this mosquito canopy around my bed. Every time I woke up, I felt like I woke up in a strange land. The roosters were the first sound that I heard, and I would resist waking up, but there was no escaping the sound of that loud *gallo*. I would stir in bed and I didn't get out of my bed until I smelled Abuelita's café. My world was waking up. Back home I didn't drink coffee. But here I loved the way it tasted. Abuelita would serve it to me with *pan sobao*. It was a pillowy soft and semi-sweet loaf of bread made in the local bakery. It was heaven. Some days it was a bit harder and that was *el pan de agua*. Either way, I loved having this type of breakfast. Basic, but oh so good!

With Abuelita, I would do all that I could to help her cook. –*Ella cocinaba a la leña.*– This fire monster served as my Abuelita's outdoor kitchen stove. She didn't like it when I got too close to the fire pit outside. I would see her feed this fiery beast with firewood. I would watch as Abuelito would cut up wood. He kept it close by the fire pit so that she could throw in the pieces of wood as she cooked. I was fascinated by everything I saw around the property, which felt like a huge farm.

The only task that I was never excited about was when she asked me to go get the eggs from the chicken coop. My second least favorite thing to do was shower inside the chicken coop. Yes, I had to shower inside a wooden shed that doubled as an outdoor shower stall and a supermarket of eggs. Abuelita did not have a finished bathroom. They had an outhouse and a hose set up inside the kitchen coop. It smelled so bad. I would try to lather up the Ivory soap bar to make it smell better and to make sure my body was clean. Here I was showering to get clean, but I was smelling chicken poop everywhere. I remember the streams of sunlight that would peek through the wooden slats of the chicken coop. I would worry that anyone could see me standing there naked and trembling from the cold water that poured out of a water hose strapped to one of the support beams in the large shed-like chicken coop. I would try my best to modestly cover myself up to get a bit warmer. The moment the cold water rushed out. Would anyone be able to see me? I would take a shower in my underwear. I tried desperately to ignore the horrible chicken poop smell that surrounded me. Instead, I focused on smelling the Ivory bar that I aggressively lathered. I would use it all over my skinny frame that was riddled with mosquito bites. The raised red swollen scabs full of pus would sting as I used the soap. I would wince and hold in the pain because I didn't want to bring any attention to me. Why did I scratch so fiercely to relieve the itch? It didn't matter that there was a mosquito net over my bed, those darn mosquitos loved my New York City blood. The constellation of mosquito bites was a testament to that mosquito love.

Sometimes, I would see some of Abuelo's farm hands walking by. I was petrified of the thought that they could see me. They were very dark men wearing straw hats strolling around with machetes. But I noticed that when I was showering, Abuela was by the kitchen back door sitting on the stoop keeping guard. There she was with a machete in her hand. Seeing her sitting there made me feel safer. She looked strong. Why couldn't my mother look that strong?

Inside the chicken coop, I remember staring at the plump hens with their cold beady little eyes and their sharp beaks as I stood very still. After I would finish showering and getting dressed, I would complete my morning task of collecting eggs for our morning breakfast. If a hen was in her nest, I usually did not bother her. I only collected eggs from the empty nests. One day, I was bold and tried to pick the eggs from under a hen and then I backed out. I was terrified at the thought that she might try to fly and land on my head. One morning, I saw a mother hen walking with her three little chicks in tow. They were her shadow. Right behind her. I immediately visualized my mother strutting in her heels, the ones that she was not allowed to wear if she wasn't with my Papi. My mother was now going to be like that mother hen with her three little chicks. Close to the Earth, grounded with the deafening chick peeps of Mami...Mami...Mami...from Vilma, Rafy, and now baby Jose Alfredo. At that moment, I decided to follow her and tried to pick up the last little chick. That mother hen was not going to have it. She protested and flapped her wings charging right at me. I was petrified at the thought of her sharp beak trying to get at my eyes. I immediately dropped the chick, and I never bothered that mother hen again.

Tío Moncho lived in Abuela and Abuelo's house. He was a weird man. This uncle whispered to himself as he carried the bible. Moncho was the family nickname for Ramon. Regardless of his peculiar way, there was something very endearing about him, and I wasn't scared of him. I was simply curious about what he was doing and why he was doing it. Every time he would walk past me, he would look at me with a penetrating hard stare as he talked about hell and his need to save souls. What the world around him would characterize as *un evangélico* was actually a chemical imbalance with perhaps a touch of schizophrenia. But no matter how odd and off he was, there was a tenderness that peeked through his eyes. I wanted to know that kind side, but his bible-toting gestures and hurried walk would make me nervous. It scared me to hear him speak with such conviction. I noticed that in the mornings, he would come into the kitchen and drink some coffee. I would peer through the cracked door and see him there. When I saw him there, I wouldn't come out until I knew he was gone. He would talk to Abuelita about talking to Jesus and laughing with his God. Abuela would just wave her hand at him like he was talking nonsense. It was her way of telling him to shut up because he didn't know what he was talking about. Upon seeing her dismiss him, Tío Moncho would stand up, hold his bible like a sword, and point it straight up to the sky as he screamed for God to save the world. In these moments, I didn't see the tender side of him. I saw the ghastly figure. I didn't understand why he seemed so angry, and why he spoke with such urgency. Was the world really going to end that day? I prayed it didn't because I wanted to be back home with my Mami.

Some days Abuelita would ask me to get *gandules* (pigeon peas) from a garden on the side of the house, and *guineos* (green bananas) from the back of the house. She would show me how to make beans with *bollitas de guineo* (grated green bananas shaped like meatballs) and it tasted delicious. *Cuando ella cocinaba arroz con gandules*, I was very excited. It meant that I would sit by the kitchen table and take out the *gandules* one by one out of the peapods. I loved working side by side with my Abuelita. We would talk about so much. I always had a million questions about my mother. I would ask Abuelita to tell me all about when Mami was a little girl. This is when I learned that Mami didn't wear shoes when she was little. She would always walk *descalza*. Abuela would say, –*Tu era la mismita como Conchita...siempre descalza.*– I loved to walk barefoot too. I felt like a free wild child. I didn't even comb my hair every day, and my grandmother didn't pester me about it. She did make me wash my face, and clean out the sleep in my eyes along with brushing my teeth. But if I didn't want to wash my hair, it wasn't a big deal. I felt so free.

I loved that I was able to walk barefoot. It was easier to try and climb the coconut tree that was very close to my Tía Guillin's house and on the other side of my Abuelita's house. Tía Guillin lived there with her husband. They didn't have any children, and she loved when I would stroll by and just sit on the rocking chair on her porch. I had never seen a rocking chair before coming to Puerto Rico. She would give me *dulce de leche* candies (made out of cans of sweetened condensed milk) and they were so delicious. I remember staying there for a little while after lunch, and then I would stroll over to my other family member's house. Her name was Yaya. She was my mother's *prima-hermana*. This paternal first cousin showed my mother how to sew, and Yaya was excited about trying to show me how to sew. There was a television at Yaya's house and she would let me watch Mighty Mouse cartoons. That was more interesting than trying to sew. It felt so strange because all of the words in this cartoon were in Spanish. It took some time to get used to, but after a while, I was catching on. When I would talk to Yaya, she would take out the sewing machine that she used to help my mother learn how to sew. She also showed me a few sequin yards of fabric that she said were made by my mother. She told me how my mother would take a bus to Bayamon to her first job as a seamstress.

After spending some time with Yaya at the end of the afternoon, I would walk back to my Abuela's house before it got dark. Sometimes, I would see Tío Moncho walking back into the house as he looked exhausted and oddly quiet. He would ask me to go with him to the mountain in the morning and I would tell him no. I wanted to stay with Abuelita. He would nod and say *–Dios te bendiga Palomita.–* The nights in Puerto Rico scared me because I heard the Coquí sounds that made it a bit hard to sleep. They were so hard to ignore. After a while, I stopped hearing them and I would drift to sleep. Sometimes, I would beg Abuela to let me sleep on the hammock in her bedroom right next to her bed. I thought it was strange that she had her own room, and that my grandfather slept in a different room. The strangest thing about being in Abuela's house was that I didn't see my Abuelo very much. In fact, Abuelo was usually gone most of the day, and when he was back, he would listen to his radio and go to his room. He wasn't as friendly to me as my Abuela. There was something about him that reminded me of Papi. His ominous silence scared me. Abuelo had blue eyes and he was very tall which was such a stark difference to my short grandmother who looked like *una India Taína* with her brown skin and her long black hair in a long braid that would go straight down her back.

I remember Abuelita asking me if I was happy that I was going to have a little brother. I was honest, shook my head, and lightly whispered, "No." Mi Abuelita leaned in and hugged me. Trying to make light of my declaration and protest, she chuckled and said, *–Aye nooooo...te cogió la falda!–* That was right. My little brothers did steal my Mommy's lap. She understood how I felt, and I thought that was amazing! I really loved Abuelita. The moment that she said this to me, I felt that I could tell her anything. I told her about the time my mom went to the hospital and what my *tía politica* said about my mother going crazy. I was so mad, and I wanted Abuelita to know. She shook her head and said *–Pobrecita.–* I told her how Papi would hit my Mami, and how she cried a lot. I told her how I didn't like him. I was bold and I didn't hold back. She was very quiet and just listened to me. Then she would just grab a hairbrush and comb my hair. I loved the way it felt. It was as if she was stroking away all the hurt that was in my little soul. It made me sleepy and in those still moments with Abuela, I never wanted to go back home. When I would realize this, I would shake myself out of it and feel guilty that I didn't miss my Mami. Then I would cry myself to sleep.

I was there for about two long months from March to May. In school, it really set me back as a reader. Not once did I lift a pencil to write, or read a book. In retrospect, I think Mami was simply trying to protect me from the fights that she would have with my stepfather. Mami was also making it more manageable to deal with an infant and a young child, than having to cope with the baby, my little brother, as well as having to take the trek of walking me to and from school each day. Today it makes sense, but at the moment I thought she was trying to get rid of me. I wondered if she had died. How was my new baby brother? What did he look like? Did she go back to Bellevue to have the baby? Did she go in an ambulance?

Little did I know that she gave birth to my brother at Lincoln Hospital in the South Bronx. As an adult today, I know that a few years earlier, the Young Lords had seized Lincoln Hospital making demands to the city and the mayor of New York City for better quality health-care for the South Bronx patients. Lincoln Hospital was considered to be more of a butcher shop than a hospital by the local Bronx residents. It was a good thing that as a child, I was not aware of this unsettling reality.

When I was an infant and a toddler, the reality of social protests and activism were swirling around me in Alphabet City, as the hippies held signs at Tompkins Square Park. As I lived in the South Bronx, the spirit of social unrest followed me. Perhaps the cry for social change mingled with the internal cries of my frustration as a child. It must have taken hold in my heart and began to sprout as a young sapling that would unfold from its seed and break ground searching for the sun. My mother was my sun. She was the center of my universe. Why couldn't I be the center of her world? I would get so frustrated with her. No matter how many times I would ask her to tell me about the baby and where it was coming from, she never answered my questions.

These were not conversations that Puerto Rican parents had with their children at the time. Abuela never told Mami, and now Mami was not going to tell me. We just didn't talk about it. It was not spoken to anyone, especially between mother and daughter.

I felt that I could talk more with my Abuelita than my mother. When I came back, I tried to do the same thing with my mom. To talk freely, to help her, and to feel the love that I felt in those moments when my Abuelita combed my hair. At this tender age, I was trying to foster a mother-and-daughter relationship where I could talk freely with her. But my mom was so quiet all the time tending to the baby and my little brother. It all changed one day when I told Mami that I loved being with Abuelita because she liked to talk with me. I told Mami that I told Abuelita how Papi would hit her. My mother gave me a worried look. It was the same look she gave me when I walked into the bathroom in Doña Hilda's house. At that moment, I learned that I could be bold and whisper my truth. I also learned that if I did speak that boldly, rejection wrapped in disappointment and disapproval would come my way. It was like a piercing knife to my heart. I didn't want to disappoint my mother. I learned that if I was going to be bold and speak the truth, it would not be considered a surreptitious affair. Speaking the truth felt uncomfortable but necessary. It was better than pretending.

Chapter Four

MAKE IT RIGHT

I t was an oppressively hot summer day. Many times in our tiny apartment, we sought refuge from the heat by sitting on our fire escape. It felt like I was back in Puerto Rico with *Abuelita* sitting on her *balcón*. But this day, I felt strange. Sometimes when I would get a stomachache, it was as though my body was protesting because I sensed something was wrong. Sometimes, I would get dizzy. Maybe it was because of the heat. Perhaps I had too many Maltas. My mom said I was anemic. To put some much-needed meat on my skinny bones, she would create this protein shake with a Malta drink that was made from a frothy malt beverage, 1 raw egg, and a tablespoon of sugar. I was so skinny from being a picky eater that my mother was convinced that this home remedy was going to help me get stronger and gain some weight.

Mami said that our neighbor Tony, my Papi's drinking buddy from *la bodega,* and his wife were going to babysit us as my mother ran to a doctor's appointment with my baby brother Freddy. A couple of weekends prior to this day, the neighbor Tony bought my little brother and me a small yellow parakeet. We were so happy with our gift. We named the parakeet Cupo. On other occasions, I visited Tony and his wife with Papi as they drank beer in the living room. His wife was always home in the kitchen. It was a sunny kitchen with a window facing the front of the building. Every time I followed my Papi to their apartment, I stuck by her side and simply watched her. She was not a conversationalist like my mother's other friends Doña Hilda y Doña Tomasa. She didn't speak to me. In fact, I didn't even know her name. She would give me the weakest smile. Instead of contending with this boring woman, I would walk over to the kitchen window to observe people walking by on Stratford Avenue. I thought it was better being there than in the living room watching a boring baseball game. She was a quiet lady who didn't smile much when I saw her in the elevator. My mother called her "*Sosa.*" I didn't understand what that meant. Maybe her name was Rosa and I misheard. In fact, *sosa* means sour.

The LP record spun round and round. Disco music was blaring on the record player with a few skips from scratches on the record. The music was playing from inside our neighbor Tony's house, which was down the hall on the fourth floor of our apartment building. As we approached the door, the music was louder, and my mother had to knock hard on the door so that they could hear her knocks. Tony opened the door, and my mother asked for his wife. He told her that she went to the supermarket to get snacks for the kids to eat. She looked at us and then told Rafy and me to go inside. I obediently did what I was told. My mother thanked him and he closed the door. It felt odd for my little brother and I to be alone with him. He wasn't a complete stranger to us. Tony was a tall, dark, and skinny Afro-Latino man. He looked like a Puerto Rican version of Felix Unger from the *Odd Couple* show on television. He smoked Marlboro cigarettes and chewed violet gum just like my uncle Tío Juan from my Papi's side of the family. He wore bell-bottom dress slacks that were very fitted on his hips and waist, along with button-down dress shirts with large collars.

In the sunny living room, I spotted a white metal birdcage by the window. There was a light blue parakeet frantically flying around in his cage with his wings flapping against the metal sides of the cage. I detested his ear-piercing screeches. For such a beautiful bird, he looked miserable on this hot summer day. Their apartment seemed huge compared to our small one-bedroom apartment. They had nicer furniture than us. They had a beautiful record player that looked like a long rectangular dresser with built-in speakers on the sides. The apartment was very neat. I figured it was because they didn't have any kids running around. The couple did not have any children and from the vibe that I felt from Tony's wife, I didn't think she liked kids. In the corner of the living room, I spied a pair of shiny black heels by the sofa. Tony encouraged me to take off my sneakers and put the heels on. They were huge on my feet and when I tried walking in them, my skinny knees would buckle and bump into each other as I tried to straighten myself up and walk properly on them. My little brother Rafy giggled at the sight of his big sister trying to be all grown up tripping with these pointy shoes.

When I turned around, I didn't see Tony and he walked away reappearing with a ball from the bedroom. What else was inside that room? I was curious. I tried peering around his shoulder and saw a small television on a TV cart with wheels. Rafy asked him if we could watch cartoons. Tony spoke English and I was learning a lot of English in school. He turned the dial on the television set and stopped it on channel 13. *Sesame Street* was on. My brother immediately planted himself right in front of the television sitting with his legs crossed happily as a clam. He was not interested in the red ball. He wanted to see Big Bird. I thought *Sesame Street* was for babies.

I wasn't a baby so I walked back into the living room to check out the bird in the cage. I was going to be an explorer now that the quiet lady was not there to give me strange penetrating stares. Anyway, when was she coming back? As I observed the parakeet flapping his wings and listening to the music in the living room, from the side of my eye I sensed Tony getting closer. He had the red ball in front of him. As he got closer, he asked with a nice voice. "Do you want to play with something?" He threw the red ball onto the sofa and when I turned my head to look at him, he wiggled out from the zipper of his pants. Tony was holding his penis in his hands. I recognized a penis from having to change my little brothers' diapers, but this one looked very different. It was big, dark, wrinkly, and quite ugly as he rubbed it hard with his hand. I got scared when I looked at his creepy smile.

I felt cornered standing between the birdcage, the side of the sofa, the wall, and Tony. Now I knew why that bird screeched. It was trapped just like me. I quickly slipped out of the heels and I told him to stop. I didn't want to play. I felt like I was on some weird loop like the LP record that kept playing over and over again. It was driving me crazy. I wanted it to stop. He got closer and grabbed my hand. He forced me to touch it. His rough hands crushed my thin little fingers around his penis. He wanted me to rub it the way he rubbed it. Then with his other dirty hand, he stroked my hair, which was in a side ponytail. He started to pull on my hair and it hurt as my head started to get pulled down closer to his ugly penis. I was disgusted. I felt like I was going to throw up. Suddenly there was this white stuff that erupted out of a hole in his penis. He grabbed most of it with his hands and brought it closer to my face. *Oh my God! He wanted me to smell it or taste it?* I desperately refused and shook my head. I said. "I'm telling!"

Tony's ugly face got very close to mine and I could smell his cigarette breath. I wanted to spit in his face to make him back off. Then he menacingly said. "If you tell on me, I will kill your bird Cupo. They won't believe you. You are a bad and dirty little girl. Look at you." I became enraged! With all my might, I punched him in the stomach and squeezed my skinny little body by the side of him. I ran straight into the bedroom to sit with my little brother. I wanted to protect my little brother. My heart was racing. Why did Tony do what he did? I didn't want him to kill my bird. It was strange. It felt dirty and wrong. What was I going to do?

Obliviously happy and content watching television, my brother Rafy looked up at me as I quickly sat down by his side. His little innocent head leaned on my shoulder. He had not heard me yell stop. He did not hear our conversation in the living room. He had not heard me run away as fast as my legs could carry me. My heart was racing. I had the oddest sensation that I could see myself from the corner of the room. It was an out-of-body experience. It was as if I was watching a movie about what was happening to me. I had the strangest taste in my mouth; it was a metallic salty taste. Did he put some of that disgusting stuff in my mouth? I was so anxious and I remember breathing really hard after running in and sitting by my little brother's side. At that moment, every cell in my body wanted to run out of that place. But I couldn't. I was trapped. Would he come in and make my little brother do the same thing? If he did, I would bite his penis off! What was I going to do? I knew Mami was not home. Where would I go? I couldn't just run out and leave my little brother behind. I prayed that Mami would get back quickly but it felt like she had just left.

I was shaking so much as I sat by my little innocent brother. I was petrified. At that moment, I felt the weirdest sensation. I peed my pants. There was a yellow puddle on the floor in between my legs. It was a warm sensation. It felt more like a release. I smelled the urine as it sat in a puddle below me. I stared at the dark blue stain on my dungaree wide-leg pants. Suddenly my brother Rafy said, "Yuck, you peed yourself." I immediately stood up humiliated and simply stood there frozen like a statue. Tony came into the room, looked down at the yellow pee on the floor, and yelled –¡Estupida!–

Now my brother could witness that he was not a nice guy. Tony walked over to me and grabbed me by my skinny right arm so hard that I felt like he was going to pull it right out of my shoulder socket. My little brother looked at him confused and started to cry pulling me away from Tony's rough grip. Then Tony sighed, released my arm, and quickly stepped out of the room. When he reappeared, Tony walked into the room with a mop in his hand. The music was still blaring. Then I got an idea. I firmly held my brother's hand and slowly placed a finger on my lip to signal him to stay quiet. Shhhhhhh!

On the fifth floor, I had created a new friendship with a girl named Lisa who lived with her mother Neldy, and her father Alfonso. They had a beautiful black and silver German Shepard named Lady. I knew that Lisa's father Alfonso liked to drink just like Papi. Sometimes when I would visit Lisa, he would be in the living room watching a baseball game with a beer in his hand. But then in an instant, I realized something very important. It was summertime, and I knew that Lisa would be home with Neldy. I made a plan to try to get as close to the door as I could to run up the stairs and get to Lisa's house. Maybe it meant having to leave my brother behind for a little while so that I could tell them what was happening. I was playing the possible escape scenarios in my mind. Even though my mother was not there to save me, I was going to save myself. Just like I ran away from that angry mother hen who wanted to peck my eyes out for holding her baby chick. I was going to run out of this horrible place. Lisa's mother could save me. Lady could save me. If he followed us, she would bite him hard on his penis. It would serve him right!

When the coast was clear, we snuck away, little by little, and I led Rafy out of the room watching closely as Tony mopped the floor. He was not looking at me and that is when I made a mad dash with my little brother to the door! I quickly unlocked the door and picked up Rafy in my arms as I charged up the steps by the apartment door. When I came to the fifth floor landing in front of the door, I frantically banged on the door like our lives depended on it. I heard the music downstairs spilling out into the echoing chamber of the hallway. As I knocked louder and louder, I heard the dog Lady barking. I was so grateful she did because it would get someone's attention inside to open the door. Lisa opened the door. I immediately pushed my brother into the apartment and hurried to close and lock Lisa's door behind me. We escaped!

Lisa looked at me perplexed. I told her that I just wanted to see her. That we wanted to play. I totally pretended like I wasn't running away from that pervert downstairs. I was going to act like nothing was wrong. Just the way Mami would act. Nothing was wrong. I was going to stay there until she got home with my baby brother. Then it hit me. What if Tony tells her that I touched his penis. What if she comes looking for me at Tony's house and he wants to play that dirty game with Mami? She couldn't fight him off. She doesn't even stop Papi from hitting her. Would he try to touch my baby brother's hair the way he pulled mine? I was so anxious there anticipating every scenario that suddenly I just pretended it was a dream. It never happened. It was a nightmare and I just woke up. I was visiting Lisa and it was all a bad dream. I was going to keep on pretending that we came up to see Lisa with my mother's permission.

Then to my surprise, I saw Lisa's father walking out of the bedroom with Lady faithfully walking behind her owner. She was just a beautiful and loyal dog. Lady came up to me, sniffed me, and then found her way back to her owner's side. Alfonso saw me in the hallway and greeted me from afar. Then he walked up to me and he patted my head and then patted Rafy's little head. I looked at him shocked. Was he like Tony? Do all men who drink pull out their penises? No. I didn't believe that. Alfonso was always so kind to me. Maybe if I told him, he would force me to go back down to Tony's house. I wasn't going to say anything. I was going to wait.

I spied Lisa's huge dollhouse in the corner of the living room, and I led my little brother by the hand to play with the dollhouse. That was going to be my escape. My brother and I played with Lisa, and Alfonso walked away with Lady. While we played with the dolls, I was so relieved that Rafy didn't mention anything about running out of Tony's house. Rafy was happy to get the Ken doll. I quickly took Ken's pants off to check if there was a penis. Thankfully, I didn't see one. It was safe for Rafy to play with that doll. I was happy and relieved to be away from Tony. I felt safe.

Then suddenly I heard a knock on the door. My world shrunk and I wanted to hide. *Oh my God. It was him. It had to be him. He was looking for us.* That is when I told Lisa, "Don't open the door!" I jumped up and raced over to the kitchen where Alfonso and Neldy were sitting at the kitchen table drinking some *cafecito*. I begged them not to open the door. That is when I felt the sensation of warm urine coming down the side of my pant legs again. I told him that it was Tony knocking. That Tony was a very bad man. I told them Tony's secret. I told them that Tony took out his pee-pee and made me touch it.

Alfonso stood up and held me firmly by the shoulders and asked, –*Vilma, ¿Él te tocó?*– I whispered, –*Sí*. Lady was by the door barking up a storm as the knocking continued. At that moment, I saw Alfonso with an angry face that I had never seen before. *Era una mirada de pena mezclada con rabia.* Neldy held me close and hugged me. She spoke English and she told me. "Everything is going to be alright."

Alfonso briskly walked to the door. He held Lady's collar as he opened it. The figure standing by the opened door was Tony. Alfonso yelled. –*¡Cabrón salte de aquí! ¿Cómo vas a tocar una nena? ¡Espera que yo se lo diga a Eddie. ¡Él te va matar. ¡Lagarte hijo de puta!*– Alfonso released Lady's collar a few inches and she looked like a horse kicking up on her back legs viciously trying to bite this stranger at the door. Tony jumped back and Alfonso slammed the door shut. He saved me! Ironically, Alfonso was home that day because he was recovering from a bad flu. But I believe my loving God in heaven sent an Earthly angel to protect us.

There was no way to contact my mother so they waited. When my mother came back to pick us up, she kept knocking on his door and there was no answer. She came up to Lisa's house anxious and looking for us when Neldy told her what happened. Mami asked me to come over to the kitchen and she questioned me. She looked terrified. I had never seen that look in her eyes. She cried and she held me close. Neldy made coffee for my mother and they talked while I was with both of my baby brothers in the living room with Lisa. I wished that I could live with Lisa. I would have Lady to protect me. After a while, we went home and then my mother told me not to say anything to Papi. – *Yo no estaba supuesto dejarte sola mi'ja. Perdoname.*– Why didn't she want to tell him? I don't want Tony ever to come to the house. He was Papi's friend. He would be back.

Later on that evening, I noticed that Papi didn't come home until very late. He was drunk. He was talking about almost killing that "summamabitch."

Later Lisa told me that her father Alfonso and Papi found Tony walking down the street and they both beat his ass up *le dieron una paliza*. I never saw Tony again. Years later I learned that they were forced to move out of the building because many people witnessed the altercation in front of the building. He was labeled as a *fresco* and his wife was humiliated. She left him and then he moved out. From that moment on, I felt safe again. Aside from Papi always hitting Mami, I never had to worry about having to touch a penis again. I always looked at Alfonso like a father, a protector, and my fairy godfather. He made everything right! It was at this moment that this little girl learned how to speak up, but to the right people.

Chapter Five

RECONCILE

S pirit of God...

Grant me the gift of wisdom to see the world through your eyes.
The gift of counsel to make difficult decisions.
The gift of knowledge and understanding to use my mind to know
you and to love you.
The gift of fortitude to have the courage to live in the faith despite the
difficulties and disappointments.
The gift of piety to be able to express my special love and commitment
to you.
And the right kind of awesome fear that makes me pause, to wonder,
and revere God's love.

This was the confirmation prayer that I had to memorize when I was ten years old. As I reflect more about it, at this young age I truly didn't understand the true meaning and depth of this moment until now. My mother gave me many gifts. But it was her gift of faith that truly modeled for me how to persevere and face trials with grace.

In the Catholic faith, you have three initiation sacraments. The first sacrament was when I was an infant. I had my baptism at St. Brigid on Avenue B in New York City. The second one was my First Communion (which was my First Eucharist) at St. Joan of Arc in the Bronx when I was eight years old. After that, I prepared to receive the third rite of passage into my Catholic faith, which was my Confirmation at the same church St. Joan of Arc. At that age, I was delving into books, and I would read all of my CCD (Confraternity of Christian Doctrine) literature also known as my catechism first communion preparation books. Reading was my escape.

It is the custom in the Catholic faith that when you prepare for your Confirmation, you must choose a biblical name that is your faith name. My confirmation name was Miriam. I remember when I first told my mom. She was concerned because she believed that Miriam was a name that was associated with bitterness or misery. But I loved the sound of that name. It sounded like a mature name. Little did I know that the root of the name Miriam is Meri, which means rebellion. Later I learned that Miriam was the teacher of the women, while Moses and Aaron were the leaders of the men. It is also the Jewish name for Mary coming from María. So my confirmation name is derivative of my mother's given name, which is María Concepción. The decision to select Miriam as my Confirmation name into the Catholic faith was no coincidence at all.

Moreover, the fact that my home church was named St. Joan of Arc is not by chance. Joan of Arc was one bold and determined woman. Regrettably, she was persecuted for her bold spirit and sadly I never learned anything about her when I was preparing for my Confirmation. Had I known, I may have chosen that name. She was a woman of certitude and she was fearless. This young girl believed in something. I was preparing to receive a holy sacrament in the St. Joan of Arc Catholic Church in the Bronx. I considered it to be divine intervention. He anointed me for the next stage of my life wherein like Joan I would have a vision to act boldly and step out in faith to defend.

During the blessed ceremony of Confirmation, it would be the moment when my heart is united with the Holy Spirit and I would receive the Holy Spirit's gifts of wisdom, counsel, knowledge, fortitude, courage, piety, and reverence for my merciful God. At this age, I was very deliberate in my decision to do my Confirmation. I also asked that Neldy be my confirmation madrina. She was the one who told me everything was going to be alright after that filthy Tony sexually assaulted me. Not once did we ever speak about what transpired that day. But I remembered. Now with my confirmation Madrina by my side, by default that would make her husband and Lisa's father Alfonso my godfather too. I loved the idea of this couple being my fairy godparents. For many years, Neldy and Lisa tried to get him to come to church. It was a losing battle. This was as close as I was going to get to having him become my godfather.

I wanted to be more of a helper of faith for my mother. I noticed that after I finished my First Communion, my mom didn't push me as much to go to the Spanish mass. But I really enjoyed it. I thought that if I could prepare for the Confirmation, that she would start taking me back to the Spanish mass, just like she did when I was preparing for my Holy Communion. I was excited about doing my Confirmation. I think that at this tender age, I was learning how to set my sights on working towards something and achieving it. Perhaps it was a way to spiritually get clean from the dirty exposure of Tony's genitalia.

I loved learning about God. It seemed like a natural fit for me. There was a duality in my world of faith. As I read the books in English, I was trying to connect the English phrases and terms from my books to the spoken Spanish words in the Spanish mass. There was another duality in my world. It was the life I had in the outside world and the inside world of my home. I vacillated between two realities. The turbulent reality, and there was the calm before the storm reality. Things weren't always so horrible with my Papi. Aside from those terrifying moments when I would peer around a corner to witness him hitting my mother, he wasn't always fighting and drunk. There were moments when he was pleasant and we would all gather and watch television in our small living room. We had a black and white television with a knob that was always broken and the only way we could turn the channels was by turning it with a plier that was always attached to it. We were always making adjustments to the antenna to try to get the best reception.

There were moments when on Saturday mornings, Papi would get up early while we watched Saturday morning cartoons. He would come back with a bag full of groceries with some fresh bread from the bakery. Papi would take out a dozen eggs, peppers, onions, cheese, and potatoes, and make a large Spanish omelet. In fact, they were gigantic and he would fill up the large fresh bread with a healthy portion of the omelet. It was so filling. I remember feeling full all day. But I will admit it felt like it took forever for him to finally finish cooking and serve us. Mami would sleep and I am certain that was a blessing for her.

I always thought Mami was a better and faster cook. Even though it took forever for him to finish making that darn omelet, it always tasted great. I remember he was so particular about cutting the onions and the peppers. Sometimes, to try to make it go quicker, I would offer to help. But he wouldn't let me. I would get so annoyed. Mami would always let me help her cook. But when he was in the kitchen I did not go in and sit at the kitchen table by the stove. I would stand outside of the kitchen and just watch him work. But sometimes, the boys would ask him if they could help, and he would let them. I felt like the ugly duckling, the extra wheel, and the annoying girl in the midst of the boys. In the moments when he was in a better mood, he would talk a lot while preparing everything, and it made me feel like he was on a cooking show like Julia Child. I wished that he were really on a television show so that he would have to stay nice all the time. He would have an audience. I wished that he could stay this way – the way he was on Saturday mornings when he was pleasant and kind to Mami. I remember asking why couldn't he be that nice all the time. Why did he have to get so angry? On Saturday mornings, he was another person. It is almost like he forgot who the hell he was during the week.

In the afternoon, I would look forward to going to church with my mother for confession. She looked so rested and relaxed. I would make a beeline into the confessional booth kneeling as I faced the screen. I didn't worry about my mother overhearing my confessions, because I spoke to the priest in English. While the priest sat in the dark on the other side of the screen, he would listen to the dark confessions of a little girl in pain. I shared with the priest that I had wished that my Papi was dead. I confessed that I hated him. I confessed that I wanted him to never come back. I confessed that I wanted Alfonso to be my father. Every time those words came out of my mouth, they scared me. But I felt my spirit lighter because I was not lying to God.

Saturdays were a moment of reconciliation in my heart not only with God but also with my Papi. After releasing the angst, the fear, and the worry that I was going to hell for feeling the way I did, I would do the compulsory number of Our Father prayers, and Hail Mary prayers that were sanctioned by the priest. Each week the numbers changed, so I figured there were weeks where I sinned more than others. I wondered if maybe he was changing too. Maybe my prayers were working. This was the moment when I learned how to become an insightful intercessor. Being an advocate for my mom involved praying and hoping for change.

CHAPTER SIX

MIND OVER HEART

I s it possible to align our hearts with our minds? Do they function in tandem or do they operate in mutually exclusive realms? Why can't the same mind that went to school and learned some tough lessons speak to the heart and tell it to wake the hell up from its clueless whimsical view of love? In the case of my heart, it is an imbecile that needs to be schooled. I believe that as a child, who witnessed so much trauma and betrayal on so many levels, my heart was fractured and perhaps broken beyond repair. Early on in life, I chose to nurture my mind and not my heart. I felt it was better to use my mind than to lean on my feelings. It was better to think, and not let my heart trap me into caring. It was better to suspend reality and to escape into a book.

Feeding the mind took effort, I never felt like a smart girl until I started fifth grade in my Bronx classroom at Community School 77. At the time, students were sorted like buttons in a sewing box. It was called ability grouping. If you were considered smart, then you were in a top drawer with the big buttons in a class labeled 5-1. But if you were in class 5-10 you knew you were in the bottom drawer. Our self-esteem as students was directly linked to the class label. As such, I felt fortunate to be in the 5-2 class with Miss Keen. Prior to that, I was in class 4-9. I don't know what happened to get me to get into this higher-performing class, but I was elated to be there. I secretly thought it was a mistake and that at any moment, the principal would come in and walk me down the hall into class 5-10.

Miss Keen was a young and pretty teacher who seemed so different from so many of my teachers before her. She was innovative and quite progressive for her time. She would cluster the desks together instead of having us sit in the usual row formation in many of the classrooms of the 1970s. Sometimes she would create a U-configuration with the desks so that we could have discussions about different things we were learning. Seeing the different seating arrangements, made it feel fresh and fun.

My favorite part of the day was when my fifth-grade teacher would turn off the classroom lights, and turn on a small lamp by her desk. The glow of the light excited me. She would read Judy Blume chapter books to us such as *Tales of a Fourth Grade Nothing* and *Are You There God, It's Me Margaret*. As she read with such expression and moving emotion, she would walk around the classroom and gently place her hands on our shoulders or our arms to keep us focused on her words. My eyes would follow her every move. I would take a mental inventory of everything she did and everything she wore. She had a stylish Dorothy Hamil haircut and on Fridays, she would wear her Sergio Valente jeans. I remember wanting to get a pair just like hers with the big V in the pockets. She was a perfect woman. A vision of beauty just like in the Breck shampoo commercials with the blonde beauties smiling an infectious smile with their pearly whites.

Seeing her collection of story chapter books made me want to read. I was able to borrow the whole Nancy Drew Mystery series from the New York City Bronx Public Library. I was so happy that the library was around the corner next to the Soundview-Morrison train station. I would reread all the books that she read to us in class. One day I spied a book titled *The Wizard of Oz* on her desk. I asked Miss Keen if I could borrow it over the weekend and she was so gracious to lend it to me. It was not a soft-covered book but a hardcover book just like the reference books that you were not allowed to take out of the library. I felt so special that she lent it to me.

The moment I got home I started reading it. I made myself a private little reading nook in the oddest of places in our small apartment. It was the closet near the bathroom all the way down the hallway from the living room. It was going to be the quietest place. With two younger and clingy brothers, it was the only place I could get some peace and quiet.

I dragged a brown extension cord from the living room along with one of my mother's sofa lamps that was always set on the sofa table and I plugged in the extension cord to an outlet that was in the middle of the hallway near the kitchen. I made sure to tape the cord to the wall so that my little brothers wouldn't get tangled up in it. The last thing I wanted was to be in a dark closet. I would push the bulk of the clothes that were on hangers to the far left side of the closet and create a little nest for myself with my mother's throw pillows from the sofa. It was my reading lair. It was my great escape. The minute I would go in the closet, I would try to forget the scary closet in my neighbor's house and remember that this was my safe closet. The place where I would visit another land. Today it was going to be with Dorothy in the Land of Oz.

Just as I was reading the first few chapters of the book, I heard my mother screaming, "No Eddie...No!" When I peered outside, my stepfather was over her with a heel in his hand hitting her on the head, calling her a *puta* for wearing high heels.

What the heck was going on this time? I couldn't even get a break to read. After hitting her and leaving her on the kitchen floor crying, he went to the bathroom and started showering. When the coast was clear, I casually walked over and put on her shoes pretending they were ruby slippers just like the ones Dorothy found. Just like Dorothy, I was going to triumph over this evil force in my house. My little heart was calcified and indifferent to this scene. It was not the first time, nor was it the last.

With a single objective in mind, I asked my mother for us to leave and go to Tio Herminio's house. It was not the first time we had gone there to escape my stepfather's drunken rages. She quickly grabbed her purse and threw a few things in a bag as she grabbed my baby brother Freddy. I held on to Rafy's hand and quickly led him out. I told them we were going to see Tio. My brother Rafy was so happy. He adored Tio so much. He was so tall and every time he lifted us up high close to the ceiling, it would give us butterflies and we would giggle. We loved him so much, and especially his laugh.

I couldn't believe it. My mother actually agreed to leave that mean angry troll behind. We quickly walked to the train and it seemed so dark outside. I was a little scared that the troll would find out we left and he would beat up Mami in the middle of the street. I kept looking back praying that he was not coming. Finally, we got to the train station and we boarded the Number 6 train.

It was only a few stops away as we got off the Brook Avenue train station which was a very dangerous area of the South Bronx. The people around there walked and looked so different. They looked like any minute they were about to slip into a deep sleep but their bodies disobeyed as they fought it in their zombie-like state with pools of drool on the sides of their mouths. Their drool in a suspended state just like their lives on pause. It terrified me, but I pushed through and pretended not to care because soon we would get to Tio's building. It was a narrow walk-up with a stoop that had graffiti and garbage all over it.

The steps to his room on the third floor were so dark and steep. I saw needles scattered everywhere. As I tried to pick one up, my mom slapped it out of my hand. My uncle lived in a boarding house where the tenants shared a kitchen and a bathroom. They were all men living in furnished rooms, which consisted of a full-size bed, a dresser, and a chair. My uncle had crammed a sofa in the room because the last time we were there, he let us all sleep on the bed and he slept on the floor. This time he would sleep on the sofa, and my dear mother and her chicks would sleep on his bed.

I remember feeling sorry for my uncle when he was giving up his bed. But he looked so happy to have us there. He was usually alone and quite disheveled. What I didn't know at the time was that my uncle suffered from mental illness. My mother called him "nervioso" but it felt that it was more than that. I would watch his hands as he would do things around the house. When he would visit us, they were always shaking. It usually was more pervasive when he would come into the house and he would reach for a beer from a brown paper bag that he brought in with him. The beer didn't scare me the way it would when I saw my stepfather carry his beer. He was always so kind to us.

There were times that I wished he was my father. Tio Herminio looked like a Borinquen Indio with jet-black hair and bronze skin. He was over six feet tall and to me, he seemed like a giant. I felt that he was my mother's defender because every time he was around, my stepfather would never behave the way he usually would with my mother. I noticed that my stepfather respected him. I wished that Tio Herminio could live with us so that my stepfather could behave all of the time.

The next morning, I followed my mother to the bathroom. After what happened to me with the neighbor, I never felt comfortable being alone with a man again. I was always by my mother's side. She grabbed some cleaning products to disinfect the bathroom. It was a miracle to see how she scrubbed the dirty tub and made it look brand new. She mopped the bathroom and kitchen floor, and it smelled like Pine-Sol. After that, she told us to take turns bathing. After I finished, I helped bathe both of my little brothers in the tub. While I was washing them with the door wide open, I noticed a man with a slow creepy gait coming towards the bathroom. He looked like one of the zombies I had seen when we were walking to the building. This strange man didn't even notice we were in the bathroom and at that moment, he tried to use the toilet. I screamed and that is when he walked out of the bathroom. My mother cursed him out in Spanish and my uncle got in his face. But to no avail. He had no visible reaction to this huge intrusion. It was like yelling at a wall.

For the rest of the day, we stayed in the room and I stuck my nose in my book devouring every sentence of *The Wizard of Oz*. I was going to be Dorothy. But in my world, there were no flying monkeys, just scary men creeping down the hall.

The next day, my mother called her cousin Isabella who had just moved a few blocks away from our apartment on Stratford Avenue. She asked her if we could stay with her and she agreed for us to come. We took the train back to the neighborhood and I was so scared that Papi would see us walking to Isabella's house. Thankfully, it was a quick walk from the train station, so we made it without running into him. We stayed in Isabella's house for a few days and I was very disappointed to miss school. I had already finished my book so I decided to read it over again. Usually, I would be interested in eavesdropping on adult conversations. But with this book, I didn't care. They all disappeared as I entered the world of the stories I was reading. I was grateful that Rafy had my baby brother Freddy to play with so that they could leave me alone. I was able to escape into the pages of my book.

I loved Miss Keen. I wanted to go back home so that I could go back to school. There was a light at the end of the tunnel. On Tuesday night, my stepfather showed up at Isabella's house. He didn't look angry. He looked very remorseful as he cried in front of Isabella that he didn't want to lose his family. He begged my mother to forgive him. I sighed and felt relieved. There is no place like home. I didn't care that Papi would hit Mami. I wanted to go back home. It was in this turbulent moment that I transformed into a mind traveler like Dorothy and both physically and mentally escaped to the Land of Oz. I learned to be like the Tin man and function without a heart. The mind was going to take me places. I just had to remember my ruby slippers.

STAGE 11: THE TEEN CRUSADER

Chapter Seven

Interpreting Heart

When my brother Freddy was four years old, my mother wanted to enroll him in the Head Start program at the Bronx River Community Center. It was a preschool program for young children living in poverty with the goal of developing pre-literacy skills before they entered kindergarten. In turn, it gave them a jump start or a headstart when they entered elementary school. My mother didn't know how to speak, read, or write in English so she needed my help to fill out the registration paperwork. Like other times that my mother needed my help, I missed school so that I could go with her to register Freddy in the program. Mami had a copy of his birth certificate and his Social Security card. When I went with her to the office, I was surprised when I noticed that my little brother's last name was not Cabán. Freddy was born in 1976, the bicentennial year that our nation gained independence from England. Likewise, 1976 was the year that I was liberated from a family secret. I remember inquiring why both my brothers had a different last name than mine. Why was my last name Cabán and their last name Ferrer? She ignored my questions and kept telling me to ask the lady if there was anything she needed to bring to help register him. It was so frustrating. The whole walk back home,

I kept asking her. Suddenly, in the middle of the street, she stopped dead in her tracks, looked me square in the eye, and slapped me silly! I could still remember that sting today. My heart ached. I could hear myself breathing. The world was quiet. At that age, I was getting taller than my mother and I felt so tiny and insignificant at that instance.

She told me to stop asking questions and that when we got home she would explain. I cried the whole walk home. When we got home, my mother walked me to the bedroom, quickly closed the door, and sat me down on her bed as she looked straight down at me. Mami explained that the man I called Papi was not my Papi. –*Él es tu padrastro.*– He was my stepfather! Was that like a stepmother in Cinderella? Is that why he was so mean to me? It was a bewildering moment. My mind was spinning and I remember feeling dizzy.

She told me the story of how my biological father left her when she was pregnant with me. I remember crying angry tears. I felt so rejected. How could my real father leave me? I was so angry that I wasn't the same as my brothers. Suddenly it was blatantly obvious why sometimes I felt that the Ferrer family treated me differently than my brothers. I thought it was because I was the only girl. But now it was crystal clear. I was not a Ferrer. I was a Cabán. I was that forgettable little girl that didn't mean anything to my father. The theme of abandonment was like a shameful shadow that followed me. No matter how I tried to run away from it, abandonment dwelled in my heart. Throughout different points in my childhood, it manifested as a stubborn rage.

Was I a reminder of the love my mother had for my real father? The father that didn't love me enough to wait around to see me. The father that my mother had to harass and go to the radio station numerous times with her baby in her arms threatening to make a scene in the building lobby if he didn't *reconocer a su hija.*

Now that I think of it without fully realizing it, this was the myste-rious father that I heard one day on the radio when I was a little girl vis-iting my uncle Herminio. I didn't understand why Tío Herminio said –*Oye...Aye esta tu Pai.*– I was so confused. What was he talking about? It didn't sound like "Papi José" was talking. I knew that my stepfather loved to sing and in jest, he would talk like a radio personality, while he spoke into a hairbrush just like a sports announcer. But that day, the voice on the radio was not his. Why did my uncle say that? It was the moment when my world stopped being my own. The moment when I felt like the ground shook beneath me and I was not the same. The moment when there was a confluence of all the possible issues related to identity, belonging, rejections, and a hungry need for affirmation came to a head for this growing young adolescent eleven-year-old girl.

The next day she told my little brother Freddy that soon he was going to attend Head Start. My 4-year-old little brother refused to go. In a very matter-of-fact tone of voice, he said that he was not going because he already knew a lot of things. He said. –*Yo ya sé todo eso Mami . Yo sé mis números y mis colores.*– A few moments later, she nodded her head, and she agreed with him! She was not going to make him go to Head Start? How was that possible?

The rest of the weekend, I remember her discussing the issue with my stepfather in the kitchen over coffee, and I would look at him from afar with new eyes. I understood why he would look so angry with me when I tried to defend my mom in those moments of drunken rage. I was the stranger in the house. Not him. He belonged there with my brothers who had the same name as him. I felt like an outsider. It was decided that Freddy would not go to Head Start, so my mother made me go with her on Monday morning to tell the lady that Freddy was not going to attend because he was going to another school. She wanted me to lie to the lady in English. I was furious. I didn't want to lie. It didn't feel right.

My mother gave me that stern look and firmly said. –*Dirle que él no va a venir y yaaaaaa.*– That lie made me so angry. Why did my mother lie so damn much? Why couldn't she just tell the truth!!! This was one of my early moments helping my mom as a language interpreter. It was one of the many moments thereafter where I would be my mother's English voice. A voice behind the voice that held my truth. A voice behind the voice that shaped the lies. Were all lies bad or were they necessary to keep me safe?

CHAPTER EIGHT

INSIDIOUS INSIDER

My mother made a secret arrangement with her brother Tío Nolin who was a builder in Puerto Rico to build her a house on the family property in Toa Alta. The house would be built behind my maternal grandparents' house. Little by little when she could send the money, he would purchase the cement blocks and the cement to begin setting the foundation and build the house one section at a time. At the time, both of my grandparents were very elderly. Abuela had developed Alzheimer's and Mami wanted to come back to PR. Her goal was to come back alone with her children and not with my stepfather. She had a plan. She was going to build her refuge from the abuse she had endured and her brother was going to make that dream a reality.

My stepfather was working in Elizabeth, New Jersey in a book binding company. He would leave very early for his two-hour commute from the Bronx to take the New Jersey PATH train to Hoboken, New Jersey, and then go on a bus to Elizabeth, New Jersey. This extra-long commute gave my mother an idea. Since he left very early, maybe she could start secretly working when the kids were at school. In order to do this, she would need my help. She didn't trust a neighbor with this secret. She trusted me, her 12-year-old daughter. Mami was able to get a job in the same factory where she worked when she lived in Alphabet City.

At the time, I was in seventh grade at Junior High School 123. Both my brothers were going to elementary school. In the morning, after my stepfather left, Mami would cook the meat for the main dish, get the boys' clothes ready, and head out before we went to school. I was responsible for making sure the kids ate their breakfast, got the cooked meat off the stove, and wrapped it up so I could store it in the refrigerator. Finally, I would have to make sure that the boys were dressed and walk them to school. Rafy was in fourth grade, and my youngest brother was going to kindergarten. It was like herding cats. At times, getting them to listen to me was quite challenging.

This extra level of responsibility meant that I was always late for school. I figured if I ran to my junior high school, I could get there faster. This is when I first started running. I would wear my sneakers and strap my backpack around my waist. I didn't mind. The faster I ran, the quicker I got to school and escaped the misery at home.

Crack was the drug of choice in my poor neighborhood. I recall running over the plastic vials on the sidewalk. I would feel and hear the cracking sound beneath my sneakers. I would take control of my breathing by taking controlled long breaths through my nose and exhaling slowly through my mouth. My legs would take strong and long strides. I developed a good flow and rhythm. I felt so powerful in my newfound cadence.

My mother was growing strong too. She was getting smart about finally getting away. We were a team! I was going to keep her secret. As much as I wanted to tell my childhood best friend, Lisa, I was scared because her father Alfonso, and my stepfather were still drinking buddies at the corner bodega. I didn't want her to say something to her mom and have my stepfather find out. This would be catastrophic for my mom. I had seen him angry numerous times, but with a secret this big, I feared he would kill her. Since I would get out of school earlier than my brothers, I didn't have to stress about being late to pick them up. I would go and get them at the school courtyard as the teachers dismissed the students.

The cover story was that Mami was taking English classes at the local Bronx River Community Center. She told my stepfather that she wanted to learn English to try and see how the boys were doing in school. At first, he didn't understand why I couldn't help my brothers with their homework, but she mentioned that I was taking advanced classes and that it took me hours to do my homework. I had picked up some old English workbooks that my friend Liz had given me because her father was learning English too. She lived in the Bronx River Projects and she was a dear friend to me since 5th Grade. I just told her that my mother wanted to learn English, but she didn't have time to go to the classes. So she gave me the workbooks that her father used. I would erase some of the pages, and try to write some words in what seemed to be like my mother's handwriting.

Her writing was very basic. Since she had only gone to school up to 2nd grade, her manuscript was very disjointed and rudimentary. She was able to write phonetically by sounding out many words. Spanish is an easy language to phonetically spell with vowel sounds that are consistently written the same way. However, in English, it would prove to be very challenging for my mother.

I was worried that my stepfather was going to figure this out. I would practice over and over with some phrases that she supposedly learned in school. "The milk is in the refrigerator. The bread is on the table. Do you want butter? Do you want some coffee? How much is this? This is my pencil. This is my pen. This is my notebook. This is my bag. This is my teacher. This is my friend." It was a litany of senseless phrases that over time began to make sense to my mom. She said that when she would go on her work break, she would try to practice with the ladies that she worked with, none of whom spoke English. She admitted that in the morning on her way to work, she would look at it and it all looked like Chinese to her. After work, she was too tired to look at it and she would try to catch a few winks as she prepared to begin her second job–being our mother. She counted on me to take out the meat and begin to make the rice.

The first day that I was responsible for doing everything by myself, I was a nervous wreck. I couldn't remember how to cook the rice! I remember my mother saying that I had to cook two cups of rice and make sure that I used four cups of water. Just double it. Got it! That was all I remembered. She also reminded me to use the *tosino* (pork fatback) and cook it in the *caldero* (pot) before pouring in the water to boil. She told me to use a *cuchara* of salt, and dutifully I did this. After twenty minutes, I was surprised that the rice looked so fluffy and ready to eat. I didn't have a chance to taste it because I wanted to make sure the boys started their homework. This day, Mami raced in. Quickly she took off her work clothes, dove into her house dress (*la batita*), and combed her hair in her usual housewife bun. She warmed up the meat and made sure the boys would see that she had her English books in her hands. I whispered to Mami, how happy I was that she was learning English. She gave me those smiling eyes that spoke our secret mother-daughter language. –*Hija, Gracias por ayudarme. Te lo agradezco.*– Then 15 minutes later, I heard my stepfather tapping his key on the door. The boys ran and cheered "Papi!" I held my breath that they didn't say anything about Mami right in front of him. They were happy to see their father. How come they didn't greet Mami like that? Hmmm. It always made me feel jealous that they had a Papi that loved them. Where was mine? But I had my Mami.

That evening, he was not smiling with the boys and he looked tired. My mom started to serve us food and as we started to eat. Suddenly, my stepfather spat his rice out and yelled –*Conjoooooooo! Tu me esta tratando de matar!!! Este arroz tiene una pila de sal!*– My mother threw me a confused glance. She immediately stood to retrieve his plate. When he threw it at her, it flew past her shoulder, skimming her head, and dropping onto the floor. I was so scared that he discovered our secret. Oh my goodness! Did my brothers notice me cooking? No, they couldn't have, they were so busy watching cartoons in the living room. I was pretending to be on the kitchen phone with my friend Liz while I was cooking. They really didn't pay too much attention to stuff like that. Instead, it was the usual roughhousing and wrestling in the living room or jumping on the bed. There was no way they saw me.

I ran behind my mother to tell her sorry. She started to make a new pot of rice. She whispered to me as she asked about how I cooked the rice. I told her that I used a spoon of salt. She asked me to show her the spoon. I did. It was the usual spoon that I saw my mother use when she worked with the rice in the pot. It was the *cucharón*. Her eyes almost popped out of her head...She said. –*Mija eso no es la cuchara...eso es un cucharón. Aye Dios mío.*– We both chuckled quietly, and she hugged me as she shook her head. It was in these nail-biting moments that I learned I could be my mom's co-conspirator. The great accomplice.

CHAPTER NINE

DYNAMIC DEFENDER

One day I picked up my little brothers from school like I usually did and when I got home, I was shocked to see that my stepfather was home. He came home sick. *–Dónde está tu madre?* I reminded him that she was going to her English classes. He criticized her and commented that she was too dumb to learn English because, after so many months, she was not getting it. I prayed silently and asked God for a miracle. I tried to do everything that I normally did before my stepfather would come home. But today I was too scared to go into the kitchen. I didn't make the rice. I tried to stay in the living room close to the front door so that when she came in, I could warn her!

The wait for my mother to finally come home seemed like an eternity. As the minutes painfully ticked by on the living room clock, my heart would race. When I heard the keys in the lock, and my mother was opening the door, my stepfather beat me to it! He wasted no time with the barrage of questions, the accusations, and the slaps. She came home at 5:30 pm just like she did every day, but this time she didn't expect him home. She was just as shocked as me. I tried defending her. Holding his arm by placing all of my body weight on it, as I hung on it like a monkey on a branch. But it didn't work. I just got shoved and flew across the living room as I fell on my back. My poor mother got a tough beating that day.

My brothers were in the bedroom watching television and I remember getting so angry. Why didn't they help Mami the way I tried to protect her? He was accusing my mother of having another man. Why was she not home? What was she doing? Why did she have her hair done? Why did she have so much lipstick? My mother did all she could to shield her face with her hands and forearms, but it was useless. That day was so heartbreaking. At one point, she got up and made her way to the kitchen to cook. She begged him to stop so that she could start cooking. As she was cooking, I stood close by sitting at the kitchen table. If he came into the small kitchen, my plan was to block him and try to stop him with a pan. I was going to do something. I was tired of him hitting her. He settled down and went into the room, and continued to watch television with the boys. Mami was crying as she began making the rice and placed the meat on the stove to warm up.

When the food was ready, she started to get herself out of her house clothes. I felt that it was safe and that she was no longer in danger. I went to the living room to do my homework. Suddenly, I heard a struggle and when I looked down the hallway I saw my mom's feet sticking out of the hallway closet as she was kicking on the floor. Her voice was muffled and she was struggling to breathe.

When I ran down the hall, I saw my stepfather straddling his legs on top of her as he sat on her chest, choking her with both hands with a tight grip. Calling her a slut. I jumped on his back and started punching his face and trying to scratch his eyes out. I pulled his short greasy hair, and I went so far as to bite his face on his right cheek as I desperately reached over his shoulder. That is when he let go! He sprang up and picked me up by my throat and he threw my body across the hallway. My head hit the corner of the wall. I had a huge bump on the back of my head. My mother begged that he stop. That is when my little brothers came out and they started crying begging him to stop by screaming *"No Papi!"*

My mother was free from his stranglehold.

I didn't care that I had a bump on my head. I would do it again. I bit the motherfucker! He was not going to kill my mother.

I remember saying, "If you touch her again, I will kill you!" He walked up to me and slapped me in my face. I just stood there and didn't move with an angry burning defiant stare. I didn't cry. I didn't move. I hated him! I was ready to die for Mami.

For the first time in my life, I didn't see him as a scary monster. I saw him as a man with a bite on his face. I was the one that put that motherfucking mark there! He stopped because of me! I was going to show my mother how to defend herself. She didn't have to take that shit anymore. I was going to defend her against this injustice. It was during this heart-wrenching moment that I learned how to become a fighter. A defender coupling actions and words.

CHAPTER TEN

KEEPING SECRETS IN A VAULT

A few months later, my stepfather had a horrible debilitating accident at the bookbinding factory. Prior to this accident, he was in need of glasses, but he refused to wear them. I remember he always would read the newspaper so close to his face. My mom would tell him that he needed glasses. He would simply ignore her and not say a word. One day, my mom received a call from one of the other employees at the factory. He notified my mom that José hurt himself when he was walking around one of the automated machines. The impact was to the side of his head near his right eye. As a result, he had emergency surgery to try to save his eyesight. After two operations, trying to restore his full eyesight to no avail, my stepfather became legally blind. The unfortunate part was that for over 30 years, he gave blood, sweat, and tears to the Dow Jones Company. All he received was dinner and a gold watch for his 25th working anniversary. On his 30th work anniversary, after that work site accident, he received a pink slip.

They let him go. They denied José worker's compensation because he was the one who neglected to wear his glasses.

I remember watching him as he lay in bed listening to baseball games on the transistor radio. He looked like a broken soul. It was the first time I ever saw him cry. He was weak and helpless. I felt so guilty that initially I secretly wished he would die. Now he was here a shell of a man. How could I have wished for this? I was riddled with guilt and went to confess my sins to the Priest. After several rounds of Our Fathers and Hail Marys, I asked God to forgive me. But with a caveat. God had to make me stronger than my mother, and not let guilt make me forget all of the traumatic things he made my mom and I experience.

I asked God to forgive him and to change Him. Perhaps now that José was hurt, maybe he would stop hurting Mami. After that, I remember calling him Papi more. My mother would try to make him feel better by playing Spanish ballads and playing the Spanish radio. From time to time when he was not high from taking the heavy painkillers, he would sing along and then experience a bout of crying episodes wherein he apologized to my mother for everything he did. That was when she would sit on the side of his bed and stroke his hair and clean his face with a damp towel. Was my merciful God changing him?

The house felt peaceful. They were not arguing as much. He would sleep a lot and when he was becoming more active around the apartment, he would feel his way around. He would wear an eye patch and this made him look like a scary pirate as he didn't shave and looked like a disheveled man. Things at the time were extremely financially hard for us. My mother would go to the local butcher where my stepfather would cash his check, and she relied on store credit from the butcher. After a month of accruing a high balance, the butcher said that he couldn't extend any more store credit. My mother told my stepfather and said that the only way to try to make things better was for my mother to work as a seamstress or to go to the welfare office. Knowing that he was a very proud man, the option of working as a seamstress would certainly be the best option that he could tolerate.

My mother went back to the bra factory that she had secretly worked at. She got a job with the same supervisor who gave her another opportunity after she suddenly disappeared and didn't return after that short stint of secretly working. My stepfather's vision was never the same after that. The best part was that he couldn't see how much money my mom made. On Fridays, she didn't bring her check to the butcher to cash for her. Mami wised up. Instead, she would go to the cash-checking place around the corner and pay the small fee so that she could keep her finances secret. She would take about twenty percent of the check she made and place it aside in a secret account. My mother had a savings account at Apple Bank near Union Square a little further south of the garment district in Manhattan. She had opened the account when she had secretly worked in the bra factory. As I worked as her co-conspirator, she would show me the bankbook. The numbers grew slowly over time.

I asked her why my name was also typed inside the bankbook, and she explained to me that I was the beneficiary of the account. If something ever happened to her, when I was 18 I would be able to have access to the money. This surprised me. A year prior, she had sent Tío Nolin over two thousand dollars to begin building the house. She was so happy. But after my stepfather got hurt, the balance of the account became lower and lower. She had to dip into her savings account to try to bring home some food when the butcher stopped giving our family any more store credit.

My stepfather's eyes healed and he had no choice but to wear glasses to maneuver about. His brother-in-law managed to get him a job as a doorman in a midtown residential building. For the most part, he opened doors, greeted guests, polished the brass railing, and cleaned the glass doors of this luxury building. He was very charismatic in this new role. The tenants really liked him. During the holiday, they were very generous and gave him so many gifts and monetary tips. Things were starting to get better for the family.

In the spring of that year, my mother gave birth to my youngest brother Nelson. Regrettably, this meant that she was no longer able to secretly work again–not with an infant. She was a stay-at-home mom.

There were so many times I would catch my mom crying, and I would try to ask her why she was crying. She would just hug me and stroke my hair. What I didn't understand was that my mother felt trapped. Mami was like a caged bird. She was probably coping with postpartum depression. The implications of this surprise pregnancy were huge! Her dream to finish building the house seemed so far away. It was a distant fantasy. Mami told me that when Nelson could begin the Head Start Program, she could start secretly working again. I would need to help her. It felt like that day would never come. It was at this moment in my young adult life that I learned about the nature of finances. Sometimes the numbers do not add up. Economic power over household finances could change a woman's life!

Chapter Eleven

OVERCOMER: FIRE ESCAPES AND ROOFTOPS

I n my senior year of high school, I had fulfilled all of my high school requirements by December. However, I still had six more months to graduate high school in June. My high school counselor recommended that I participate in a cooperative program that involved taking business classes at my high school for one week. Then I could participate in a paid internship for a company in downtown Manhattan, where I would work every other week. It would be in the Accounts Receivable department at the Williams Company, a branding and marketing company that specialized in real estate marketing. My internship was doing data entry of the checks that would come into the Accounts Receivable department. It was a monotonous job and I had to be vigilant about accurately entering the check numbers and total amounts. A few times I was rushing, and they called me into the supervisor's office. As an intern, I learned quickly to make sure I double-checked everything before submitting any work.

It was the first highest-paying job that I had aside from my tutorial work at the community center (in my sophomore year of high school). I enjoyed working in Manhattan. I worked those 40-hour weeks twice a month and I felt that I was vacillating between two worlds—as a high schooler and as an adult professional grinding to make money. I worked hard to look the part. I borrowed some of my mother's clothes so that I could look more professional. It was mostly her skirts that she wore to church and I would roll them up and wear stockings. I would even use her high heels and her sweaters and blouses. Some of the clothes were from her skinnier days before having the babies. They were classic clothing in muted clothes so I was able to get away with it. I felt like a grown-up woman.

Before the famous J. Lo was riding on the 6 train, I was that brave Bronx girl from the block. Preparing to get off my next train stop, I would quickly make my way to the double exit doors. The quick blur of station posts would come into view, as the train slowly pulled into the Morrison-Soundview train station. Every time I got off the train, I made sure I stuck close to the crowd. As we shuffled to ascend the subway station steps to the street level below, there was safety in the flow.

On Fridays, the shuffle was quicker. As a dressed-up young lady looking quite pulled together, I had to brave the perverts going back home. Walking with a quick pace down Westchester Avenue under the elevated train station, I would spy the sun hiding behind the rooftops of the South Bronx tenements. This would require that I armor up emotionally and heighten my senses. I would get ready to survey the asphalt landscape before me. Walking to my building, I would pass by the *bodega*. It was two buildings away from the place I called home. I detested the *bodega* with the usual rat pack of men huddled in the back of the store, sitting on boxes and drinking away a week's worth of money. They were kicking back liquid courage to face their miserable lives. It usually dwelled in a can of Miller or Budweiser beer or sometimes it was in a bottle of Heineken chilling in the store refrigerator. Was he among them? He usually was, especially on a Friday night.

The street block where I lived was like a pinball machine of unpredictable ball traps where I dealt with the hissing and taunting catcalls of –*Oye, Mami iiii* and the lewd gestures of men jeering –*Mami tu estas buenaaaaa*. They wanted me to be like the pinball that frantically bounced back and forth in the eyes of these dirty men. Sometimes I would cross the street to avoid them. However, this evening I remained unmoved and indifferent. Passing right by them. This pinball evaded their dirty levers. My steadfast eyes steered away from their perverted stares. Then just like the frustrated blow of a pinball player hitting the side of the machine (desperately trying to get the ball stuck in the corner to react) the dirty old man says –*Mami si tu era un caldero de arroz, yo me como hasta el pegaooooooooooo*. I just kept my eyes ahead. My face grew more and more stoic and statuesque. I said to myself, –*Lo siento sucios*. No reaction here.

The voices faded away, as I set my eyes across the street. Taking stronger steps that dug my heels into the sidewalk, I grew tense and I did not waiver. Spying the usual crowd of suspects that loitered in front of the building, I nodded my head and said to myself, "I am almost home." Every bold and purposeful step brought me closer to my final destination.

Once I passed through the building entrance doors, the majority of the time, the elevator was out of service. This was a common sight and occurrence. So I made a beeline for the steps. I ascended four floors to my door before I took out my keys. I leaned my ear against the door and listened in. Hypervigilant as always. Yes, it was the usual background noise of the television blaring, and my three little brothers wrestling in the living room. But I didn't hear him. He was not home. I suspected my mom was preparing dinner. I thought I could smell it. The moment I opened the door, the fragrance of my Mami's cooking wrapped me up in a warm hello. I was temporarily happy. The peace that I experienced was always short-lived. It was always a matter of time before it would end, and *El Diablo* would tap ta-ta-ta-ta-ta on the door with his beer bottle. On Friday nights, sometimes that ritualistic tapping usually came after 10 o'clock. So I had time to relax and enjoy being home before every cell in my body would become tense again.

My beloved mother, stuck at home, was usually in the kitchen. I always loved my mother's scent as I hugged her and greeted her with a –*Bendición Mami* .– She always looked proud of me, as I would come in and sit by the stove at the small kitchen table. There was always a symphony of pots full of rice, beans, and some carne. Taking off my warrior attitude and hanging my book bag on the back of the kitchen chair, I would help her with the *ensalada*. As I would cut the lettuce and tomatoes, I would tell her about my day. I made sure to leave certain parts out, especially the *sucios'* words. Each day I saw her, my mom looked more and more tired.

Every strong step I took to walk home, I wished my mother would take, but in the other direction, away from my stepfather. Sometimes, her strength would miraculously reemerge in those moments after a tough altercation with my stepfather, where she would rebelliously whisper in my ear –*Hija, estudia y ve a la escuela para que ningún hombre pueda dominarte y humillarte.*– (Daughter, study and go to school so that no man can dominate and humiliate you.) Those empowering words prompted me to seek the power of a college education. So I applied to different colleges. To my surprise, I got accepted.

Perhaps if she continued her education, Mami could have gained access to more options. I recall my mother's shameful eyes, as she spoke of her regrets. This could have enabled her to get away and stay away from this painful situation. Was that really possible? My abuela and great-grandmother were battered women too. During my mother's upbringing in her small rural town in Puerto Rico, it was just a bad argument between husband and wife. No one would get involved. In my mother's case, being in an abusive relationship was what she knew. It was her normal. However, for this daughter, it was not the normal that I wanted. I am quite certain that for many of my apartment neighbors, it was the normal and usual sounds behind my apartment number D11. No one would call the police. In order to make that happen, I would take matters into my own hands. I had developed the

art of listening and observing to assess how bad our Fridays were going t
o be.

The moment he would come home, I could immediately sense his
mood. A slow shuffle down the apartment hallway, quickly told me
that he was too drunk to fight and he would soon fall asleep. A whistle
as he entered the apartment, meant that he was in a good mood and
that he didn't drink too much. He would probably watch the *Late
Show* and laugh as he saw *The Honeymooners* on our dilapidated television set. Now when I heard the tapping of the beer bottle on the door,
my heart would race. I knew that it was only a matter of time after he
ate, that he would start talking about the "somma-a bitches" at work.
Anything could set him off. I would try to keep my little *hermanitos* a
bit quieter in the living room and convince them to watch television
with me. As I sat on the living room sofa, I silently prayed and hoped
that my mother would pick up on these darn clues.

My heart begged as I thought, *Mami don't start asking questions.*
Don't start asking about the rent money because I knew all hell was
going to break loose. First, he would demand that my mom warm up
the food sitting in the pots, obediently waiting for him to come home.
If the food was too cold, it was a slap. If the rice was too salty, he
would toss it across the kitchen. The moment I heard the commotion,
I would frantically race to the bathroom and lock the door behind me.
Over the years, I learned not to get in the way and try to physically
defend my mother, because I would get the brunt of the kicks and slaps
as he called me a troublemaker and a *malcria.* So I learned to make a
mad dash to the bathroom.

El Diablo probably thought I was retreating and hiding. But oh,
how he was wrong. This daughter had a plan. I was going to leave
the apartment and it was NOT going to be through the front door. I
would turn the water on in the tub, and then face the silver accordion
window gate while taking a deep breath. It had a small Master key
padlock that was missing the key. My mother kept the key in the
bedroom side table which at this moment wasn't helping me at all.
However, I was a master at picking the lock open with a bobby hairpin.
Unfortunately, through the years I had developed so much practice,

that with my shaking hands I learned how to open it. Over time my hands stopped shaking. I was able to do it with my eyes closed. In those moments, as I picked away the pain, I prayed for God to protect me and to help me not get caught.

As I stepped up and straddled the edge of the bathtub and the top lid of the toilet, I would bring myself up to the window ledge. I would push my torso through the narrow bathroom window, as I held myself up with my arms desperately crawling to the other side onto the dark cold building fire escape. Standing four floors above ground level in the pitch-black darkness, I would quickly turn around, close the window, and pray no one would try to go to the bathroom as I made my temporary escape. Feeling my way up the stairs that were lit by the lights spilling out of the neighboring apartments, I climbed each floor and held on tight to the metal fire escape railings that were rough from rust and peeling layers of old paint. Sometimes my hands would get caught in the sharp edges of that peeling paint and I could feel my hands wet with blood. Always looking up. Always trying to control my breathing.

As I reached the top floor, it was the metal ladder steps that would bring me to the rooftop that always scared me. As my head slowly cleared the top of the ladder, I wondered if there was someone up on the roof shooting up heroin or smoking crack. Was I going to interrupt them? I hoped not. Were the guys from the block smoking pot up there? I hoped not. In either event, I would casually and quietly walk past them with racing steps toward the rooftop door. In those moments when I made it back inside the building, I felt safer but I could hear him yelling at her. Making my way down the marble building staircase, I could hear Mami crying once I quickly ran down past the fourth floor. Finally reaching the lobby, I would mentally regroup and calmly stride past the everyday characters in front of the building.

Without bringing too much attention to myself, and without skipping a beat, I would briskly walk to the corner of the block trying to spot the usual Friday night neighborhood cops walking the beat. They were always gathered by the pizza shop. There I would step up to them, and quietly make an appeal with my eyes. Not saying a word. The moment they would see me, they would ask "Is he at it again?" and I would simply nod. Mission accomplished. They would finish their conversation. I would quickly race back home to retrace my steps. I prayed that no one was near the rooftop door impeding my return. With each step back down toward the bathroom, my heart raced faster as I prayed that I could quickly and safely get back inside my apartment.

My stepfather, who was still in his rounds of slapping and hitting my mother, had no clue I was the reason for the police knocking on the door. I was the one interrupting his rounds of hate and drunken rage. Before he could notice I was in the bathroom too long, I would quietly slip by and get past the bedroom. Finally, I would make my way back into the living room. I would pray and count the minutes that I would hear the thunderous and rescuing knock on the door. *Please make it come soon, God!* Which it usually did, followed by the familiar series of questions. I would pray that the cops didn't betray me and say that I told them anything. As usual, my mother denied that there was a problem. Followed by the ceremonial escort of my stepfather "taking a walk." Why did my mother not say anything? Why was she keeping this horrible secret? Why did she always let him back in again? I was simply tired of this scene.

Ultimately, I chose to listen to my mother. Feeling frustrated, angry, hurt, and partially relieved, I decided that I definitely wanted to go to college. It was the toughest decision of my life. A part of me was trying to get back at my mother for not leaving. A part of me was so angry with her because I was the one who had to leave and not El Diablo. As her rescuer, I felt defeated. Even though I was strong, I longed for the moment that my mother would be stronger. As I think about this Bronx girl's actions, I feel that at that moment they were in vain. However, this is where I learned to strengthen my muscles as an advocate and become an overcomer.

CHAPTER TWELVE

SELF-ADVOCACY VS. SELF-PITY

In the fall of my senior year, my high school counselor advised me to apply to different colleges. I told him that I didn't have money for college. Maybe if I started working with the company that I did an internship with, I could possibly go to college in a few years. He encouraged me to apply to the different City University of New York (CUNY) and State University of New York (SUNY) colleges because he believed that I would qualify for federal aid and Tuition Assistance Program grants. My counselor helped me get the application fees waived so that I could apply to several colleges. I remember that I didn't want to go to college in the city. So I only applied to SUNY schools such as Cobleskill, Plattsburg, and New Paltz.

I dreamed of going away upstate to college, to a new calm space I could call home. Our Bronx apartment was so tiny and crowded. I simply don't know how we did it. There were four kids in our one-bedroom apartment. I didn't have my own room, and I slept on a sofa bed in the living room. Prior to that, I slept on a small cot that we stored in the hallway because our bedroom was full of three beds. There was a full-size bed for the adults and two twin beds for my little brothers. Meanwhile, for many years, I slept on a cot in the hallway near the bathroom and the bedroom. It felt like my own little room. It had two narrow long walls and immediate access to the bathroom and kitchen. I made the best of it. So when my mother purchased a full-sized sofa, I felt like a queen. When I was 12 years old, I got chickenpox. Out of necessity, my mother went to the local furniture store and got store credit to be able to bring the sofa home. She would pay twenty dollars a month so that I could have my own place to sleep. She didn't want my other little brothers to get chickenpox, so this was a way to contain it and quarantine me to the confines of the living room. I was like a pig in the mud sleeping alone on my full-size sofa be d.

As a senior, six months away from graduating, the thought of going to college away from the Bronx, away from my overcrowded apartment, away from the drugs and the shootouts, and away from the hopeless situation with my mom and my stepfather seemed like an eternity away. When the time would come, I would finally be able to have some much-needed peace in my life.

Even though I loved my little brothers, they were so annoying. When they weren't trying to do their WWF wrestling moves on each other or all ganging up on their big sister, they followed me everywhere I went. Many times they lingered to see if I was doing what I was supposed to be doing. If I was on the phone too long, they would tell me to stop talking so much. If I was at my friend Lisa's house on the fifth floor, they would come knocking on her door to get me and insist that my mom sent for me. Many times it was a lie because they just wanted their big sister home. They loved me and at the time I was so caught up in my teenage head with my teenage drama, that being around them was a nuisance.

I was just trying to seek refuge away from the hurt. I would spend a lot of time at my friend Lisa's apartment number E1 or my other friend Daisy's apartment on the 6th floor in the same building. If I wasn't with them, then I was practicing with the Golden Charms Drum Corp

Color Guard as we rehearsed for the next parade or exhibition. Music and exercise were my escape. I knew at that young age that I needed serenity because at times I felt like I was going crazy. Soon I would have the chance to have my own small bed in a dorm room where I only had to tolerate one roommate. It seemed so workable. Sharing a room with a stranger would be better than sharing a room with my whole family. I wanted to be on my own. I noticed that the only way that the girls I knew around the block got to leave their homes was if they got pregnant and were disowned and kicked out by their parents. The other and rarer situation was that they had gotten married and left their house to live in their own apartment with a dead-end job. I didn't want that. I wanted to work on my future. I didn't need a man to do this.

On different occasions during my junior and senior years, I used to stay over at my friend Ivonne's house on the weekends. This was a big deal for my mom. She only let me sleep over at my cousin Letty's house or with my aunt Lola in Bridgeport, Connecticut. The fact that she let me stay with my high school friend meant that she trusted my friend's family a lot. She liked Ivonne. Mami thought she was a hard-working dedicated student (which she was) but Mom didn't know that she had a boyfriend. Had she known, I would not have been able to stay over her house. Ivonne shared a room with her sister María, but since her sister was in college, she was lucky to have it all to herself. I loved going to her house. There was so much room and she didn't have a bunch of little brothers pestering her and following her every move.

One weekend in the early fall, my friend Ivonne invited me to see her older sister María attending college at SUNY New Paltz. I told my mom I was going to Ivonne's house, but instead, we caught an Adirondack Trailways Bus to New Paltz, New York. We were going there on a Saturday and coming back early Sunday evening. It was close to a two-hour trip from the Port Authority Bus Terminal in New York City to the New Paltz bus station. It was the first time that I had ever gone that far by myself away from "the block." I had gone on day trips to Bear Mountain Park with the church and traveled to do different color guard and cheerleading exhibitions with the Golden Charms, but they were always chaperoned by church members or the Drum Corp adult leaders.

This weekend, Ivy and I were traveling solo like a bunch of college students. It was so liberating. We stayed in her sister's dorm room in Bliss Hall. At the time, it was the only female residence hall on campus. I remember calling my mom from a payphone down the hallway on the first floor. At the time there were no caller ID capabilities on the phone, so she couldn't tell that I was calling her from close to a hundred miles away. That was quite bold, daring, sneaky, and so dishonest. I was rebelling so much. Thankfully, my time in New Paltz was a calm weekend with her sister who was a senior in college. She was a very studious college student who took her learning quite seriously. Ivy's sister was trying to encourage her sister to follow in her footsteps. Regrettably, Ivy was not interested because she was in love with a high school senior named Paul, and she wanted them to get married and live together. She didn't have any plans to go to college. I thought Ivy was nuts. There was no way in hell I was getting married. I was not going to get stuck with a man. College was my way out. I was grateful to experience a taste of what college life upstate had to offer.

When I told my mother I was applying to different colleges, she insisted that I only apply to colleges in the city. She would say –*Una señorita no se va de la casa hasta que se case.*– I had to wait to get married to leave my home? Oh my goodness, this couldn't be! So I did what I had to do to keep my secret and not fill out any forms for the CUNY colleges. My mother couldn't read the applications and I was confident I would not get caught. My stepfather was legally blind and he would have difficulty reading the fine print, so I was safe from his prying eyes. However, my brothers could rat me out if they got a hold of the forms. So I carried them with me in my book bag everywhere I went. I was always carrying my backpack. It was my companion. Then I started getting acceptance letters from all of the colleges that I applied for. I was so relieved when I received the acceptance letter from SUNY New Paltz. I was going to attend the same college as my friend's sister. I did it!

Now the moment came that I had to figure out how I was going to pay for college. I knew that my counselor said I could qualify for financial aid, but I didn't know how to fill out the financial aid applications. Thankfully, Mr. Vega was very helpful and he sent me home with the application so that my mother could sign it. There was no way that I was going to give her that form. *What if she refused to sign it? What if she noticed it was not in the city?* I couldn't take the chance. I knew she wasn't going to go for it. So I did what I had to do. I had my mother sign the form thinking it was information for the city colleges. I remember taking out her social security card and telling her that I needed to get a copy of it to submit it with the application for the city colleges. Hoping she didn't ask me too many questions, I was relieved that she didn't.

It was at this scary moment that I learned how to take extra measures to advocate for myself. It was official. I was a college student. Due to the financial challenges at home with my stepfather working as a doorman making very little money, he insisted that my mother stop working as a seamstress. He was the man of the house and he was going to provide. Having that low income helped me qualify for federal financial aid and a state grant from the Tuition Assistance Program. Moreover, I was accepted to the college as a part of the Educational Opportunity Program (EOP) which was a program designed to help economically disadvantaged students who also faced academic challenges. It was an academic program that would help capable students who did not have the financial resources and academic preparation to realize their academic potential. Attending one of the worst high schools in the Bronx qualified me for this program. Dealing with such poverty in the South Bronx made me a strong candidate.

Instead of starting college like the general admission students, I had to start in early July to take four weeks of remedial courses before officially starting the fall semester. I was terrified to tell my mother that I got accepted. How was I going to break the news that I was leaving home? Could I actually do it? My plan was to sit her down a week before I was scheduled to arrive at the EOP orientation program. I showed her the acceptance letter and lied to her saying that none of the city colleges accepted me. I never applied so how could I get accepted? I left that key detail out of my explanation.

Instead, I began to tell her more about the college. I mentioned that it was only a bus ride away. It was 75 miles away from my Bronx home. I explained to her that Ivonne's sister María was a student there and then my mother's face changed. She seemed relaxed and more accepting of this news. At that moment I cried tears of happiness and told her that I wanted her to come with me to see the college.

The next day we took a day trip with my little brother Nelson who was five years old. We took the long bus ride together. I remember that my mother packed us a few sandwiches. I carried them in my backpack along with some snacks for my little brother. We talked the whole ride and for the first time, I felt that the distance made my mother feel free. I was free again just like how I felt the first time I snuck away to New Paltz with my friend Ivy. My beloved mother kept mentioning how beautiful the trees looked. I remembered that on a few occasions, our church had organized a few bus trips to Bear Mountain Park. I reminded Mom that Bear Mt. Park wasn't too far from New Paltz. Again I lied because it was actually about 40 miles away, but I didn't want her to worry that I was too far from home. I was wrapping my reality in comforting blankets of white lies and stretched truths so that I could get away. I knew what I needed. I was being resourceful. Instead of always helping my mother, I was going to start helping myself. My mind was starving for a new place to grow. It was a risky move, but necessary. Without her knowledge, she had co-signed my release papers as the key to my new life and my new world away from the Bronx.

STAGE III : THE COLLEGE ACTIVIST

CHAPTER THIRTEEN

BURNING DESIRE

The first few days in my new college home were mixed with feelings of wonder, bewilderment, homesickness, and culture shock. I missed Mami's cooking. The foods served at the food hall were nothing I had ever experienced such as chicken cordon bleu, lasagna, pasta, and wild rice. This was unbearable! I had to cook to remain sane. I managed to get my hands on a few cooking utensils and a small bottle of Goya Adobo to try and cook some meals. It helped me remember home. Unfortunately, I couldn't afford the expensive bus tickets back home, so I had to make do with what I had. I would walk into town about two miles away from the dorm so that I could go to the local supermarket and I could buy a few items.

It was a bit scary walking through a town that didn't look at all like anything I was used to back in the Bronx. I had never seen so many white faces before. Back home, I was used to the racial landscape changing on the train as it went past 96th Street into midtown Manhattan. But here I was truly the minority. Every time I saw a brown face, I wondered if that person was Puerto Rican like me. The best part about being at New Paltz was that a few of my high school friends also attended the college. Sonia and Mary were very good friends, but we were not roommates. We all lived in Bliss Hall on different floors.

I wished that I had them as roommates. Instead, I had an Italian roommate named Danielle who was an avid soccer player, and she wasn't friendly at all. She seemed very snobbish and her parents had set her up with every possible amenity you could imagine she could ever need in a dorm room. Based on what she had on her side of the room, I imagined that her family was very well off. Meanwhile, I did not have matching curtains with a comforter set, refrigerator, microwave, stereo system, or word processor. I had sad-looking mismatched sheets and pillowcases with a few old frayed towels that my mother was able to spare from the house. Along with a few hangers of clothes and a dresser with empty drawers.

I was embarrassed that my side of the room looked so poor. But honestly, what other choice did I have? I couldn't start working because I was taking twelve credits and a math remedial course. I just would not have any time. So I made the best of it, and I waited for my financial aid refund check that would come by mid-semester. When it did, the first thing I bought was a nice comforter set with a matching pillowcase.

I was so happy. It was the first bed that I had in which I didn't need to fold up and put away. It was mine. It wasn't a rusty cot that had to fold up and hide in the corner of the only bedroom in our small apartment. This bed was all mine and I loved to sit on it and read. Sometimes it was impossible to do that every time she had her rock music playing. I would just try to tune her out and show her that her rude behavior was not phasing me. Didn't she know who I had to deal with for the past sixteen years? She was going to be a piece of cake. A nonissue.

By mid-September, I was going through an identity crisis. What I didn't realize was that I truly was not alone. There were other students like myself who missed home and we were gravitating towards each other in the hopes of replicating the cultural nucleus that made their spirits feel centered. Tied together with our love of House Music with hits by TKA, Lisa Lisa and the Cult Jam, and of course Frankie Knuckles. I wanted to be a "Diamond Girl" stuck in this faraway place.

One day I was going to the dorm after class to pick up my friend Mary. We had different class schedules, but we always checked in for dinner at the Hasbrouck Dining Hall. This was before cell phones and text messages. I had to actually go and physically find a person to talk to them. If they were not in their room, you left a note on paper or on a dry-erase board on their door to alert them you were looking for them. Going to the dining hall was all the way across campus, and it seemed like it was a universe away from our residence hall.

Mary introduced me to her roommate Rae Torres. I was delighted that Rae was Puerto Rican too! She was a petite, vivacious Latina powerhouse and I admired how eloquently she spoke. In fact, she was a spitfire! Everything that came out of that young woman's mouth was spirit-filled with conviction and strength. I wanted to be just like her. I wanted to talk like that smart *Boricua*. After spending a few days sharing meals and talking about our lives, Rae mentioned that there was an organization called La Fuerza Estudiantil Latina that she was interested in joining. Her father was a professor and a former activist and she was fortunate to have his guidance as she attended New Paltz. I remember longing to have a similar relationship with my real father. She mentioned that her father was remarried and that she had half brothers and a sister.

It made me want to know more about my real father. But emotionally I just couldn't go there and be disappointed. I realized that I couldn't change that. But I could change who I was. Even though I viewed myself as a brave and bold young lady, I wanted to be wiser and stronger. This young warrior named Rae was going to play an instrumental role in establishing my new self. I was going to join her. Even though I didn't have a clue about being a member of a political social college organization, I was going to do my best to learn.

As it turned out, the president of La Fuerza Estudiantil Latina was a junior and her name was Liza Lopez. She was a fellow Educational Opportunity Program student and a political science major. I was quite impressed that she wanted to become a lawyer. I had never met anyone like her. Liza and Rae had very similar traits. I remember just staring at them in awe as they spoke to the organizational members about a conference that they were planning in the spring. Liza mentioned that she needed two vacant cabinet positions to be filled. She needed a Vice President and a Minister of Education. Rae raised her hand and shared her interest in the VP position. While she sat next to me, she took my hand and raised it up, nominating me as the person who would be interested in the Minister of Education position. "Did you know that Vilma wants to be a teacher?" The only word I recognized in that whole exchange was the word education. I had no idea what the position entailed, but I certainly was not going to admit it in front of so many people! So I humbly nodded and mustered the courage to say I was interested. They all voted and next thing I knew Rae was Vice President, and I was the new Minister of Educational Affairs for La Fuerza Estudiantil Latina.

As a part of my work, Rae and I had to look through the organization's archives to catch up on the history of the organization. We sorted through former conference flyers, minutes, financial budget reports, article clippings from the college newspaper *The Oracle*, and conference agendas and logistics from former conferences. They had a publication *Hermanos Unidos* that featured articles about former organizational events.

Rae called her father and shared the good news that we had joined the organization. He mentioned that he was fascinated that La Fuerza Estudiantil Latina's organizational structure was modeled after the Young Lords' organizational structure with different positions like the Minister of Political Affairs, Minister of Cultural Affairs, Minister of Financial Affairs, and Minister of Educational Affairs.

I feared that I was in over my head, but I was going to brave through it. In retrospect, it astounds me to imagine how two young 18-year-old women were able to get on track so quickly after graduating high school. Oh my goodness, we had to coordinate such an aspirational lofty goal. A few months later, we were sitting at the registration table in the Student Union Building getting students to sign up for the conference and firming up last-minute details for our speakers.

One of our conference speakers was the renowned Pedro Pietri who was a Puerto Rican poet. He was one of the founding members of the famous Nuyorican Poets Café (NPC) in the Lower East Side of Manhattan. The place where I was first raised as an infant was literally three blocks away from the NPC. This was the first time I had ever heard of a Puerto Rican man writing and publishing poetry. I remember Pietri reading poems from his book *Puerto Rican Obituary*. They were very controversial, to say the least. In the 1970s he was an active member of the Young Lords Party. His poetry offered a voice for Nuyoricans that dealt with poverty and poor living conditions. In one of his poems, he must have said the word fuck over 10 times. Many people were taken aback and admittedly shocked by the language (how ironic that three decades later, that same book became a gift from a loved one). But at that moment I met the voice that sparked permission in my spirit to wake up the scared little girl in my 18-year-old frame. In retrospect, what a great honor it was to be face-to-face with that poet, greeting him as he prepared to present at our conference.

It was at that moment, that my world from the Bronx came over and reached for me in that faraway place called New Paltz, New York. Seventy-five miles away from the living conditions that he spoke of, I felt that I could truly identify with everything he said. I was so impressed that he said yes to us when we asked him to come. This was a historic moment indeed! My creator in heaven was aligning stars and shaping pathways to lead me in the direction of literary inspiration and political awareness. A seed for activism was planted. I was so caught up trying to survive in the Bronx that talking about politics or my rights as a Puerto Rican was never on my radar. It was like a fog was lifted, and I was able to think clearly and begin seeking answers to many questions that I had about my being and my innermost fears. I was searching for who I was and what I wanted to become.

The following year La Fuerza Estudiantil Latina morphed into the Latin American Student Union to mirror the work of the Black Student Union. I resented that we changed the name of our organization to an English name. We should have stayed with our original Spanish name. But the politics on the campus were changing and it was important to begin creating language bridges to have our work be more public on campus. The original name of the student organization was in Spanish, and if you didn't speak Spanish you would not understand what the letters F.E.L. represented. Rae continued to work closely with Liza and transitioned to carrying the baton as the LASU president as Liza prepared to do an internship at SUNY Albany. I remember traveling with Rae and Liza to a LASU conference at the SUNY Albany campus. This is when I realized that the work we did in New Paltz was a part of larger organizational work across different campuses.

It was so inspirational and humbling to be around so many change agents who were on fire for raising socio-political awareness. My curiosity about Puerto Rico was heightened. Rae was very helpful in telling me more about my history. Her father was an activist during the 1960s. She was a history major because she wanted to be a history teacher. So I was in the right place at the right time to get more in touch with myself and my history. I was going to learn more about HER-STORY. I learned about the history of Puerto Rican advocates who were brazen to wave the Puerto Rican flag from the Statue of Liberty and about the Young Lords in the 1970s who were starting to fade with the political changes in the late 1980s.

It was the first time I learned about social protests outside of the civil rights work that I learned in elementary school. The theme of "we shall overcome" didn't seem to apply to the Latino diaspora. While taking the Black Studies course, I felt frustrated that I wasn't learning about my island's history and about the key political figures who were trying to make changes on the island. It was a topic that was not on the table.

I felt it was important that we had to work to learn more about Puerto Rico and my people's history. I was clueless. I learned about what a Taino was. It was when I learned that I come from a mixture of Spaniards, African slaves, and Taino indigenous Indians. I was enthralled with learning more about this. But now that LASU worked broader on its mission to support Latin American students, Puerto Rican students had to share the agenda with students from the Dominican Republic, Colombia, and other Latin American countries.

Ultimately, the LASU work was about Latino pride, and the work had to continue. Consequently, I remained active with this organization. It was in these early college years that helped me begin the process of learning how to collaborate well with others. This was a crucial skill for a future advocate.

Chapter Fourteen

RALLY CRY

By the beginning of my sophomore year, the Latin American Student Union began to branch out. Some of the Latinas in the organization were interested in breaking off and propagating a new plant of social awareness on our campus. They came up with the concept of creating a Latina organization. I joined them and I had the great honor of becoming one of the founding members of Latinas Unidas. It was a college organization that was centered on Latina empowerment and raising awareness about issues that related to our identity as women and the obstacles we faced in regard to domestic violence and machismo.

I remember getting very emotional after one of our meetings, and that is when I confessed to Rae about my home life living with a batterer and how my poor mother was still coping with this. It had changed a bit now that things had changed for my stepfather in terms of his vision and health. He was drinking less and my mom would describe him as *mas tranquilo*. But nonetheless, I worried. I knew that now that my brothers were getting older, they would probably be more defensive and protective of my mother. She was suffering from high blood pressure and they were very loving and more attentive with her. My mother mentioned in a letter that they would help her out more around the house. Rae would try to calm me down and tell me to focus on creating something that was going to help things change for our future with our upcoming spring's first annual Latinas Unidas Conference. It was a wonderful distraction.

Our Latinas Unidas organization was growing. I was working with a larger group of talented and inspirational Latinas like Lu and Jo who were developing beautiful friendships with Rae. They offered such great ideas and our think tank sessions were powerful. They shared our fun-loving sense of humor, our silliness, and our get-back-to-work drive. They were also very well-spoken and kind women. I had never been around so many smart and considerate beings. I remember missing them terribly during the holiday breaks when I would go back to the Bronx. I realized that my circle of friends back home didn't seem interested in politics, much less in the details of the conferences back in New Paltz. My neighborhood friends were thrilled to see me back on the block. We would hang out together and go window shopping at Southern Boulevard, or go to Conways with the little money that we had and try to buy a shirt or two. We would do each other's hair and simply enjoy hanging out and listening to music at each other's houses. But the tenor of our conversations didn't touch upon the ideas that my heart yearned to talk more about. I was sensing that my relationship with my childhood friends Lisa and Daisy was growing distant and that hurt so much. It was my fault. Why did I have to go away to college and be the one to change? Maybe if I tried to change them, and help them see more about where I was, they would want to go to college with me. They simply were not interested and I accepted this.

Just like my mother who refused to have things change by leaving my stepfather, these friends were not going to change either. It was a pattern that I saw everywhere. Similar to my friend Ivy, my friend Lisa was in love and she wanted to marry her boyfriend Tony. Daisy was very close to her mom Rita, and she wasn't interested in leaving home. She admitted that when her cousin Jackie went away to college, her cousin proclaimed that it was so hard and lonely being away from home. I sensed that Daisy was not going to venture out and take such a scary risk. It was understandable. I had more of a reason to leave. I was trying to get away from the violence I saw at home. But now that things were calming down, what was my excuse? Maybe things could change.

I could come back home to the Bronx and attend a City University of New York college. I was so conflicted.

The Latinas Unidas in New Paltz became my new sisterhood. I simply couldn't wait to come back and have our upcoming spring conference. Working hard as a college activist and student kept me busy. However, I wasn't busy enough to run away from what I had left behind. There were a lot of painful memories and trauma that I had pushed down deep. Life back on campus was an escape. I was socially thriving. Maybe a little too much. In fact, I was entering quite a rebellious season drinking almost every day from Wednesday to Saturday. I would join a group of friends walking over to the local bars in town and frequent the P&G's sports bar on Wednesdays, the Thesis Bar on Thursdays, Joe's dancing bar on Fridays, and a party on or off campus on Saturdays. Sometimes we would have some wild escapades into the city and go to different clubs and crash at a friend's house in the city. The Limelight, Copacabana, Latin Quarters, and Studio 54 were calling our names! Party On! All of our crazy shenanigans were starting to spin out of control. By the end of the fall semester, I got worried because my cumulative average dipped.

I was trying to escape the pain. I was very angry with my mother. In retrospect, I may have been feeling resentful that I didn't have a mother figure to guide me. The highest grade that my mother attended was second grade. She truly didn't have a true sense of what I was experiencing as a college student. I understand now that my mother couldn't give me what she didn't have. But at this age, I was in a state of frustration and pent-up anger. Drinking was my way of coping. I never had the opportunity to process and heal from everything I had experienced. Never attending any counseling or therapy sessions, my pain was like a huge bullet that was ricocheting rapidly in my spirit. I was slowly becoming unhinged, and I was self-medicating to find a way to cope with the hurt.

To make matters worse, I received the news that my favorite uncle Herminio Cores had passed away and nobody in my family wanted to tell me because I was in school. I missed his funeral! How was this possible? What was wrong with my family? Who behaves like that?

They did not know how to behave like normal people and share what was happening. Why was everything a secret for my mother? I was sick of it.

My Educational Opportunity Program counselor Vernon Jones was very concerned. He had a serious talk with me. Mr. Jones reminded me why I decided to come to college so far away. I had confided in him by sharing what I dealt with at home. He said if you get kicked out of school, you will be back there with your stepfather or worse trapped in a relationship trying to get away from your life there. That sobered me up!

I tapered it down and dialed it back to partying only Thursdays through Saturdays. Recovering from my hangovers on Sunday and Monday. I don't know how I kept my grades decent considering how much time I wasted socializing. But I did somehow. Having a strong photographic memory was a tremendous help. Once I read my assigned pages a few times, and wrote down some notes, I was able to mentally recall facts with great ease. This was my saving grace. My friend Mary was concerned. She reminded me that I had to stay focused. She didn't drink and she was a very committed student. Mary would remind me to study for my tests and to finish our writing course papers that I totally dreaded.

As our coursework was getting more intense, I needed to regroup. The drive that I found in organizing myself to rally and support LASU and Latinas Unidas, I channeled to focus more on my studies. The thought of failing and going back to the Bronx terrified me. My friends Rae, Mary, and I locked arms and became each other's accountability partners making sure we created study groups in the student lounge. There were many nights we crammed for tests and writing papers. We were on a mission and even though I dated a few people, I would quickly break up with them the minute I sensed that I was getting distracted, or worse...that they wanted sex. I was still a virgin and I was not going to let a man pull me away from my dreams. I was going to stay on track and keep my eyes on the prize.

The following 1989 spring semester, I took a Women's Studies course. Oh my goodness! How it broadened my perspective on women's issues! I was able to identify with issues related to women's bodies that I was never able to discuss with my conservative Catholic mother. These delicate sexual topics were simply not discussed in my home. Many of the themes shared in the course helped me become more self-aware about what I wanted as a woman. For the first time, I saw myself as a woman...a young woman with a huge future. It was up to me not to waste the great potential that was ahead of me.

Latinas Unidas had one of the highest-attended Latino conferences in SUNY New Paltz history. Aside from the LASU conferences and FEL conferences, we were focused entirely on Latina women's issues, which was historic. My friend Rae's stepmother Vivian did a phenomenal job presenting about domestic violence and women's health. Rae had invited Vivian and a few other professional women from her network. They presented a few other topics centered on women's rights. It became a mentorship exchange of seasoned professionals reaching out to support this young cohort of college Latinas. We were making strides in changing the socio-political landscape on our campus. We were a larger network of Latinas who collaborated so well.

I remember meeting Jo and not only was she very bright, but she was a prayer warrior. She was instrumental in organizing some of the sessions. Jo openly spoke about her faith and I admired that so much. I still remember the gorgeous gigantic stage centerpiece balloon arc that we all created with the purple and white balloons. It transformed that reception hall. I had never seen anything like that in my life. This conference was huge. Purple was the perfect color because it represents royalty. We created this Latina kingdom. Stitching the pieces of our Latina hurts and lives together. Stitching together our hopes for a better kingdom of future promises. I felt honored to be a part of this dynamic circle of Latinas creating such a powerful space for learning.

The Latina voice was loud and fierce! Rae wrote an article in the college newspaper about the perils of Greek Life for Latinos on campus. I was so proud to read that article. It was the first time in my life that I read something published written by someone I knew so well. I was extremely proud of her. It was a very controversial topic because so many of the Latino friends we had were actively seeking to pledge for sororities or fraternities. I was never interested in pledging. It didn't make any sense to choose to be controlled, hazed, ridiculed, and part of this organization that said you were a Greek brother or sister, but they treated you horribly in the initiation process. It simply was not for me. I was a GDI, a God Damn Independent. It reminded me too much about the way my stepfather humiliated my mother. This strong Latina was not going to fall into that trap!

I was thrilled to be a part of the first annual Latinas Unidas Conference. I was proud as a Latina, as a woman, as a college student, and as an EOP student. Latinas Unidas received a lot of positive feedback from the conference participants, the community, and the Educational Opportunity Program. In fact, many EOP students were active in our organization along with the Latin American Student Union. The director of the program Tom Morales communicated how happy he was with our efforts. We left a footprint and blazed a new Latina trail.

It was an exciting time for me as a sophomore in college. I didn't want to go back to the Bronx in the summer. So instead I signed up as an EOP peer counselor and residence hall assistant. I was going to work with the new generation of EOP students. With this summer job, I was going to have my own room! I couldn't believe it. Finally, after almost 20 years, I was going to have my own room! It may have seemed like such a small thing, but for me, it represented my independence as a woman...as a powerful Latina. I chose to attend both summer sessions and I earned 12 college credits. I was making my own way and I was making up for lost time when I was a bit unfocused. It was in these social awareness moments that the heart of this advocate learned she had a passionate spirit yearning to be free. I wanted to empower others to stand free in their Latino identity.

Chapter Fifteen

LINGUIST

Learning a new language, other than Spanish, seemed so intriguing to me. When I was a freshman at SUNY New Paltz, I signed up for Italian courses for the first three semesters of my undergraduate studies. Professor Urbino was my Italian professor for all three courses. He believed in immersing his students in Italian. This meant he did not speak a word of English throughout the whole class. I remember many times trying to speak in Spanish, and he would say very firmly. "Signorina Cabán...questo non è un corso di spagnolo. Questo è un corso di Italiano!" With that, I would straighten up and push hard to not utter a Spanish word. His face was stern, but his eyes were so kind. He was a short Italian man who always wore a suit to class. Professor Urbino took his work seriously and he was a true professional. He created a learning space where we felt comfortable taking risks. In fact, he would give us conversation exercises where we would partner up and pose a question to our partners, and in turn, they would respond using some basic vocabulary that we had learned in the previous lesson. It was very engaging and quite interactive. I loved going to my Italian classes.

At the end of the second semester, he mentioned that there was a study abroad program in Urbino, Italy. I thought this was such an amazing opportunity. My financial aid would cover my tuition and fees, but it would not cover travel and the incidental costs of studying abroad. It seemed like such a faraway place. Perhaps it was too far. So I filed away that dream in the recesses of my heart and mind. I prayed that one day when I got older, I would have the great opportunity to visit different parts of Italy like Venice, Florence, and Rome.

In the meantime, I took my final Italian class with the same enthusiasm and fervor that I did when I first took the class. I had taken a French class in high school and spoke Spanish. Now with a second Latin-based language, I was able to deepen my understanding of the Spanish language. I knew that if I wanted to be a world traveler one day I would need to have a few languages under my belt. Ever since I was a child watching television and the Feed the Children campaigns, my dream was to travel to Africa and help feed needy children. In order to do that, I would need to be more comfortable learning different languages. As the girl from the Bronx, I had never left the block other than taking the train to my senior job at Williams. I wanted to leave the borders of my small little world in the city. I wanted to break the code for another language and break apart from my world in the Bronx.

It was Professor Urbino who mentioned that the United Nations hires language interpreters and knowing several languages could open that door. It was the first time I had heard of the place called the United Nations. This was before the time of the Internet, Google queries, and the World Wide Web. I went to the Sojourner Truth Library on campus and looked it up in the Britannica Encyclopedia. I found the history of the United Nations quite interesting. The notion of so many nations working towards world peace seemed so hopeful.

In my first year of college, I declared my major early. I knew that I wanted to be a teacher. But maybe one day, I could help children who couldn't go to school and build brand new schools around the world. I found Africa to be an exciting part of the world. In my Black Studies courses, I learned how so much of the history I learned was so Eurocentric and there was a world to explore within the African Diaspora. For the first time, the word African didn't seem like a destitute place, but it was a place full of history and strength. Black pride was something I witnessed among the Black fraternities and sororities on campus. I longed for that strong identity within my Puerto Rican roots. Regrettably, there wasn't a Puerto Rican Studies Department on campus. I had a shift in my own thinking when I felt that it was important to make remarkable accomplishments and be one of the first Puerto Rican women to do it. Learning languages was my way to becoming a global *Puertorriqueña*. Maybe after I become a teacher, I could work with the United Nations and be a language interpreter, or travel around the world to teach English. It was the first time that the global seed of change was planted in my heart. Unbeknownst to me, it was a seed that was slowly germinating. Over time, I would revisit this global dream later on in my life.

Sign language was a language that kept following me. After I had learned sign language from Ivonne and her sister, I didn't want to forget what I had learned. As a living language, you must use it or you most definitely will lose it. I was thrilled to see that American Sign Language 101 was available to fulfill the language requirement. So in my sophomore year, I gladly signed up. I was pushing the bar, but it was worth it. I had a heavier courseload doing my liberal arts courses, Italian, as well as American Sign Language. I was learning two new languages, Italian and American Sign Language, but I had such a n affinity for languages. It was not challenging at all. Sign language was activating another part of my brain that was not auditory. It was such a strong visual form of learning. Considering that I had such strong visual memory, I was able to observe and remember the litany of signs that the professor modeled for us. Every time he would ask for a volunteer, I would quickly raise my hand without any hesitation.

As an overzealous student, I remember asking the professor where I could go to learn more sign language after class. Earlier in the semester, he invited the class to attend several cultural events for a deaf association in Poughkeepsie. It was the Mid-Hudson Valley Club of the Deaf. Poughkeepsie was across the Hudson River and it was over a 45-minute drive to get there. At the time, I didn't have a car so I couldn't attend unless someone else was going to Poughkeepsie. The Poughkeepsie Mall was a popular venue for college students who wanted to get out of the college town for a few hours. But it was much further away than the Newburgh Mall which was about 20 miles away.

So if someone was heading out to the Poughkeepsie Mall, I would ask them to drop me off at the meeting and I would grab a ride back with one of the students. It was risky. One time I was the only New Paltz student at the association meeting, so I took a bus back to campus. It was a long ride, but totally worth it. Sometimes, I seized the moment to join up with other classmates, and I went to the Christmas holiday party.

I was elated to be able to use my sign language with the members of the organization. I loved to be in that world of kind eyes, expressive faces, and gestures that spoke volumes beyond the basic signs that I was using. This Deaf community was so inviting and many of them had children. I was shocked that so many Deaf couples had hearing children. But the majority of people who were at the association gatherings and meetings were deaf. It was fascinating to know that I was able to communicate and there was not one spoken word. Similar to the way that I was able to speak to my mother with a look when I saw things were going to get ugly with my stepfather or how I was able to read body language when he entered or left a room. I was able to tap into this underworld of unspoken language and connect spiritually with people who were welcoming me into their world. It was an honor to be there. It felt like I was a hearing ambassador. I wanted to demonstrate that I wanted to learn as much as I could about their world and that I was being respectful in learning about their language. Race was not an issue. Color was not an issue. The fact that we signed the same universal language broke so many barriers. But there truly was a subculture here. I had a peek into that Deaf world.

My ASL instructor taught us how the Deaf community had a strong cultural identity. Deaf pride was not about having a handicap or a hearing deficit. The Deaf community has a historic contribution to our society and just like we honor other cultural identities, it is important to understand the issue centered on having a Deaf identity while learning ASL. There was a spectrum of language that I was dealing with as I signed up for this Sign Language course. I learned how to use English Sign Language (ESL) to finger-spell proper nouns and names. I learned from my professor that ESL took up too much space in academic settings and that Deaf students resisted it because ASL was so much more conceptual and the use of space within the gestures spoke more effectively than the drawn-out ESL signs. This language was developed by hearing people to make the ASL fit within the spoken language around sentence structure. Therefore signs for articles (a and the) and prepositions (of) showed possession and the composition of something. When I would use the ESL the Deaf people would sign that I didn't have to sign those and chuckled. There was the spoken language, the book language, and the living language within the Deaf community.

I learned the phenomena of a sublanguage of home signs. It was how I received the gift of my name from a deaf person. She was the president of the club. I shared in sign language that I had learned some ASL when I was in high school from a friend. She asked if they were deaf or hearing. I mentioned both. She asked what they called me. What was my name? I didn't understand her question. I fingerspelled my name V-I-L-M-A. She in turn made a V sign in a wavy pattern away from the top of her head to her shoulder. She was describing my waving hair. I was Vilma with wavy hair. That is the moment when it was not about learning sign language for the sake of meeting a language requirement. It was the moment I was trying to replicate from learning sign language with Ivonne and her sister. No matter how much I thought they liked me, they never gave me a home sign for my name. Even though Ivy and I were friends, I was not IN. I was the hearing outsider. It was the moment I scratched the surface. I learned that signing was different when hearing people were present. I mentioned this to my instructor, and he had a broad approving smile. He was proud that I made the connection. I was curious about the history of learning in the Deaf culture. Aside from the classic Helen Keller story, I didn't know any other history about the Deaf culture and community.

It was my mission not to just learn their language, but to understand Deaf history and the medical implications of technology in support of the Deaf community. I was familiar with a TTY because the instructor brought one to class and showed us the device. This was 1988 and at the time the most expensive piece of equipment I had seen was an IBM electric typewriter and a fancy word processor that one of the girls had in the dorm. In order to type up my college papers, I would go to the writing lab that had computers with floppy disks to store my documents. Seeing the TTY was a rudimentary form of today's form of texting but it was using telegraphing technology. It was ingenious.

One evening while having dinner with Rae and Mary, I shared how things were going for me in my Sign Language class. I tried a social experiment. I signed it for them. Rae's eyes were wide open. I signed how I witnessed the phenomenon of deaf parents with hearing children. This is when my friend Rae shared that her grandparents were deaf. However, her father was not deaf. Over 25 years later, Dr. Dr. Andrés Torres wrote in his book *Signing in Puerto Rican* about his experiences being raised as a hearing child with two deaf parents.

This coincidence really struck me. Perhaps God was talking to me and this was a sign. I wanted to learn so much about the Deaf culture. Was I supposed to be a teacher for the deaf? As a hearing person, was this even possible? Could a hearing person be capable of teaching deaf students? I didn't know, but I sure was going to find out. My source was going to be my Sign Language instructor. I remember meeting him during his office hours, and we spoke for a lengthy amount of time about the challenges of being a hearing person in the Deaf culture. Being so stubborn and willful as I was, I was enticed by the challenge and made it my personal quest to learn as much as I could.

That academic year, I took two courses and a June session summer course. With three American Sign Languages courses under my belt, I felt more proficient. So I signed up with a temp agency in the city to work at Beth Israel Hospital in lower Manhattan as a sign language interpreter for the outpatient psychiatric department. When they didn't need me to translate, I would work in the Ambulatory Care department working with files and registering patients. It paid extremely well. Rae mentioned that there was a Deaf school close to the hospital. Later I learned that there was a large Deaf community in the area. This made so much sense. It was the reason why they needed sign language interpreters.

I was excited to be closer to this community. Conversely, it also meant that I would be home with my family in the Bronx. As much as it made me happy to spend time with my little brothers and my friends Lisa and Daisy, I was not happy about seeing my mom look so sad. Our relationship had changed. It felt distant, just like the 75 miles that were between us when I was at college. I noticed that my mother had gained a lot of weight and now that my little brother Nelson was in school, she was working as a seamstress again to supplement the income that my stepfather made as a doorman.

At this point, my stepfather was legally blind but able to get around with his thick glasses. He had cut back on his drinking but was irritable all the time. My mother's hair was cut very short, and she mentioned that she did that so that my stepfather wouldn't have his jealous tirades. She was proud that I was working and more curious about my sign language experience. I had introduced her to Rae and she liked her very much. I had mentioned to my mother that Rae's grandmother lived in that area near the hospital. That made my mom happy to know that there was someone close by to my job in case I needed anything. Mothers worry so much. What would I need? I didn't get it. I do know that having a place to 'go to' was always important to her. In retrospect, I get it now. As a woman she wanted me to have options and to have an out. With this summer job serving as a sign language interpreter, I was able to do just that. Have options.

This summer was all about financial freedom and the summer I met a special person. Through a mutual friend, I met William Rivera. He was a nice guy with a funny sense of humor who was close friends with my high school friend Maribel and her husband Carlos. One day after work, I ran into Maribel on the train. She was excited to see me. We had taken the same cooperative business courses at the high school and after she graduated she was offered a job as a secretary in midtown Manhattan. That Friday, Maribel invited me over to her house for dinner. I was looking forward to spending time with her and catching up. Just like an evangelist trying to bring folks to church, I was trying to get Latinas to sign up for college classes. This was my ulterior motive when I accepted her invitation for dinner.

Little did I know that she was playing Cupid. She invited her husband Carlos' friend Willie to come over too. We all had a lovely time
conversing and laughing mostly at Willie's jokes. I really liked this
guy. He seemed so kind. When I told him I was a student at SUNY
New Paltz, he wanted me to know more about what I was studying. I
mentioned that I wanted to be a teacher, but that I was curious about
teaching the Deaf. He found that very intriguing and he wanted me to
show him some signs. Right at the dinner table, I did an impromptu
lesson and of course, the first thing they wanted to learn were all the
curse words. It figures. So I obliged.

As I was preparing to go back to college, I will admit it was hard
leaving Willie behind. We were mutually interested in each other. We
made a plan to be friends and to talk from time to time. Personally, I
wanted more, but I didn't know if I was ready for a serious long-distance relationship. I was going to play it by ear. He was impressed
that I had worked so hard in the summer to save my money for my
first car. He said that when I was ready he would help me look for
my first set of wheels. By the end of August, I did just that. I saved
$1,400. Willie played an instrumental role in helping me find the car.
We drove all the way out to Pennsylvania to get this deal. It was a blue
1982 Oldsmobile Firenza. I was going to start my Junior year of college
with my brand-new used car. It was a symbol of my independence.
By the end of this crucial sophomore college year, I learned the power
of learning multiple languages—Italian, Sign Language, and the new
language of long-distance love.

CHAPTER SIXTEEN

BRAWLER-SHOT CALLER!

B y my junior year in college, I was coming into my own. Finding my way, and totally devoted to my studies. After completing over 60 liberal arts credits, I was now focusing on my coursework to fulfill my minor in Communication Arts, and my major in Education. This was the year that I felt I was ready for something new. After living on campus for two years in Bliss Hall (a female residence hall) I was ready to step out into the world. So a couple of my friends Rae and Jenny decided to live off-campus and get an apartment. When they asked me to join them, I was elated and more than willing to become their roommate. I used the housing stipend that I would normally get for living on campus, and I applied it to that semester's rent.

Independence took on a new form. We were three independent ladies living off campus like free adults. We found a large apartment in the Village Arms Apartment complex on Route 32, which was about two miles away from campus. I was so happy to have my own car. I couldn't believe it. It was a big deal to have my own car. My other roommate also had a car, and between both of us, we would carpool to campus. We would all chip in for gas. It was an exciting time for us.

As *tres damas independientes*, we were striking a stronger balance of taking our coursework seriously as well as having a more balanced social life. We were hosting social events in our new off-campus apartment as well as going to different parties in town and on campus. As three very vivacious and lively positive women, we were extroverts. Jenny was a psychology major, and Rae was a secondary education major. We were studying service-oriented fields. So mingling with people was something that came very naturally to us. I don't know how we kept our grades on point, considering how social we were. But we had a way of helping each other and keeping each other on track.

At the time, my relationship with Willie was slowly evolving in spite of the long distance. Through letters and phone calls, we remained connected. More importantly, I was able to handle this type of relationship because school was my priority. I appreciated that he was comfortable with this long-distance arrangement. I wasn't receiving any pressure to see him or for him to come up to see me. It was a friendship that was naturally evolving into something more serious. Willie was five years older than me so that made me a little nervous because I didn't want to fall in love too quickly. I figured someone older would want that. I needed to study him and see what he was about. If I got any hint of him being too controlling or macho-man he was going to be out of my life quickly.

He was raised by his grandparents Guillermo and Conrada Soto along with his mother who was a very hardworking single mother. Just like me, he didn't know too much about his father and he appreciated his mother María very much. Willie had just come back from serving in the army and he started working with his uncles in a printing press as a printer. I was impressed that he worked very hard to have his own place which was in the same building as his mother and grandparents. They were a close-knit family. This was very important to me. The grandfather had passed away a few years prior to him coming back from the army. As a son, he seemed very concerned about his mother's well-being and that made me feel safe with him. He was a man who respected women. The fact that he seemed very proud of me as I went to college was an excellent sign.

Meanwhile, back in New Paltz, I got to live with my single room-mates. Sometimes when you are hanging around people who are in a relationship, it can remind you that you are single and they are not single. They have someone and you do not have a significant other. This was not the case with Rae and Jenny. We were all free-spirits ready to face the world. We were locking arms like Charlie's Angels and facing the world together. Single ladies can focus on their future. I was always focusing on my future.

My mother used to tell me –*Hija sigue pa'lante y no te amore. Sigues siendo una señorita sola sin compromiso.*– She wanted me to keep going and not fall in love. Remain a young lady without any romantic involvements. Did this mean that she never wanted me to get married? Did this mean that she wanted me to stay a virgin forever or did I have to wait to have sex until I got married? My mother never spoke directly with me about such delicate matters. It was always *indirectas y refranes* with her. Passive and indirect statements that went around in circles. She spoke in code all the time. Sayings shared among generations and generations. –*Hija, dime con quién andas y te diré quien eres. Mejor estar sola que mal acompañada.*– Tell me who you are with, and I will tell you who you are. And her favorite was –*El que coje consejo llega a viejo.*– Those that take advice, live long. I had to infer a lot.

I was not going to tell my mother about my new boyfriend Willie. I didn't want to take a chance that she would think I was in a *compromiso* which sounded too much like compromise in English. I was not going to compromise my future. Nope, that was not going to happen. No way. Officially I was still a single woman without a ring on my finger so I believed it was my prerogative to come and go as I pleased. At the time, the singer Bobby Brown who was dating Whitney Houston had a big hit single called "It's My Prerogative" and that was my single ladies' anthem. I would sing it free and loud.

My roommate Jenny was active on campus as a Kappa Sweetheart and hanging around a lot of the Sigma Rho fraternity guys which I really did not like. They walked around with such bravado and I was not feeling it. The Greek fraternity and sorority lifestyle was not my cup of tea. I didn't understand why she was a part of the Kappa

Sweethearts. She seemed like just an independent woman with her own mind. The group mentality of this organization didn't align with my independent streak. Every time Jenny, Rae, and I went out to the local pubs, the guys in her affiliated Kappa Sweetheart fraternity would go out of their way to seem intimidating to the guys we would talk to. Even if it was harmless chatter, they would give our newfound friends the stink eye.

At the time, Rae had broken up with a guy she was dating for about two years. He was away at law school in Albany, but his cousin was still a student at New Paltz. We called him a super duper senior. It was time for this guy to graduate already! He looked like an old man. I really couldn't stand this guy. Everything about him struck me that he was an abuser. I could smell it a mile away. A part of me was scared of him, but I never showed it. I just would ignore him and pretend I didn't see him.

One night, he saw us at the bar while we were having a great time singing Queen's *Bohemian Rhapsody*. There we were *las tres amigas*. Free-spirits standing up on chairs swinging our beer mugs in unison. High up in the air forgetting about every care in the world, our voices sang in synchrony like no one was watching. Her ex-boyfriend's cousin came over to her with a serious and disapproving facial expression. He asked her why we were there. He tried ordering us around and told us to get down. We ignored his ass. Apparently, he thought he was supposed to be our keeper. Hell No! We won't go! Rae was five feet tall, but she had the presence of a six-foot woman.

Afterward, we came outside to get some air from the extremely crowded P&G's sports pub. The knucklehead harassing Rae approached her again. As a drunken and belligerent fool, he got in her face and called her a *puta*. She was stunned by what he said and it took a few seconds for her to react. What the hell? I wasn't going to let this guy harass her like that. So all 5' 6" of me stepped up to him and the girl that was standing next to him. She had blond, big 1980's hair. I remember seeing her on campus. At that moment, my eyes were fixed on him. My stare was like a laser, and I got into autopilot mode just the same way I would with my stepfather when he would slap Mami and speak in a menacing way to her. I snapped and that second I lost it. I was closer to the girl than I was to him and I told her to get the fuck out of the way. I shoved her to get to him. I was going to sucker punch him. However, the blonde pulled back her arm and made a fist which made full contact with the left side of my jaw. POW!

What the hell just happened? I didn't see that coming! For a split second, I thought I got hit by him. Coping with the stinging pain on the side of my face I questioned why the hell she was defending him and hitting me. He was a dog. I lost it, I lunged at her in full fury. Every ounce of me that was full of bottled-up unprocessed rage was now focused on getting back at her. There was a big crowd outside. A few people who witnessed this held me back and held her back. Meanwhile, this idiot was still in Rae's face talking so much bullshit. I felt helpless and I couldn't stop crying angry tears. I felt so powerless. Why were these idiots holding me back? I was totally immobilized by their stronghold. Had my mother seen this deplorable scene, she would have been mortified because that was not how she raised me. But I stood up for Rae and myself. In spite of the scandalous and shameful bar fight, I felt proud of the fact that I fought back with every ounce of strength in my being.

Eventually, Rae made her way through the teeming crowd and checked up on me. She was horrified when she saw my face. It was red and swollen! I had so much adrenaline rushing through my veins that I didn't feel a damn thing. The next thing I knew, I was walking away from the bar and heading toward the Police precinct. It was two blocks away from Main Street which was in the center of town or "bar row" as we liked to call it. Rae and another mutual friend walked behind me asking me where the hell I was going. I said I am going to the precinct to report that bitch for sucker-punching me. Rae didn't think that was a good idea. But no, I wasn't going to let that bitch get away with that. Ironically at that moment, I had amnesia that my initial intent was to hit her man. With a puffy face and a bruised ego, I mustered up the courage to walk into the precinct.

At that moment, if there was any trace of drunken stupor left in me, it immediately dissipated as I spoke to the officer in a calm and poised manner. I said that I was there to file a complaint against a girl who hit me in the bar. He asked me her name and the mutual friend who came with us told the police officer that her name was Tammy. She mentioned that Tammy was roommates with one of the girls from Latinas Unidas. Coincidentally Tammy was dating that idiot that was in Rae's face. This was all I needed to know. The New Paltz Police called the College Campus Police. Together both law enforcement agencies helped me file a formal complaint and press charges.

The next morning, I drove to the city and met up with Willie to have a good cry. He was very concerned. I was complaining about a clicking sound in my jaw. Every time I opened my mouth too wide or I would chew food, I would hear the clicking sound. Later that Saturday, he took me to his dentist in New Rochelle. His best friend's fiancé was a dental hygienist and she highly recommended the dentist that she worked with. I was so grateful that I visited the dentist. The dentist confirmed that I had TMJ (Temporomandibular Joint Syndrome) which essentially was a misaligned jaw due to Tammy's fist clocking me like a punching bag. As a courtesy to Willie, the dentist's office made a payment arrangement with me that at the time seemed like so much money. The bill was close to $900. I had never seen those numbers on a bill with my name in my entire life. Willie offered to pay for me and place it on his credit card. However, I was adamant that he was not going to do that. I was going to figure out a way to pay. Then it hit me. When I went to court against Tammy, I was going to present the judge with my dental fees. She was the reason why I was contending with TMJ.

A few weeks later, I was standing before the judge in the New Paltz Town Court. It dawned on me. All those years I had witnessed my stepfather hitting my mother and no matter how many times I snuck out of the apartment to get the police nothing ever happened to him. I had seen cops come and go from our house and nothing changed. The main reason was that my mother never admitted that he hit her. This time, I was not going to be quiet. I was going to be bold and speak up. I was standing up for myself. I found my voice. I wasn't going to remain silent about someone hitting me. Tammy showed up in court with that ugly man by her side. I don't think it helped her case because he looked like a thug next to her. Considering they were a biracial couple in a town primarily not ethnically diverse, I felt that was not going to help her case at all. I remember digging deep to not get nervous. The boxer came out of me and I was ready to go toe to toe in the courtroom instead of the ring. I was going to fight with my words.

It helped that Rae came with me to the court to speak as a witness. I didn't have a lawyer. I couldn't afford one so I was going to represent myself. I shared with the judge that the reason why I was coming to court was to seek justice for the way Tammy punched me. I shared that she was a trained female boxer. I shared that she had full intent to hurt me because the same fist that she uses in a boxing ring as a weapon, she used to punch me on the street. In closing, I asked the judge to help me get justice and that Tammy had to learn the repercussions of her actions. Taking her fists to my face knowing full well that she could have broken my jaw was assault and battery.

What the judge didn't know was that this Bronx girl used a thesaurus the night before to find the most eloquent way to say that Tammy beat my ass. She had to pay for hurting me. The coup de grâce was when I brought a picture that I had taken of her parked car with miniature red and white boxing gloves hanging from her rearview mirror. I snapped a picture of the car and the license plate to show that it was her car. After I presented the pictures, I pleaded with the judge that I needed help paying my dental bill due to Tammy's punch to my jaw. The dentist wrote a letter describing my condition and that a punch to my jaw was the reason why I had developed TMJ. I confessed to the judge that I was scared Tammy or her boyfriend might retaliate and hurt me, or my friend Rae.

At that point, the judge reassured me that this would not happen and that he would file a restraining order on her so that she could not come near us. If she did, she would be in contempt of a court order. After I presented my case, the judge spoke very firmly to Tammy and he ordered her to pay me every cent that I paid on dental bills. The judge reproached Tammy for her behavior and she asked if she could break up the payment into installments. The judge agreed.

It was in that instance that I felt vindicated. I had a voice. I learned that a woman can follow proper legal channels to change things. In addition, the realization hit that if I had not controlled my anger, I could have been on the other side of this mess. That scared me. I had a renewed sense of hope that the law could protect a woman. I had never seen that happen to my mother. How many times did the police come to address the noise coming out of my apartment, but nothing happened? They just would encourage my stepfather to go for a walk, and then later on when he sobered up, it was like nothing had happened. This time it felt so different. I spoke up and something changed. It felt great to be able to speak up in such an intimidating space like a courtroom. I remember Rae saying how proud she was that I spoke so well and how I defended myself. Instead of defending myself with fists, I used my voice. It felt amazing. It was at this key moment that I learned that I can fight for my rights, not only with my words, but with the judicial system.

Chapter Seventeen

REMORSEFUL RESILIENCE

In the middle of my junior year, I received a disturbing call from my brother Rafy. My mother had suffered a stroke. She was in the hospital. The minute I heard this, I made a quick drive back to the city. I missed all of my classes. I called Willie and left him a message on his apartment answering machine. I imagined he would get the message the moment he came home from work.

In the 1990s, things were less immediate. Everyone had to wait...not like today where it would have been a quick text message. Waiting was a painstaking process that helped to develop resolve and perseverance. Receiving that call created such an overwhelming sense of urgency in my heart. I wanted to be by my beloved mother's bedside. I was terrified that she had died, and worse that they chose not to tell me. I begged my brother to tell me the truth. He told me she was at Jacobi Hospital and that my mother was unconscious. He was very worried too. He had just graduated high school and he was home with her when it happened very early in the morning. I believed him. The drive home was the longest two-hour drive of my life. Why did I have to go to school so far away? Now that my mother needed me, I was not nearby. I abandoned my mother. I left her alone. I was coping with an overwhelming amount of guilt with every mile marker that I drove past racing back to the city.

The moment I arrived, I saw my mother sleeping in her hospital bed. She looked so peaceful as she lay there with tubes in her arms and nose. I learned that my mother had suffered a mild stroke due to her high blood pressure. Mami was coping with partial paralysis and in time she would recover with physical therapy. It was heartbreaking to see her with a feeding tube because she was not able to properly chew or drink until she got stronger. The right side of Mami's face looked so droopy. She didn't look like herself. I was terrified to see my mother this way.

While visiting the hospital with my brother, I learned that my mother was getting ready to go to work when she suddenly felt dizzy and collapsed on the kitchen floor. This must have been such a terrifying scene for my brother Rafy. My stepfather was home because they had laid him off as the doorman of the midtown apartment building. He was receiving unemployment benefits and he was the one taking my little brother Nelson to school. My brother Freddy was in Junior High School and he had just been accepted to a special program. As a high school student, he would receive the wonderful opportunity to participate in an elite boarding school experience in Simsbury, Connecticut as a part of the ABC (A Better Chance) program. My mother was happy that he had this great opportunity, but she also felt that it would help to have fewer mouths to feed at home.

As a mother, having two of your children away from home must have been so scary for her. However, having three growing boys could eat you out of house and home. My mother and stepfather couldn't count on getting any more store credit from the butcher on Westchester Avenue because he was retiring and it was going to be under new ownership. The pressure of coping with less money earned from my mother's seamstress job and my stepfather's unemployment check must have placed tremendous strain on my mother. I remember my mother complaining about the huge rent hikes in the apartment. The country was still recovering from the tail end of the Reagan Era. The higher inflation made it so challenging to make ends meet. As a family, we had experienced tough times like this before, I remembered the fights and the many slaps that my mother received because she didn't shut up about not having money. Did this happen again? I didn't ask my brother, I just imagined that it occurred.

As I stood in the hospital lobby using the public telephone booth, with a stack of quarters that I had from paying the interstate highway tolls, I called my college advisor and told him that my mother was in the hospital. Mr. Jones had a copy of my schedule and he was going to contact all of my college professors. He told me that he was certain they would work with me to complete my assignments later and that I needed to focus on being there for my mother. Mr. Jones said that it was too early to decide if I needed to take a leave of absence, but that I should call him in a few days to give him an update on her condition. The thought of not going back to school was paralyzing. However, the fear that my mother would not be her normal self after this stroke was even more frightening.

After pleading with God, kneeling down by her bedside, and sobbing, I made a pact with God. I asked him to forgive me for being such a horrible daughter abandoning my mother the way my father abandoned us. I was just angry with her that she wanted to stay, but I now understood why she nobly chose to stay. Mami wanted to make sure her children had their father. I didn't have my father and she didn't want that for her *hijitos*.

In that instance, Lord God touched my spirit and I felt a sudden sense of calm. I heard every sound in that hospital room clearly. It was like having super-bionic hearing. My mother's breath, the nurse station hustle and bustle down the hall, and the sudden stirring in my mother's bed. I was relieved that when my mother woke up, I was there to see her reaction. She was so happy to see me.

After a few hours, they removed the feeding tube, and a physical therapist came by to assess her. Thankfully, the extent of the mild paralysis was treatable and she would need physical therapy to help her recover with better mobility in her right hand and arm. I was able to stay for a few days and visit with her all day. It was nice to have that time together as mother and daughter. I missed this so much.

With the time and distance between us, our relationship was estranged and it always felt so awkward talking to her at home. I was always trying to measure what I would share with her. I couldn't tell her about my boyfriend because I didn't want the *cuidado* speech. I felt that I couldn't talk to her about school and that she wasn't able to relate to what I was experiencing as a college student. So I kept our conversations centered on updates about my friends Daisy and Lisa. I would ask her about her job and how things were going for her. I would ask her if my stepfather was behaving better and drinking less. She would tell me about her elderly friend Doña Tomasa who lived by our church St. Joan of Arc, and how she was helping at the church to help with the food pantry on Saturdays. I admired her so much for doing that. After working crazy hours during the week, she would find the time to help others. How did she do it? I will never know. Perhaps it was her form of therapy and meditation sorting food and organizing materials. Later I learned that my mother was not only a volunteer at the food pantry but also a recipient. This broke my heart. Why didn't she ask me for help? Why didn't this self-absorbed daughter ask her mother if she needed help?

Mami enjoyed it when I spoke to her about school and how I was learning to be a teacher for the deaf. She thought this was wonderful. However, Mami was worried that I was missing too much school and she wanted me to go back to SUNY New Paltz. So I was a good girl and listened to my mother. I told her that I would see her the following weekend. So that Friday, I went back and caught up on all of my course assignments as I crammed them all in over a weekend. I was able to remain focused because I knew I would see her the following weekend.

After spending such a wonderful time catching up with my mother, I felt so guilty that I was keeping a tremendous secret from her. I needed to tell her about Willie. Here I was asking God to bring back my mother, and I wasn't being honest with her. I felt that if Mami met him, she would immediately like him. The fact that his mother lived right up the block on Stratford and that they both went to the same church was a wonderful coincidence. Then to boot, Willie's mother was named María. I found that to be such a great sign. Maybe one day both of the Marías could meet. So the following weekend, I didn't delay it any longer. I asked Willie to come with me to the hospital because I wanted to present him to my mother.

When I walked into the hospital room, my mother was sitting up in a chair and she looked ten times better than the last time I saw her. I was relieved and so happy. Willie was walking behind me and she thought he was there to see the lady who was in the next bed. When I told my mother that the man next to me was there to visit her, she looked confused. I imagined my mother was going to have a serious face. But she did something that truly surprised me. Mami smiled and welcomed him. That evening we stayed for 4 hours talking and Mami gave Willie the proverbial third degree. I was pleased that with every answer, my mother looked more and more relaxed. I was so grateful. Everything seemed right in my universe. I had my mother back. I was fearless in revealing my new love to my mother. I was ready to go back to college and finish what I had started.

I launched my spring '91 semester with full force. I completed all of my communication arts classes along with my different language requirements. I had my sights on life after my undergraduate studies so I wrote a letter to the admissions office at Gallaudet University in Washington, DC. I wanted to learn more about the University and the housing options for a Master's program. I was trying to finish as much as I could so that I could complete all of my coursework by January 1992 so I had a few months before my commencement in June to prepare for a move to Washington, DC. It was an exciting time for me. Things with Willie were getting serious, but I was comfortable with that because the distance was a great buffer for me. He surprised me with a special trip to the Bahamas for my college spring break. It was the first time I had left the country and the thought of going to a foreign place was exhilarating. I got wonderfully lost on that Bahamian adventure chasing Bahama Mamas while being beach bums and getting a gorgeous tan. Life was wonderful. So this is what it means to be a grown-up? It was the first time I had experienced going on vacation. I loved it. I loved Willie. I loved life. I loved that there were so many great options before me.

When I returned from the trip, I contacted the Lexington School for the Deaf in New York City near Flushing Queens. I was interested in applying for a four-week unpaid internship where I would assist a fifth-grade teacher during the month of June. Considering that it would be the end of the school year, I knew it might be a bit challenging. I was trying to fit in as many observation and field hours as possible so that when I applied to Gallaudet University, it would show that I had some field experience.

Instead of staying with the family, I decided that I would spend the time staying with Willie. It would help me get to know him better. Although we had a wonderful trip together and we got along so well, life is not a vacation. I needed to see how he behaved after work, in the morning, managing bills, and dealing with life's pressures. Willie didn't know it yet, but it was my test to see if he truly was the one for me. I truly loved the way he treated me, but a part of me was terrified that it might be a façade. My biggest fear was that he might change at some point. If things did, I had an exit plan. I had to go back to New Paltz to attend the second summer session which was during the month of July to the beginning of August. It was a good four-week plan. I felt that I could handle four weeks living with him. Another reason why I chose to be with him was to be closer to my mother. This way I could visit my mother on the weekends. I would not tell her that I was literally a block away from her from Monday through Friday. I would just tell her that I came by to see how she was doing. My plan over the course of my internship time in the city was to bring Willie over to my mother's house so that he could meet my little brothers and my stepfather. I hoped that it would go well and we would not experience any awkwardness.

My internship at the Lexington School of the Deaf was truly an eye-opening experience. The learning curve was quite steep in trying to communicate with students as well as pay attention to pedagogical strategies that the teachers used. After learning everything that I did with my ASL professor, I was horrified to see that the majority of the signing between teachers and students was primarily English Sign Language (ESL). This was so contrary to what I learned from communicating with deaf people who signed with me in the Mid-Hudson Valley Deaf Club. ASL is a language in its own right and by dissuading the students to only sign the English Sign Language structure, they were in essence suppressing their true Deaf culture language of ASL. It was like someone telling me to only speak English because we are in America. In a learning institution designed to serve Deaf students, there was a need for us as hearing people to use their native and maternal language which was ASL.

There was a strong focus on ESL at the Lexington School for the Deaf. All the language theory and cultural norms that I learned upstate did not seem to apply in the school. Many of the students were able to read lips when I spoke in English or didn't know how to sign a word in ESL. I learned through various signing conversations with teachers and students that the family members wanted the students to assimilate and not to sign and there was a lot of shame centered on the students being deaf. The ASL movement of Deaf pride and identity was not honored by this school system. I did witness the students using ASL signs and some signs that I didn't recognize. The first question they would ask was if I was deaf. After that question, I immediately felt like an outsider. I felt the same sensation that I experienced when I arrived on my college campus.

Many of the students were Latino, with the majority from Puerto Rican descent. I had learned from the hearing teachers that most of the students had some emotional disturbances due to issues centered on their home language. Things got even more complicated when I learned that many of the students had family members who only spoke to them in Spanish. The hearing family members refused to learn sign language. I couldn't fully imagine the level of frustration that these students felt having a legitimate way of expressing their conceptual ideas in school and with their peers, but not being able to do so with their loved ones at home. The Deaf students must have felt so alienated by their families. This would help explain their level of frustration and emotional outbursts. How could family members do this to their deaf loved ones? Unless they were embarrassed and showing tough love that the deaf child had to confirm and survive in the real world. These students did not have Cochlear implants that would amplify sound. These Deaf students were living in a silent world where they were silenced. I felt this was so ignorant and quite arrogant. I tried to wrap my brain around this reality for so many of the Deaf students. As they navigated the hearing world in an English-dominant New York City culture, I couldn't understand why ASL was not the primary language in the classroom. ASL was the true Deaf language.

Essentially, they had to become experts in four types of receptive languages; ASL, ESL, reading lips in English, and reading lips in Spanish. I realized that I was in for a serious ride and I felt inept. Perhaps I was in over my head.

By the middle of my internship at Lexington School of the Deaf, I was experiencing nausea and not feeling well. While attending the Puerto Rican parade one weekend, I fainted from the heat. I thought that I was nauseous because I was still dealing with the side effects of heat exhaustion. I called Rae who was still at New Paltz attending the first summer session. I told her how I was feeling. She suggested that I take a home pregnancy test. When I heard those words, it was like four walls of the room were closing in on me. Oh my goodness. What was I going to do? At the time, I was taking my birth control pills. But during our trip to the Bahamas, I wasn't very consistent about taking them. Could it be that I had too many Bahama Mamas and the alcohol compromised the effectiveness of the birth control pills? I didn't know what to do. The anguish of not knowing was eating away at me. I couldn't hold any food down and I still had two more weeks to finish up my internship. I tried my best to push through and eat mostly crackers and drink as much water as I could.

On the last Friday of my internship, and just a few days before getting ready to go back to New Paltz, I decided to go to Duane Reade and take a pregnancy test. I was supposed to see my mother on Saturday before leaving. I was hopeful that I wasn't pregnant and that I had just developed a bad stomach virus or flu. Well, I was wrong. I was pregnant. The toughest thing to do was to tell Willie. When I did, he looked just as surprised as me. But he hugged me and said that he would stand by any decision that I wanted to make. I cried for hours because I was so scared. *What was I going to do?* We did the mental math and figured that I must have been close to 10 weeks pregnant. There were times that I wasn't consistent about getting my period due to stress. So the fact that I didn't get my period didn't surprise me. Now I had to figure out my next move. My world was spinning.

The next morning, I called my mother to confirm that I was going to bring Willie over. She had cooked us lunch and she was very happy to have us visit. I was sure that my mother had spoken about him. But this was going to be my brothers' first time meeting him. While Willie and I were in the living room answering my little brother Freddy's questions (So...what is your job? How much money do you earn in an hour? Why do you like my sister? Do you realize how ugly she is in the morning and you still like her??) my mother was finishing up the food in the kitchen. When I first came in, I had left my purse on the kitchen table. Unbeknownst to me, Mami looked in my purse to see if I had lipstick that she could borrow. Instead, she found an ortho-birth control packet and the minute she saw that she stopped looking for my lipstick.

She called me over to the kitchen and I left Willie to fend for himself against my little brothers. My stepfather was not home and I was so grateful that he wasn't because when I walked into the kitchen I read my mother's face. She looked furious and very upset. She told me in a calm and low voice –*Siéntate*. As I sat down, I saw the birth control pack in her hand, my heart almost stopped. I focused on my breathing and looked straight into my mother's eyes. She looked so disappointed. I asked her to please sit down so that I could explain. When she asked me if I was having sex with Willie, I nodded and then I told her that I had something very important to say. Not only was I sexually active, but I was pregnant. My mother looked at me in total shock. –*¡Aye, que cantaso!* It was a tough hit for my mother. In that instance, I wanted to take back the words that came out of my mouth. Not only was I terrified that I shattered my mother's image of me, but I was scared that she would have another stroke again.

I rushed to her side and tried hugging her. She held me and sighed with a breath of resignation. –*Hija, que se va hacer? Pues, lo que Dios quiera. Sabes que tienes opciones y que Dios te va cuidar.*– Did my mother just ask me what I was going to do? Was it God's will? Did I know that I had options and that God would take care of me? What the hell was she talking about? Could anyone in this house speak directly for once?!

My mother stayed in the kitchen for quite some time after that unilateral talk of her talking in code and her daughter sitting there in stunned silence. She gave very little eye contact to Willie, but she was cordial and pleasant. I saw a broken promise in my beloved mother's eyes. It was more than her disappointment. It was true fear. Perhaps I took her to the place where she was 22 years earlier or maybe when she was pregnant with my last little brother during one of the hardest economic times for our family. Either way, I could see that she was still dealing with a myriad of emotions and she chose to be quiet. Willie was not sure what had occurred. I whispered the news and he looked scared, but he also kept up appearances in front of my brothers. We were in for quite a ride. In the meantime, I was not going to let this set me back. I went back to New Paltz to complete a summer session of needed coursework. Time was truly of the essence.

A few weeks later, I went to Our Lady of Mercy Hospital near E. 233rd Street and there it was confirmed that I was pregnant. I was due at the beginning of January. It was at that instance, I decided I wanted to be a mother. Our Lady of Mercy Hospital was going to extend a huge measure of mercy over my unborn child's life. I was going to figure out a way to fit my surprise miracle into my last year of college. Abortion was not an option for me. I had to make a sacrifice to make room for my miracle. It was at this time that I also came to terms with the fact that I wasn't going to become a teacher of the deaf. I was not going to move to Washington DC to attend Gallaudet University for my graduate studies. I was going to figure out the best way to become a teacher of hearing students. I was willing to let that dream die because now I had a new life inside me growing.

I wasn't married to Willie, and I didn't want to get married just because I was pregnant. He asked me and I told him to wait. I needed to see if he was a good father before I felt comfortable about him being a good husband. This warped sense of logic made a world of sense to me at the time. But what I was truly fighting was the fear of being stuck in a marriage like my mother. This young expecting mother prayed that God would provide the right answers in His time. I didn't have health insurance. So for the first five months of my pregnancy, I could not afford neonatal care. I tried to eat as healthy as I could and get through the morning sickness.

I was in my final year of college, but thankfully eligible for financial aid. I moved back on campus and lived in Bliss Hall as the only Prego (pregnant girl) on campus. I was quite a novelty around the residence hall getting larger and larger by the month. I graciously weathered through the awkwardness knowing that it would be a temporary situation. I would give birth after finishing my last semester of my methods courses. I lived on campus Tuesday through Friday. My roommate was a shy international student from China who was studying engineering. Ying Yue was very polite and I was certainly happy to have her own room Friday night to Tuesday morning. Every time she saw me come back, she would say how much bigger I looked. I would smile but cringe on the inside. Oh my goodness I felt huge. Over the course of my pregnancy, I gained 50 pounds and that was not fun.

In order to qualify for student teaching in the spring of '92 I had to complete 18 credits of courses, which meant taking six intense methodology courses. It also required passing my New York State teaching exam so that I could apply for a provisional teaching license. The pressure was on. I had to figure out a way to complete all of my courses in that Fall semester so that I could begin my student teaching in February. How was I going to do this?

One weekend when I came home to be with Willie, he gave me the tough news. He shared that he got laid off. He was so worried about how we were going to make it with a baby on the way. I told him not to worry and that we were going to figure it out. I told him that I came from tough stock and that our baby was going to be a survivor. So on Monday, I did one of the toughest things that I ever had to do. I swallowed my pride and thought about my child's well-being. I went to the Department of Social Services and applied for welfare benefits.

I didn't want Willie to go with me. I chose to go alone. I needed to eat healthier and find a way to have money for the things that we would need.

They registered me to participate in the WIC program which is the Women Infants and Children program where the mothers receive waivers to purchase staple items that offer them extra calcium and nutrition for their growing babies. I remember seeing women in the supermarket in my old neighborhood using them to buy raisin bran cereal, milk, cheese, and baby formula. I remember getting angry because I had a longer wait in the checkout line because the cashier was double-checking the items that were listed on the waiver, which looked like a blue check. I would roll my eyes and sigh out loud saying come on already. Now I was going to be one of those women. I was going to be one of the women going to the cashier's place to cash in their welfare check on the first of the month. It didn't matter. If I had to be one of those women, I promised myself that it would be temporary. After I graduated from college, I would not be on welfare anymore. I was not going to be the classic Bronx Puerto Rican girl from the block who got pregnant and a second or third-generation welfare recipient. I was going to be different.

The blessing was that I qualified to receive the down payment to get my own apartment. It was a small apartment on White Plains Road near the Parkchester number 6 train station. It was the first time I had my own name on the lease. After I got the keys, I spoke with Willie and he decided to move out of his place and give his apartment to his mother while he moved in with me. It was a tiny little apartment. The narrow bathroom door was about six steps away from the front door of the apartment. I would joke and say that every time I turned the key to enter the apartment, I swore that I heard the toilet flush. It was a sunny apartment. The walls were covered with a soft creamy peach color and the wood floors were recently sanded. They looked so warm and beautiful. It was going to be my baby's new palace. We decided that the baby's crib would be in our bedroom so we converted the original living room to our bedroom with the French door and lace curtains.

The first time that my mother came to visit us, she cried. She begged Willie to take care of her daughter and not abandon me the way my father left us. He cried when he heard that story, and he told her that he loved me very much and that he was going to be a great father to our child. He told her that he wanted to marry me, but that I am stubbornly saying no until after the baby is born. My mother just threw me a disapproving look, and I broke her gaze. I was going to stick to my guns. There was no way a man was going to marry me simply because I was pregnant.

My commute to New Paltz early on Tuesday mornings and my return back to the Bronx on Friday evenings were getting more and more challenging as my belly extended out closer to the steering wheel. My used car was my only connection to both worlds. As I drove the 75 miles, I would get lost in thoughts of my baby. My neonatal appointments were always scheduled on Mondays so that I wouldn't miss any days of school. When I was seven months pregnant, I found out that I was expecting a baby boy. I knew exactly what I wanted to name him Christopher William Rivera. Christopher is the patron saint for children. He would also be named after his father and grandfather. I wanted to hyphenate my son's name Rivera-Cabán, but his father was not having it. Then the more I thought about it, my biological father didn't deserve to have my son carry his name.

In the middle of December, my dear friend Rae organized a surprise baby shower in the New Paltz College President's guest house. It was a quaint cottage setting with a beautiful circle of girls that I knew from my life in New Paltz. Many of them were fellow classmates and friends from LASU, FEL, and Latinas Unidas. It was such a beautiful expression of their love and encouragement. A few weeks earlier, I shared with Rae that I was having a baby boy, so I received many gifts that would welcome my newborn son. In my math methodology course, my fellow classmates threw me a surprise shower on the last day of the semester after presenting our math teaching units. Many of my classmates were impressed by how far I was traveling to finish school. I knew that I didn't have a choice. I had to get my teaching degree and certification so that I could try to land a teaching position in New York

City for the 1992-1993 school year. It was going to be tough, but I was not going to give up. My final day of school was December 20, 1992, and 15 days later I was having contractions ready to welcome my son into the world.

After 13 hours of labor without any pain medication or epidurals, I finally was able to give birth to my beloved son Christopher William Rivera. The moment I was able to cradle my son in my shaking arms and look into his beautiful eyes, I knew that my life would never be the same again. It unlocked something in me. It was like a veil of doubt was magically lifted from my world. Clarity and a distinct sense of purpose came over me. This moment revealed my truest self. It showed me who I really was and I knew that I had to be the strongest and best mother that I could be for my son. There was no obstacle that was going to deter me from offering my beloved little prince everything that he needed to be healthy and happy. I was Christopher's mother. My final year of college was a transformative experience. This young woman became a mother and teacher. The heart of this advocate was beating strongly in tune with the heartbeat of my beloved son and his devoted father. We were ready to step out into the world as a family.

STAGE IV:
THE PUBLIC
SERVANT

Chapter Eighteen

DO OR DIE

I gave birth on January 5th and 28 days later I started my final semester of college, which was my professional practicum. This utterly exhausted brand-new mother had to face student teaching during the first critical months of her newborn's life. I was going to miss so many firsts, but ultimately it would all pay off. My student teaching placement was in Congers, New York located at the Congers Elementary School. It was in Rockland County, and it was a 45-minute drive from our apartment in the Northeastern part of the Bronx. It felt like a universe away! As a 23-year-old mother, I had a determined spirit. The mind was willing, but a post-pregnant body was lagging behind. To this day I don't know how I was able to summon the strength to complete my student teaching requirement. In retrospect, I had physical youth, stamina, and a desperate mother's heart on my side.

Congers was a predominantly white affluent community and the sight of a young Latina as a student teacher was a rarity. During the first eight weeks of my student teaching placement, I was in a first-grade classroom. The teacher's name was Wendy Wondra and she had a warm welcoming smile with a stylish and hip short hairstyle. Wendy was a mid-seasoned teacher who earned her master's from the progressive Bank Street College in New York City. It was the first time I heard about the college. She raved that her graduate school experience there was enthralling because it was such a progressive college. It was nestled in between Columbia University and Barnard College in the upper west side of Manhattan. I was curious to learn more about it.

I learned so many insightful, dynamic, and impactful teaching strategies from watching Wendy at work. She promised me that she would jam-pack my student teaching experience with as much as she could so that when I had my own classroom, I could teach with a constructivist approach. I remember learning about this progressive pedagogy in my methods courses. But now I was going to have the chance to marry educational theory and practice.

However, my second placement was with a very traditional and older fifth-grade teacher who made it very difficult for me to teach. My student-teacher supervisor had to come in several times to talk to her and encourage her to give me more instructional opportunities. The waspy fifth-grade teacher's number one complaint was that I had a very heavy Bronx accent and that I was a poor teaching example. I overheard her telling one of the male white teachers in the hall that she thought I was a poor speech model for the students. As I walked around the corner and she spotted me close by, she didn't stop talking. It didn't phase her at all that there was a strong possibility that I heard everything she said. This woman just gave me an indignant look and simply continued to talk to a teacher near her about an upcoming school trip they were planning. I never felt that my presence was acknowledged. They never said hello or good morning. When I would try to greet them, they simply would look at me and not respond. I felt invisible and I couldn't comprehend why they were being so dismissive and rude to me.

When my student teaching supervisor came in, the fifth-grade teacher recommended that I take elocution classes before getting my teaching certification. I was devastated. After getting some constructive criticism and tips from my student teaching supervisor, I worked on the pronunciation of certain words that were red flags for the fifth-grade teacher. I was mindful to work on words that ended with /er/ and instead of saying "I will ax my students some questions." I made sure I enunciated every sound and said "A-S-K." It was the first time in my life that anyone told me that I sounded different. I felt like a failure.

During my lunch hour, I would try to shake off the doubt and fear of this woman and go down to visit my former first-grade cooperating teacher Wendy. This gracious and generous thirty-something progressive white lady would sit down with me and share teaching strategies to make a few of my fifth-grade Social Studies and Science units more engaging and student-centered. This was a very progressive approach at the time but it was in tandem with the Whole Language Approach of teaching. I knew I was taking a risk. But I had proven educational theory and practice on my side.

Wendy originally came from Brooklyn and she told me not to worry. She said that she had to work on her Brooklyn accent when she first started teaching there. I cried on her shoulders and she said to not be anxious about that old hag. I would chuckle as tears streamed down my face onto her nice blouse. She smelled like flowers and Wendy was truly a breath of fresh air. I thanked God for her compassion and her belief in me. I was standing in so much self-doubt that I felt I was drowning. My post-pregnancy hormones were everywhere. I was starting to lose my hair from the drop of estrogen and all of the stress of these final weeks of student teaching. I will never forget Wendy's words of faith and encouragement. "You will complete your student-teaching with shining stars." To this day I am grateful for her belief in me. It was a pivotal time in my life when I could have turned away from teaching. I could have given up.

I wanted my student teaching advisor to observe dynamic lessons that ultimately would inform a future recommendation letter for a teaching position. Every time she came in to observe me, she always offered glowing reviews and constructive feedback. My mind and heart were open and vulnerable. It didn't matter. I had to persevere so that I could graduate and qualify for my provisional N-6 New York State Teaching License. One day after a successful lesson and a visit from my advisor, the fifth-grade teacher came to me and said that my advisor was not living in reality. She wasn't going to have her students be my guinea pigs. She wanted me to stick to the content in the Social Studies textbook and stick to the scope and sequence of teaching points in the manual. I drove home crying the whole ride second guessing myself as a teacher. On the outside, I would let this bitch win. I would do as she said, but on the inside, I vowed that I would never treat a fellow teacher the way she treated me. I vowed that if I made it into this teaching profession I would only offer support and encouragement to any teacher that I worked with.

The discrimination did not end there. At the end of the school day, I had a few students who always refused to clean up after themselves. When the teacher asked them why they were not cleaning their desks, they earnestly said that they thought I was there to do that because in their house they have someone that looks like me that does the cleaning. Did I just hear what they said? Oh my goodness, this was a new level of discrimination that I had never experienced. The only time I witnessed a housekeeper was on the *Brady Bunch Show* and *The Jeffersons* sitcoms. The housekeeping staff wore aprons. I would go to school dressed modestly professionally, with my hair neat, and a little bit of makeup. I purposely didn't wear bright red lipstick because I didn't want to seem like the hot Latina all done up. What were these kids talking about? What was wrong with them?

When I spoke to the fifth-grade teacher, she smiled and said that I had to excuse her students. "They live very sheltered lives. Many of them have nannies, Mexican landscapers, and house help." Did she just say that out loud? Yes she did! At that moment, I wanted the Earth to crack open and swallow me up. I felt so small. I was in flight mode and not fight mode. I wanted to run back to the Bronx where I saw people like me and people who sounded like me. It was very unsettling. I am ashamed to share that after she told me that, I simply nodded and said it was ok. Why did I betray myself? Why didn't I say something? I think I was utterly stunned and couldn't find the words. If there was one thing that I learned from my mother that was extremely helpful in this situation, it was the steady grace and even facial expressions that I had to maintain throughout these humiliating experiences. I was going to be the queen of grace because, in a few weeks, it would all be behind me. It was temporary. I was doing this for my son.

It was heart-wrenching to leave my precious newborn Christopher. My mother took care of him for only two days of the week on Tuesdays and Thursdays because she still had limited strength after her stroke. She was thrilled to be able to spend time with her first grandchild. In addition, Rae's mother Nilsa lovingly offered to help me out three days a week, Mondays, Wednesdays, and Fridays. It was on my way up north in the Bainbridge area of the Bronx. I will always be indebted to her for her support. I couldn't afford to pay a babysitter, and out of the kindness of her heart, Mama Nilsa watched my son three days a week. Every day I had to take my son to a different place and I would drop him off at 6:45 am so that I could get to the school at 7:30 am. I would carry that heavy car seat with Chris still in it over 5 flights of stairs because the elevator never worked in my mother's building, and Mama Nilsa lived in a walk-up apartment building that didn't have an elevator. It was grueling, and this was my post-pregnancy workout to lose the 50 pounds that I gained.

Every time I dropped him off, I couldn't wait to come back and hold my baby. But I needed to arrive early to help set things up in the classroom and to demonstrate how committed I was to teaching. I was the first one there, and the last one leaving. I did not dare leave before my cooperating teacher left. It was a sign of respect that I valued my time there as well as a sign of dedication to the profession. I heard that if teachers left too early, they were not taken seriously. It broke my heart and I would feel such awful piercing pain that I am sure it was an anxiety attack. I would smell him and stroke the top of his precious little head. He was always sleeping from the car ride, and I was thankful that he didn't see me go. He had a full head of pin-straight jet-black hair with the warmest little eyes that got lost in my loving stare. Nilsa and my mother said that he was such a good baby. He had such an easygoing temperament and he hardly ever cried. The best part was that my dear son was the same at home. He slept the whole night and loved to fall asleep on my chest, as I would take catnaps on the sofa. When he slept on my chest, I felt like I was cradling a miracle.

This little angel was inside my belly as I was dealing with the stress of 18 college credits and a community so far away. To this day I do not know how I made it to the Dean's List with a 3.84 average. I was very hard on myself and I wanted a 4.0. Considering that I was the only pregnant girl on campus, I think that unofficially I earned my 4.0 because I truly was on my A game. For the first time in my life, I felt settled in. Our little apartment was our safe world. It didn't matter that we were on welfare, unable to pay for babysitting and just barely making it by buying diapers, and food. But we were a family together working hard for our future. His father Willie was getting frustrated that his only job opportunity was a temporary position working at a printing press, so he took it. It didn't pay much, but at least he was able to work. The printing industry continued to deal with drastic changes because so much of the technology that was used for printing was changing due to the advent of printing software on the early Mac computers. He was feeling defeated and wondering how we were going to make ends meet. I tried to tell him not to worry because deep in my heart I knew things would get better once I was able to attain my teaching certification.

The moment arrived when I successfully finished my student teaching! My graduation was a week later and I was so grateful that this chapter of my education was finally over. Receiving my graduation gown made it all feel real. I was going to my commencement ceremony. My intention was to carry my beloved son on my hip as I walked down the aisle. He was with me during the last year of my college experience and our soul ties are what got me through this most challenging season of my young academic life. Thankfully, I was able to do it for a small portion of the procession. When I finally approached the stage, I had to hand Chris over to his father so that I could have both hands free—one to shake the college president's hand, and the other to receive my diploma. My legs were shaking as the realization hit me that everything that I had sacrificed was all about coming to this life-altering milestone. My mother and Willie's mother came to my graduation. I remember seeing the pride in their eyes. I was the first one in my mother's family who had graduated from college. This was a significant accomplishment for the Cores-Ayala legacy. At that moment, I was not a Cabán...I was my mother's daughter, *La Hija de María*.

CHAPTER NINETEEN

FORT APACHE DREAMS AND BRONX TALES

After graduating, my number one priority was to get a job. My heart ached because I really didn't want to leave my son's side but I had to make money. I was so happy to have my time with Chris. He was five months old and such a happy and easygoing baby. Mama Nilsa and my beloved mother had given him everything he needed. Love, attention, and security. His smile would pull on my heartstrings every time he looked at me. Mother and son had time to bond. The June weather was splendid and I enjoyed going for strolls with him. It was time for this new mother to catch up with her five-month-old son. But in these blissful moments of mother and son time, anxiety would creep in and I would become very concerned about getting a teaching job.

If I was going to work for the New York City Department of Education, I had to get on the ball. The first stop was to go to the Board of Education office located at 65 Court Street in Brooklyn. I had never gone to Brooklyn and the thought of navigating the subway system to get there was quite overwhelming. I was so grateful that I had a stroller and that I had shed some weight from my teaching stress and running around. So I felt fit and stronger to go all over New York City with my son on the subway. I thought, *No había de otra.* I really didn't have a choice. I was going to do what my mother did with me, go on the subway.

I went and did the formal application process and got my finger-prints done. Afterward, I went to the Barclay teacher store to browse around and see what they sold. The first thing I wanted to buy was a lesson plan book. I had saved up all my change and quarters so that I could have money saved for the fingerprint fee as well as for a few teacher tools. Everything in that store was so expensive, but I made the sacrifice and purchased a lesson plan book. It was an act of faith. I was declaring my belief that I was going to get a teaching job and this was going to bring me one step closer to having it. The ride back home was surreal. The last time I was on a train, I was commuting from my internship at the Lexington School of the Deaf. I was going to be a teacher for the deaf. Now I was a new mother seeking a teaching job for the hearing. I prayed that I didn't make a mistake not moving further in going to Washington, DC to attend graduate school. I felt guilty and morally conflicted.

When I walked back into our apartment building, I decided to check the mailbox. I was praying for a surprise check, but it was empty. I closed my eyes and said a prayer. I asked God to step in and show me the way. I didn't want to live on public assistance. I had a college degree and I wanted to use it. As I closed the mailbox, the apartment door next to the row of mailboxes opened up. It was an older lady I had seen various times. She was always sharing hellos and compliments about my dear son. She looked down at him and spied the Barclay Educational Store bag. The lady asked me if I was a teacher. I told her that hopefully, I would be because I just graduated. She mentioned that her best friend was a principal at a school in the South Bronx. My heart jumped. She told me to give her my résumé so that she could give it to her. Apparently, she was a retired teacher who used to work in the same district as her best friend. I asked her if she had a free moment because I had just finished writing up my résumé. She accompanied me back to my apartment on the fifth floor. I gave her a few copies of the résumé and she told me she was going to see her later this week. I was so grateful for her offer.

A few days later, I received a call to come in for an interview at Community School 234 also known as the Family School near West Farms in the Bronx. I couldn't believe it. My neighbor made that interview happen. The lady on the phone was the school secretary and I was so nervous as I told her that I would be delighted to come in and meet the school principal. I didn't have any money to buy clothes for an interview, but I had some nice maternity outfits that I wore while I was pregnant. I had lost a lot of weight in the past five months due to higher activity, and simply eating less because our budget was so tight. We simply focused on making sure Chris had his special formula and diapers. There was very little money left for extravagant spending on food. So instead of eating three meals a day, I ate dinner with Willie when he came home from his part-time work at his uncle's printing job. Those were real lean times, but in those fasting months, things were truly taking shape in preparing the way for my teaching career.

I eagerly showed up at the Family School ready to conquer the world. It was an elementary school surrounded by a large asphalt yard with rusty gate fences. It was the only standing building that wasn't burnt to the ground. So many other buildings around it were abandoned. When I walked in, there was a school guard that made me sign in. Upon entering the main office, I was greeted by the school secretary who had a stern and serious face. She shared that the school principal wasn't ready to see me yet and to please take a seat. Up to this point, I was so nervous wondering if this was going to be my home school. After student teaching in such an affluent suburban school where no one looked like me, I was longing to be surrounded by those who spoke Spanish and had brown skin like me. Somehow in my head, I thought I was going to be received in a more welcoming manner.

This Bronx-raised new teacher was longing to go back and give back to her community. But hey we're in the Bronx and the welcoming committee was totally no frills....heck nonexistent. However, sitting in that hard metal chair circa 1940s gave me the chance to observe. I was fortunate to get a vibe from life in the main office. It was lunchtime and teachers were coming in and out getting their mail and talking with the secretary. A beautiful Bohemian-styled woman strolled into the office. Who was this woman? She looked so cool. This woman with long black hair to her waist and a sunflower clip holding it back from her face. She had stylish wide-legged pants with a casual yet elegant top. For a moment I thought she was the principal because she walked into that office like she owned it. Her confidence and her smooth style changed the air in the space. She made a stylish beeline path into the principal's office. She spent a few minutes inside and then when she reappeared, she walked across the office towards me as she was heading to the office exit. She paused and looked and me...smiled and kept on walking.

A few moments later, I was greeted by the principal and we walked inside her office. The interview went very smoothly. She asked if I was familiar with Whole Language instruction which was all the rage from New Zealand and their approach to teaching literacy. Thankfully, I was familiar with and very comfortable speaking to that methodology because my English Arts methods professor spent an exorbitant amount of time speaking on the subject and modeling the use of large texted big books to model the reading process for students. Instead of using the antiquated traditional basal readers like See Jane Run that was so common in the 1950s and still there when I was a child in the South Bronx in the 1970s, this principal was able to get large education grants that afforded her to bring consultants from New Zealand with a litany of educational materials and workshops to train her staff. Tons of books were ordered so students had access to real books. The goal was to teach thematic units using a variety of children's books that would captivate learners. It was about integrating English language arts with other content area subjects.

I felt like I was in a sweet spot to speak about this innovative methodology. My student teaching experience with a former Bank Street graduate and a firm believer in the Whole Language movement fully indoctrinated me into this teaching philosophy. The coy and somewhat reserved college graduate transformed into a fiery and passionate professional eager to show this school principal what I knew and what I was all about. By the end of the interview, she shared that I was hired and told me she wanted to show me around the school. In that instant, my heart was racing and my palms were so clammy. Everything I had been working so hard was coming to a head. I was going to be hired as a per diem teacher and not on a tenure teacher track. I was desperate for a job and didn't know what that fully meant at the time, but I was thrilled to be able to teach in my beloved South Bronx.

There was a true dichotomy between the inside of the school and what was on the outside of the West Farms Bronx dilapidated tenement building. The school was beautiful with freshly painted walls and art murals. When she walked me through the hallways, she proudly shared that she was able to get artists in residence from Parsons School of Design, and she had educational consultants from the progressive Bank Street School of Education in collaboration with Columbia University and Teachers College.

I felt like at that moment, I stepped into a new world...full of pedagogical wonder. I was shaking. I clasped my hands together to try to exude confidence, but it was my only strategy to hide that they were visibly trembling. Finally, she walked me to my classroom. The children and the teacher were not there, because they were on a field trip. I felt so fortunate to be able to see the room that I would teach in. Even though the hallways were gorgeous, this classroom lacked interest and it needed some serious tender loving care. She told me that she would love it if I could come in the summer and decorate to personalize the space. My response was, "Absolutely!"

The principal said that she wanted to introduce me to my next-door neighbor as well as my mentor teacher. Her name was Sandy Johnson. Her students were not in class and she was preparing some teaching materials. Next door was the mysterious lady from the office that had full command of the air and space around her. Sandy sounded genuinely pleased to meet me. As I thanked her for being willing to be my mentor, she offered to meet with me when school was out so we could plan. It was surreal I had crossed the finish line and stepped into the professional world of teaching. It was at this key moment that I learned going the distance literally and figuratively was worth every arduous, painful, and rewarding step.

I felt so fortunate to find a teaching position in Bronx County which had over 430 public schools during the recession of the early 1990s. The New York City Board of Education was in the midst of re-structuring education and this school leader was leaning on corporate grants and collaborative initiatives with different universities to make up for fiscal shortages. This innovative space was fertile ground for a brand-new teacher. I was stepping into the future of my public service career.

AWAKENING THE CHILD ADVOCATE BEAST

R ealizing my dream as a teacher was extremely gratifying. Never in my wildest dreams would I have guessed that teaching in the South Bronx would require every ounce of strength and fortitude. Being raised in the city, I felt that I had what it took to be that tough cookie that could handle anything that would come her way. However, I discovered that my advocacy voice would continue to strengthen as I worked with economically disenfranchised children who battled a wide range of societal and community hardships.

The first thing I did prior to having the students arrive was to paint the classroom walls with an inviting lavender. It was in the midst of a stifling hot August in a classroom without air conditioning. The custodian thought I was crazy, but he didn't offer to help. I bought fabric for window treatments and sewed my own curtains. I created throw pillows and other decorative items, purchasing the fabric on a credit card that I had no business using. I wanted my classroom to speak to the children that were entering their second home. My new mentor Sandy was the same way and we would hunt for specials and discounts trying to purchase things for our classroom. Our classroom budget from the district was a trivial one hundred dollars and I could only purchase items from the Barclay Store in Brooklyn. With such a small purchase order account, I quickly realized that after purchasing the larger pencils, primary lined paper, and some construction paper, I was not going to have a lot of materials to work with. I remember Willy sharing how sad this was that teachers had to spend so much money out of their pockets. We made an appointment with his accountant and the accountant told me to save all of my receipts for any work expenses. I doubted that paint and window treatment fabric would be a valid expenditure, but I wanted my students to immediately feel safe and welcomed.

From the moment I met my first-grade students, I immediately was brought back to the realization that I was that same poor student sitting at a desk trying to learn to read almost 15 years earlier. All the theory and practice courses I took didn't align completely with what was in front of me. More than anything, I realized that as a child I didn't feel seen. I was the little girl who didn't speak English too well, being raised in a home where we only spoke Spanish. My mother tongue was nowhere. Not heard or written on the chalkboard or on the pages of the basal readers that I held. I felt like I didn't have a voice. My job was to help my students channel their beautiful voices to speak to what they liked, what they needed, and what they wanted to learn.

I leaned on my instincts and used the training that I received from the consultants at Bank Street College of Education. Their mission was to help teachers at my new school create a holistic approach to learning that helped students make connections from their world to the learning environment. So I ventured out to do just that. I got very creative making math manipulatives that students could touch and count with by taking white beans and spray painting them gold and shimmery so that students would use them to do their addition word problems. I created a Barney's Cafe fitted with a little green and white canopy hanging from the ceiling on a tension rod so that students could pretend they were going shopping and ringing up items to add. Armed with some beautiful large books purchased by my school principal, I did all I could to make interdisciplinary connections in math, science, social studies, and writing. My students couldn't get enough of the books and I wished that I would be able to give them more. I purchased books from Scholastic and went to book fairs using money that could have been used for gas or the babysitter, but I was desperate to create a learning space that made my students fall in love with learning.

By the winter of that year, we were humming like a well-oiled machine. The students were stretching their reading skills and I would write on any writable surface, getting butcher paper from the local grocer to make charts that I could hang and kids could read throughout the room. A print-rich environment is what I wanted to offer considering that our book selections were so limited. I tried to model that every time we would take walking trips to the library. I had them hold their books close to their little hearts because they needed to show everyone in the neighborhood that they loved reading.

When I came home from work and picked up my little boy Christopher from the babysitter, I would read my little man some of the books that I would read to my students. From being months old to a one-year-old, life seemed to fit just right as we did our best to raise our little boy living from paycheck to paycheck. I remember the day in August after that interview when I reported to the Welfare office declaring that I wanted to terminate my WIC benefits and the check that I was receiving when I was in desperate need of feeding my newborn son. I proudly shared the letter from the New York City Department of Education and my per diem placement at my new school. The caseworker shared that I could have the benefits extended for three months so that I could have money for a babysitter and I proudly told her that it would not be necessary. I wanted to earn my living and I didn't want to depend on a welfare check. She looked at me shocked and shrugged her shoulders while she loudly stamped some paperwork with a red stamp case terminated benefits. That thud resonated in my heart and at times I would hear that sound when I would open the refrigerator and it was very empty. But thanks to Willie's mom and my mom who would cook and send food, we managed as best we could. I ignored the hunger pains and just chalked it up to being on a diet and trying to lose the baby weight that I had gained. By February, I was slimming down and in need of new clothes, but I would just roll up the pants and wear large tunic shirts so that you couldn't tell too much that my pants were so big.

By the springtime, my little angels were reading everything they could put their eyes on. Spring love would blossom and the little cards and pictures would stream in from my students. It was such a glorious time and I was feeling so accomplished and successful.

One day one of my students, Octavius, came in and sang the song "I Want to Sex You Up" by Color Me Badd. There he was singing and gyrating his hips in a very lewd manner up against his first-grade classmate while standing online in the classroom to go to recess. Mentioning that he was ready to sex someone up! Talking about rubbing down on the little girls.

Upon hearing those words, I literally stopped in my tracks. As I was ready to open the classroom door to lead my students out, I took a deep breath and walked over to Octavius. I told him that I needed a helper, and if he could please hold the door for me. He was very happy to do so. Meanwhile, the little girl's face in the back of the line was in shock and she looked like she was about to cry. I knew that it was not the moment to say anything in front of the children. I held her hand...asking her if she could be our line leader and help me hold some teacher papers that I had to bring to the office. Nothing in the teaching methodology courses had prepared me for such a delicate moment. It stirred me up so much as I thought about my own childhood and dealing with sexual advances by someone I had trusted. So at that moment, I chose to be a queen of grace and move that little one away from the culprit of her shame.

As I led the class out of the building onto the courtyard, I asked one of the paraprofessionals to watch my class as I pulled Octavius to the side to speak with him privately. I asked him where he had heard that song and shared that what he was singing was not appropriate for young people. He said, "My father plays it all the time." He became defensive. I asked him to not sing it in front of other young people again and to not dance that way in class because it makes the kids in class very uncomfortable. He looked at me quite bewildered and said, "Ok teacher."

As I walked to the office thinking about how I was going to broach this topic with his grandmother, I just asked God to give me the words to raise this topic with the grandmother who was raising him alone. His mother was a drug addict who had abandoned him and his father was incarcerated. So I know his Grandmother had a full plate. Then to make matters worse, she was legally blind and had trouble with her mobility. I didn't want that older woman to have to make a trip to school to talk about this, so I chose to call her and speak to her about this matter over the phone.

When the phone rang, I heard a man's voice answering the phone. I introduced myself and I asked to speak with the grandmother.

The male voice said. "I'm his father. What's up?"

I shared the details of the incident and he hung up on me. I was stunned by this response and chose to try and call the grandmother at another time. I focused on making my photocopies for the remainder of the week and then went to pick up my class. As I walked to the playground to pick up my students for recess, I had Octavius as the line leader because I wanted to keep a close eye on him.

As we entered the building and made our way to the classroom, Octavius's biological father was standing right outside my classroom door. The moment he eyed his son, he quickly pulled his belt off the belt loops and started to hit him repeatedly yelling and cursing. "What the fuck are you singing in school?! Huh?"

I tried to block the little boy from the tough blows and got a few on the side of my leg as I blocked him. I pleaded with the father that this was not the way to handle this and that my poor students shouldn't witness this behavior. I begged him to leave and handle this as a family matter. He left with Octavius and I felt helpless. Needless to say, I couldn't stop feeling guilty that I had brought on this horrible scene by making that phone call. What was I supposed to do?

I tried to put on my best teaching face and keep my voice steady and calm as we continued with the remainder of the afternoon. After I dismissed the students, I tried calling the grandmother, but no one answered. So I made two phone calls. One to the local precinct and to the Department of Child Welfare. It was a long afternoon in which I had to help the local police make a report. I was terrified that the father would hurt the little boy. I went home that evening feeling defeated and cradling my little boy. Smelling his hair. Holding him close and feeling his little heartbeat as he slept peacefully in my arms. I promised that I would always keep him safe. I was deeply grateful that Christopher's father was the most loving father in the universe. He was devoted to his little boy and I prayed that someone would be protecting my student that evening.

The next morning as I parked my car on the sidewalk in front of the school building, I spied Octavius's father walking towards me as he crossed the street. What did that man not yell at me? He called me a bitch. He kept saying, "I know it was you bitch that called the police. I know it was you bitch!"

I asked him if he wanted to come into the school so we could sit down and talk and he said. "FUCK YOU!"

As I walked away my heart was racing. I was terrified that I would feel a punch on my back or feel him pulling on my hair to stop me. But it didn't happen. Instead, every day after I left the school building, he was leaning against my car on the driver's side near the back fender and he would say with the most sinister smile "Hi." When I would arrive in the morning after parking my car and walking away, he would say. "You have to be careful parking in this area. Anything can happen. My those are nice tires you have."

I would smile and give him the toughest look I had and say "Good Morning" or "Good Afternoon." This carried on for weeks and I was so scared about telling Christopher's dad. I didn't want Willy worrying about me. I would ask the school custodian to walk me to the car after school and that helped to deter him. He wasn't always out there when I would come out.

It was at that time that I realized that I couldn't stay at this school. I had my running shoes on. The way to deal with this menacing behavior was to leave. I was scared to tell my principal because I was worried that I never told her about making the call to the police or the Department of Child Welfare. I knew that I had every right to advocate for this child, but I wanted to be that responsible teacher who had a handle on things. But clearly, this was out of my hands and it was totally out of control. It was at this moment that I learned the key lesson of advocating for a child. However, doing this is only truly effective when you lock arms with your leaders and surround yourself with support.

CHAPTER TWENTY-ONE

MOVE TEACHER MOVE

I n life the only constant thing you can count on is change, and boy was CHANGE coming my way! On so many levels. Listening to my inner voice and leaning on my instincts led me to the next chapter in my young teaching career.

At the time, Christopher's godmother Rae was teaching in Port Chester, New York. She told me that teaching in Westchester County was a different universe. She was going to attend a Southern Westchester Boards of Cooperative Educational Services (BOCES) job fair in White Plains and she encouraged me to refresh my résumé and to attend. I gave it so much thought as I contemplated what I would leave behind. I was scared and I wanted to run. But this would mean that I would have to leave my new mentor. Our relationship had morphed from a mentor-mentee relationship to thick as thieves "work besties." It would mean not having the consultant support from Bank Street College. It would mean that I would be in another school with another principal who didn't know me. My current principal was so supportive and she trusted me implicitly with her eyes closed. I guess the reports from the consultants were quite favorable and she would always be in my room taking pictures of what I was doing with my students to get other teachers in the school to follow suit. My mentor was an instructional leader too and I was learning so much from her. Would I be able to teach in another school in Westchester without her? I was so scared. However, the moment came when I made up my mind to attend the job fair.

As I approached the school after driving up a long driveway that revealed a beautiful rustic stone building that looked more like a castle than a school I realized that maybe I was ready for this new chapter in my life. The school was called Highlands and perhaps God was delivering me to higher ground so that I could elevate my teaching craft and be ready for the next chapter in my profession. I asked God to give me the words during the preliminary screening interviews conducted by school principals and district human resource directors all over the southern Westchester region.

It was like a cattle call. The gymnasium was full of prospective hires and prospective employers. White Plains Public Schools was hosting the event and when I saw the long line of people waiting to interview for that district I felt discouraged. I decided to stand online and interview with Bedford Schools and Chappaqua school districts. I had no clue where these districts were located, but I felt confident that I did very well. Then I saw the line for White Plains and it was still long. But I decided to stand in line and wait. Rae had already interviewed and was walking around getting information from some vendors.

Finally, it was my turn to interview across a table with a long line of other applicants behind me. Stay centered Vilma. You've got this! I had the chance to read the ID badge of the person that was going to speak to me. Her name was Dr. Jeanne Vissa. She had the most endearing smile and a welcoming handshake. The moment she spoke, I recognized the accent. It was a Bronx accent. After introducing herself and sharing some pleasantries, she went right into the interview questions. I anchored my feet firmly on the ground and steadied my racing heartbeat by clasping my hands in front of me. Many of the questions she posed seemed so familiar regarding pedagogy centered on the Whole Language Approach and the importance of child-centered learning. Theme-based teaching and hands-on math learning were the key questions. I rattled on my answers like I was in 5th gear all by joking and smiling. That five-minute interview became a twenty-minute interview. After she spoke with me, she shook my hand and pulled me closer so that I could lean in. She said, "Vilma, you will be hearing from me. You would be perfect for our school."

Two weeks later I was sitting in an interview room with ten people in a conference room at the Chappaqua high school. I did very well and was posed a tough question: How would I feel about being the only Hispanic teacher in the school? I was stunned by that question. I answered. "My goal is that when children, parents, and staff see me that I seek to be a global teacher...not just a Hispanic teacher." The moment I spoke the last word of that sentence, it was resounding in my mind like a bullet ricocheting in my heart. I felt like I was betraying myself and that this was certainly not the place for me. Where was that call from that awesome principal in White Plains? The one that said I would be hearing from her? What was I doing? I graciously stood up and thanked them for the interview. I prayed that they wouldn't call me back. They never did. Little did I know that eight years later, this town would be the future home of the Clintons. This Bronx girl was not ready for such a move.

Instead, I received a life-changing call from Dr. Vissa. She wanted to meet with me at the end of the week. She apologized for the short notice. I jumped at the chance and geared up to interview for a kindergarten position at Church Street Elementary School. I brought my A+ interview game face with a portfolio of pictures, student samples of work, and a glowing letter of recommendation from one of the Bank Street College consultants Dr. Wolfe. I was ready! Upon entering the conference room and seeing a room of 12 people sitting at that rectangular table, I knew that I had my work cut out for me. The Chappaqua interview primed me for this scene. Poised and centered, I conveyed not only my thoughts on effective teaching practice and the most recent findings of educational theory, I also spoke about being a young mother of a toddler and my desire to find a home community where my son could group up in and where I could grow professionally. Oh boy! That Chappaqua interview was truly my dress rehearsal!

The next day, I got a call from the principal that she was confirming my strong candidacy with the director of human resources and that I would hear from her office for a final interview. I couldn't believe it. I was so close! The final weeks at my job were so tough. I was conflicted and guilt-ridden because I was terrified about stepping out of my comfort zone. But I knew that I needed to do this. I couldn't have Willy worrying about me and I needed to be safe for my beloved son. He needed his mother safe too. The following weekend I bought a navy blue shirt and blazer from JCPenney and opted to recycle the pink blouse that I wore for the last interview at Church Street School. I was ready for the call and the interview.

It came the following Monday. By Friday of that week, I was walking into a beautiful white estate called the Education House off of North Street in White Plains, New York. It looked like the house of a rich and famous person. What was I doing here in this affluent neighborhood? Was this the actual address? Did I read it wrong? But no, it was the address. It was such an intimidating location. I really had to dig deep to settle my nerves. I brought the leather portfolio that I had shared at my interview as well as the recommendation letters from the Bank Street consultants and my mentor Sandy. It was now in God's hands. What was I going to be asked? I prayed I had the right answers. As I waited inside the beautiful hall at the base of a regal red carpeted broad staircase, out of the scene of *Gone with the Wind*, I looked up and said a prayer. "God if this is for me...I receive it. If it is not for me...I receive that too."

The interview went super smoothly and by the end of the interview, she just wanted to know when I would begin my master's for state certification. I shared that I was just waiting until my little boy got a bit older so that I could begin. I shared that my goal was the Spring of 1994. It was the Spring of 1993 and I prayed that my response wouldn't convey the message that I was not serious about pursuing my permanent teaching certification. Immediately after that, she shared the salary scale information and I discovered that I would make seven thousand dollars over the $24,000 salary that I was earning working in the Bronx. I was blessed beyond measure. This would turn out to be the biggest choice that I made after the moment that six years earlier, I decided to go upstate to college. Now I was teaching upstate in a different county which seemed more like worlds away. Was I ready for this?

CHAPTER TWENTY-TWO

BLEEDING HEART

The pressures of being a new teacher, mother, and aspiring graduate student seemed so overwhelming at times. But with the help of colleagues, teaching partners, mentors, and friends I was able to get through it with grace and poise. They were my models of how to do this. I landed in one of the most innovative magnet schools in the district. They launched so many initiatives that were quite progressive for the time. Led by a motivational leader, we took on inclusive teaching practices for special needs, supportive hands-on constructivist math educational practices that broke away the societal barriers of inequity in math education, and the use of technology and science to spearhead thought-provoking, engaging, and child-centered learning units. As a new teacher, I was nurtured and placed on such fertile soil to grow and thrive. My new school, Church Street School, was a diamond in an urban city school district in the heart of Westchester. The moment I met that new principal and she hired me truly was the moment that my professional life took off.

With the leadership support of my new principal, after a year of teaching in this new school, I was sent to California in the summer of 1994 to be a part of a policy-changing equity mission developing new standards for learning mathematics. Within this new standards movement, I received guidance that helped me learn strategies for creating a leveled playing field for all students. The National Center for Restructuring Education, Schools, and Teaching (NCREST) was a research hub for educational leaders across the country. In a cross-country analysis of learning standards across different states, it was discovered that there weren't any consistently communicated and executed learning standards. To level the playing field within urban, suburban, and rural schools, school districts had to tighten up the scope and work toward a higher set of learning standards both in the learning of English language arts as well as mathematics.

Having the honor of traveling to California to participate in my first professional conference in San Diego was such a huge moment for me. I got to see that behind the curtain of Oz was truly a machine of different educational leaders, officials, and district leaders working to shape what teachers should be teaching. This restructuring initiative was spearheaded by teachers and teacher leaders. With the help of teachers across the country teaching to these new standards, capturing images and videos, and meeting to share what they learned and shared, I learned so much. Dr. Vissa had so much faith in me. She encouraged me to continue my "action research" as she called it and to enroll in the Bank Street College Math Leadership program.

By 1995, I had matriculated with the Math Leadership program at Bank Street College working to earn my master's in educational leadership. It was a 45-credit program with 30 credits in math education and 15 in supervision and administration. After sitting with my principal for a post-observation meeting, she shared that I had great potential to participate in future educational leadership opportunities. With a phone call to the director of the Math Leadership program at Bank Street and an immediate appointment thereafter, I was led by two phenomenal women who truly believed in me, Dr. Vissa and Dr. Dubitsky. the directors of this innovative and highly prestigious program.

It was an extensive process of attending graduate courses during the summers and throughout the school year. I managed to get through it with the help of my mother who would babysit my dear son Chris. However, my relationship with Christopher's dad did not survive. Although he was a remarkable father to my son, I felt that our life trajectories were heading in two different paths and I didn't feel happy in that relationship. No matter how much I tried to stay in the relationship, I just was not happy. I was in such a serious and intense mode that Chris' dad just couldn't connect with me. It wasn't his fault. I was just in another mental space and in the zone as I call it.

After a somewhat peaceful breakup I signed up to be a single mother, graduate student, young teacher leader, and trying to survive living in the Bronx and commuting to Westchester County. One day as a way to decompress, my friend from high school Monique invited me to go bowling with her and a few of her work colleagues. I placated her and finally went. It was at that moment that I met my future husband and life partner. James Vazquez had just thrown a strike down the bowling alley and our eyes locked. There he was throwing that bowling ball like a true pro and remaining in his strike posture waiting for all the pins to fall before yelling, "Yes!"

It was a fast and furious romance. He had two little girls from two former relationships and marriages. One of them lived in South Carolina and his youngest daughter lived in the Bronx. He warned me that there might be some baby-mama drama from his exes. But I really liked this guy and I didn't know what I was heading into. Before we knew it, we moved in together into a small apartment in Yonkers, with the vision of buying a house in Orange County, New York.

James was a hard worker, ambitious, and wanted to do anything he could to provide for his new family. Now my son would have a consistent father figure along with his bi-monthly weekend visits with his biological father. I would have a solid encouraging man that understood my passion to excel. We would live the American dream. When I signed up for my Master's program, he would take me to class, pick up my son from the babysitter, feed him, bathe him, and then pick me up from class so we could enjoy a late dinner. He loved to play jazz music in the car as we drove up the west side highway after indulging in some Papaya Gray hotdogs from 76th Street. The music would relax me, and I felt so taken care of. Together we could do anything. We could conquer all obstacles and challenges. There were many spinning plates, but I felt alive and I figured it out. I felt that there was great promise in my school district. There was a lot to still learn. Earning my master's was necessary to change my provisional license to acquire my permanent teaching certification.

CHAPTER TWENTY-THREE

EQUITY AGENDA

After earning my master's degree from Bank Street College, I was encouraged by my college advisor and mentor to teach a few graduate courses. My son was a little older, and with James' help, I was able to teach evening courses at the college. The drive from upstate New York to the Upper West Side of Manhattan was pretty smooth because it went against the flow of commuter traffic. This was a saving grace. Finding a parking spot on Riverside Drive by 112th and 114th was always easy.

I would walk the streets shared by Barnard students, Columbia University students, and Bank Street College students with such pride. Being a young Latina scholar and working to prepare the next generation of teachers was a great honor. Here I was at the young age of 29 looking more like I was 19. I remember the first time I taught a math education course in the Spring of 1998. I tried my best to dress the part by wearing slacks and a cardigan. One time I had come in early to set up the lecture hall and left my syllabus and copies at the front table by the podium. I sat in the back of the hall to take a small break and just observe my students as they entered. I wanted to take in the moment.

There I was sipping my Diet Coke and looking at my watch when a student walked up to the back and asked me... "What do you know about this Cabán lady? Have you seen her syllabus? She is asking way too much."

I smiled and said. "I have heard she is a very fair professor." She shrugged her shoulders and raised my handouts with silent disapproval. At that moment, I walked to the podium to greet my graduate students. You should have seen her mouth drop as I spoke. She didn't know where to put her face. I smiled a warm smile. The mortified student tried to make it up to me by being an engaged course participant.

By the end of the semester, she apologized for her presumptuous statement and gave me a glowing course evaluation stating that my progressive strategies would help her be the best teacher she could be to her students in the South Bronx. My mouth dropped when I read that. I assumed this white young woman would be teaching in the suburbs. Here she was working so hard to earn her degree and teach in New York City. It was a key moment when I realized that we can't function by perception alone. Making presumptions sets us back both socially and professionally. We were both striving to change education for all.

A few months later, I was signing a contract for a promotion with White Plains Public Schools. In this historic and new position, I was going to be the district's first Math Instructional Specialist working with five elementary schools, a Pre-K program, and a newcomer program located in one of the larger middle schools. With the support of my former graduate school professors, my Math Leadership Program advisors, and mentors I had an arsenal of consultants and resources at my fingertips.

Math equity was on my professional and personal agenda as I worked coaching teachers in their math teaching practices. It was not easy at all. The teachers did not understand the intention and scope of my work. With time, as I developed instructional coaching relationships across the schools and across the grades, I was able to identify some systemic barriers to quality math education for our economically disenfranchised students across the district. I was working to close the minority achievement gap at a time when the educational law shifted to Bush's No Child Left Behind Act (NCLB). However, there were many children left behind in homogenous teaching and ability groups. There were high flyers and then those on the bottom. Ironically it was not just about being left behind, it was about leaving them to stay below. The brown faces of children across the district who were failing in mathematics were truly inequitable and a disgrace.

I was grateful to have the support of the district educational leadership to organize and set project timelines that would slowly throw out antiquated teaching resources and bring in teaching resources, curriculum, and assessment practices that were about supporting our most struggling students. The work started slow with my instructional visits and demonstration lessons highlighting hands-on learning, and constructivist teaching practices. Convincing principals to release a team of grade-level teachers to debrief and share additional resources was not welcomed. Once I was able to dispel the collective perception that I was there in an evaluative capacity, I was able to promote more capacity-building opportunities. I began creating a culture of learning among the staff. It was a huge feat. But I signed on with an eager heart. As I served as a teacher, school-based math lead teacher, and district-appointed math instructional specialist, I was able to develop positive professional relationships centered on positive collegial interactions and project collaborations.

I strongly believe that change shouldn't be about one person. It has to be about the collective. In my work with over 200 teachers, I was able to witness excellent math teaching and I would invite those teachers to be a part of a cadre of math lead teachers. It was not easy convincing my assistant superintendent of curriculum and instruction to extend a budget to offer more professional development from Bank Street College and the National Council of Teachers (NCTM) math conferences. Thankfully I was given a modest budget to equip these teachers as math leaders in their schools. With the help and support of other math lead teachers, I created several professional development tools that were produced by the local district which included teacher training videos and summer school curriculum guides. Capturing images and actual teaching practices in a series of different professional development videos which were produced by the district's television media specialist, we focused on instruction that created a learning environment for promoting math equity. It was so gratifying to plan and develop this work.

The next pivotal step was chairing a committee of 11 math lead teachers to begin aligning the district's kindergarten through fifth-grade curriculum with the NCTM standards. With their feedback, suggestions, and exemplary lesson writing we were able to position teachers to have a delineated scope and sequence of curricular content that they could teach to.

Rolling out NCTM standards-based math programs was the next huge step. My superintendent of schools and the board of education supported me as we received funding to purchase the Investigations in Time and Space math program. The purchase of this math program along with all of the hands-on math manipulatives and computer software that supported the learning made a huge dent in changing the landscape of teaching in our district. Math scores on the New York State math assessments were increasing and exceeding the scores for English language arts. However, there were marginalized students who were still not making academic gains.

I was able to organize a Math Equity Conference with different community stakeholders from White Plains which included the White Plains Youth Bureau, El Centro Hispano (an advocacy community organization), district leaders, different administrative staff, teachers, and parent leaders. Creating capacity for change begins with coming to the table to identify where we are failing our students. Where are we coming up short? It was noted that in order to create change, there had to be accountability standards not only for our students but for our teachers. With the No Child Left Behind law, there were accountability systems that were in place in schools to track student progress. Now we just needed to create an interval and district-wide math testing system that would help forecast which group of students were in need of additional math support prior to state testing so that we could begin academic intervention strategies. The fact that these conversations were happening in 2003 was avant-garde. I was grateful

for the faith that my district leaders had in me to spearhead that charge.
Once we had data that we could hone in on, I developed different
math test preparation conferences and grade-level meetings so that we
could attack certain areas of deficits with a few targeted instructional
practices.

There was a small cohort of students that were under Title 10 state
funding. They were our homeless population that resided in a local
homeless shelter in the center of town. I realized that if there was going
to be a change to address this marginalized group, I would have to
create a program that would reach out to those children living in the
shelter. By then, I had been with James for close to 10 years, and he
was so used to me with my grandiose visions, but when I was going
after work and on Saturdays to do the family math workshops, he was
not a happy camper. In retrospect, I understand this. But at the time,
I needed to place my mission first. Making interactive math games
that focused on developing numeracy concepts took many hours of
hands-on crafts and planning. Purchasing materials for distribution
took many of my Sundays so that I could go out to the shelter on
Mondays. This way they had the games for the whole week. With
a modest budget to purchase pizza, I would entice families to come
out and listen to me about ways we can play with math and learn
with math. Those moments were truly my most memorable ones as
a teacher and community advocate. It was in those moments that I
realized that the scope of my work was limited as a math instructional
specialist. I had to think broader.

Dr. Marvin Cohen from Bank Street College had received a grant
from the National Science Foundation to create a professional development program called Math For All. He came several times to observe
me and film my lessons working with students with special needs.
Afterward, we would debrief and film the interviews. It turns out that
many of the lessons and sound bites from my interviews became key
components of their professional development math training semi-
nars. With the support of the NSF grant funding, they were able to
acquire a publisher with the Corbin Publishing House. So out there
somewhere in Chattanooga, Tennessee some young teacher is seeing

a Bronx-raised math educator and advocate talk about Math for All. How awesome is that?! I am profoundly appreciative and indebted to my Bank Street family and mentors for playing such an important role in the development of this national math teacher resource.

It was a conversation with Dr. Cohen after filming that convinced me that I had to go after the next transformative phase in my educational journey. I had to pursue my doctorate of education so that I could strive to make a larger impact. These were seeds planted in my spirit by three wonderful women who contributed to my personal growth. Dr. Vissa, Dr. Dubitsky, and my future building principal Dr. Klemm. In order to do this, I would have to step down from my leadership role and transition back into the classroom. It was not an easy decision to make, but it was nonetheless a necessary one. Dr. Klemm was the principal of one of my favorite schools where I worked as the district math coach. I knew she would continue to support my professional growth. Dr. Vissa retired and was living in Philadelphia and I missed her so much. So many times when things got tough, I would ask myself, "What would Dr. Vissa do?" Then the toughest blow came when Dr. Dubitsky shared she was retiring. She encouraged me to pursue my dream. She said, "Honey, if at my age of 65, I can still learn how to play piano and bike 10 miles a day, at the age of 35 you can do this with your hands tied behind your back." That was the wind that helped me lift my wing to a higher plane...a bird's eye vantage point that this lady was just getting started.

My vision was not to make a state impact or a regional impact. My goal was to make an international impact. That night I prayed to God and spoke the scripture of 1 Chronicles 4:10, "Lord, oh that you would bless me and expand my territory." It was at that moment that I had the courage to boldly declare a larger vision. At the time, there was a sense of social justice urgency stirring in my heart. I believed that education was the great equalizer and no matter what I did to try to level the playing field of math education, there were some systemic systems in place that were not allowing for math equity for all. My goal was to pursue my doctorate and explore this inequality, this miseducation phenomenon, and pull away the shroud that kept so many of us from seeing a way to support our most vulnerable student population.

Chapter Twenty-Four

QUESTIONS LEAD THE WAY

P ersonally, a lot was going on in my relationship with James. After coping with the pressures of a demanding job as well as seeking to balance home life and work life, James and I made a healing decision with the help of pastoral counseling to seek resolution. We were together for close to ten years when we finally decided to get married. It was a fall wedding in a small chapel with only 40 guests. Ridgeway Alliance in White Plains had a small chapel and our Pastor did the nuptials. It was an exciting new beginning as a couple and a family.

My maid of honor was Sandy, my professional mentor and now my dear friend. In her duty as a maid of honor, prior to walking out into the chapel, she asked me a pivotal question. "Chica, are you sure you want to do this? You know you don't have to get married."

I chuckled and said, "Girl, we are not doing this now."

That question lingered in my heart for so many years after that. James met me as a kindergarten teacher who had grown in so many areas both educationally and professionally. At every bend in my journey, I always felt like I was fighting to be me, and boy did we fight. I figured that once we got married, he would settle down and accept my nature to grow, my passion to expand, and my desire to make a difference. I thought it was just a matter of time before which I would be able to bend the arc of his will to help him see that I had a larger calling on my heart and spirit. However, we hit a very tough breaking point a year after I got married when I applied to the doctoral program and I was accepted. He couldn't understand why. I earned my master's and made decent money. Why the hell would I take on the burden of going to school again? He was complaining that I was neglecting my duties as a wife. I resented him so much for that.

My reaction to his resistance was to dive deeper into my studies and chase after excellence. I was asked to teach a graduate course at Manhattanville College by the student teacher supervisor Jeanne Connor. She had placed a few Manhattanville Fellows who were career changers. They would observe my lessons as I worked with my 4th and 5th-grade students. Word got back to her about my teaching practices, and she encouraged me to teach a course in the Spring. That was when I realized that earning my doctorate could position me in the future to teach graduate school full-time after I retired. That would come for about another 15 years, but I was always a planner. So having my doctorate would be a plus. This was going to be my winning point with James. I could earn more money and we would reach our goal of retiring to Florida a more attainable reality.

I was 35 years old with an adolescent son and retirement seemed so far away. But that is all that James spoke about. In the meantime, I had my hopes and dreams and I was trying to be the best model for my dear son Christopher, who at the time was on the varsity wrestling team and the junior varsity football team. Between games and commuting to White Plains, where he attended school instead of upstate, I didn't know how I was going to pull it off attending doctoral courses. But with prayers, extra coffee (which I didn't start drinking until this time of my life), and late nights of reading and writing, I was able to pull it off. At times, it would take a toll on my health, my marriage, and my home life. My days started at 5:00 am preparing for an hour commute with my adolescent son and then high schooler.

During the winter, it was tougher as my son had to be at the high school for early qualifying weigh-ins for his wrestling tournaments and matches. I would go in early to prepare for my lessons and daily teaching responsibilities. After school, I would take a thirty-minute nap and then gear up for the next part of my day which was centered on all of my doctoral coursework readings. Next, I would rush off to the high school to see my son's football games in the cold bleachers, sneaking in some more reading during the time my son was on the bench. It was easier when my son would have home games or home wrestling matches because travel time was dramatically shorter.

My favorite moments were truly driving home with my son Chris. For an hour, I would connect with him about his social and academic life. It was mother-and-son time where all of life's pulls and pressures were suspended as we bonded. So many beautiful conversations about his dreams and aspirations. His questions about me growing up in the Bronx and living in poverty. Sometimes I would talk with him about what I experienced in high school and see what a beautiful difference my son was having both as a student and a young student leader. I was so proud of him when he would share the things he was planning as President of the Student Government at the high school. I was always impressed by how mathematics and science were so easy for him. He loved it and I was grateful that my son had so many extraordinary teachers. As a parent, I was proud of my school district. As a teacher, I felt grateful for all that I learned to become a better teacher. However, it was very conflicting to see that there was a large group of economically disadvantaged students who were not getting what my beloved son received.

My favorite courses were centered on research methodology and the use of qualitative data and quantitative data to paint a research scenario. I realized that the situation of inequities in math education was extremely complex. It would require a combination of both research methodologies to take a more comprehensive look into the inequities. The intensive work of taking three years of doctoral courses was not always easy to handle. When I started working on my doctoral dissertation, I began to hone in on my research focus. The problem that I explored was the low math achievement of local economically disadvantaged elementary students as well as the limited nature of professional development for teachers directly working with low-math achievement fourth graders in my district's school-based supplemental educational service after-school math program.

I wanted to hone in on a local problem that was replicated throughout the country in both suburban and urban school settings. My local problem started to unfold approximately eight years ago when I served as a district math instructional specialist within the school district. In that role, I collaborated with educational leaders and teachers to design district-based and school-based math professional development opportunities across five elementary schools, an early childhood preschool program, and a transitional program for new immigrant elementary students.

During this time, the local district responded to the United States Department of Education's No Child Left Behind Act of 2001 wherein school districts received legislative mandates to demonstrate educational reform efforts that could yield higher rates of academic success for all students. The ultimate objective of NCLB was to close the minority achievement gap between socio-economically diverse students wherein said students must demonstrate proficiency on state standardized tests by the year 2014. In spite of implementing higher math learning standards for students, the local problem continued as I served in the role of a school-based math lead teacher and fourth-grade elementary school teacher. Although my district was in the midst of implementing the standards-based math program, a marginalized population of economically disadvantaged students continued to demonstrate low mathematical proficiency on state and district math assessments. As an educator and school-based math lead teacher, the experiences I gained by directly working within the context of this local problem were favorable in conducting a doctoral project case study.

Prior to the launch of the study, I participated in a local district-based and state-mandated initiative wherein testing data were collected and analyzed to report on the quality of math instruction as well as monitor student math achievement. One of the primary objectives of using this district-wide database monitoring system is to help educational leaders track standardized math testing results from the New York State Standardized Mathematics Assessments for third, fourth, and fifth-grade students. The longitudinal school testing data for the past three years revealed a significant math achievement gap between economically disadvantaged fourth-grade students and students classified as "not disadvantaged" as demonstrated by the New York State Standardized Fourth Grade Math Assessment. Statistics collected from successive *New York State School Report Card: Accountability and Overview Reports* focused on different student groups within the local school setting. The numeric data revealed that in the past three years, there has been a 10% increase in the number of students demonstrating math proficiency on the New York State Standardized Fourth Grade Math Assessment. However, a significant number of economically disadvantaged students demonstrate low math achievement across a span of three years. Economically disadvantaged students were students who were eligible to receive free or reduced school lunch.

In the role of math lead teacher, I reviewed the standardized assessment findings and identified a significant number of economically disadvantaged students not making adequate yearly progress in the learning of mathematics. Regardless of the enforcement and accountability measures of NCLB, research suggested that many school communities were not in compliance with developing, administering, and evaluating supplemental educational services. These were SES services that offered standards-based learning experiences outside of the traditional academic structure of a school day expressly designed for the promotion of academic success. Many times there were after-school programs, but they could also include early morning tutorial services. It had been close to ten years since the release of the NCLB educational mandate, and standardized testing trends revealed that an academic achievement gap still existed among socio-economic subgroups. School learning communities had to take more innovative steps toward educational reform to eradicate educational inequities marked by a minority and socio-economic achievement gap.

Conducting that study within my school district required the support of not only my building principal and school colleagues but also the full support of the district superintendent. They were very proud of my efforts, and every time they saw me during different professional development opportunities workshops, they would also share how grateful they were that I was working to place our school district on the map. Teaching in White Plains opened up a new universe to me. I learned quickly that my presence was needed in a community where students didn't always see themselves. Being a Latina teacher who spoke Spanish was a welcoming sight for newcomers and students who immigrated from other Latin American countries. In our teaching profession, we learn the art of suspending our home lives, trials, and tribulations, to be present in the moment that we are cradling someone else's child with their set of dreams and aspirations bundled up in the hearts of their precious children.

This realization really hit me hard when 20 years after teaching a third-grade student, this young woman actively sought to find me teaching in another school within the same school district. She was serving as a substitute teacher and gearing up for a new profession as a counselor. It brings me to tears just thinking and writing about this. If she only knew where I was at the time personally and professionally while I was her third-grade teacher.

Michelle Espinosa recapped the profound impact I had on her young life. She remembered coming from Colombia at the tender age of eight years old. Being so scared coming to a new school. The moment she learned I spoke Spanish she described how she was so relieved that if she could understand something, she could ask me to explain it to her. She shared how much I meant to her. Michelle described a scenario that I had totally forgotten. It was the last day of school and when she realized that she wouldn't see me for the summer poor Michelle began to cry uncontrollably. When it was time for dismissal, students would normally walk themselves to the bus circle to board the buses. That day I realized that little Michelle would need some more encouragement. I gave her two envelopes with my home address asking her that if she wanted to write to me in the summer, she could certainly reach out to me. I had just moved to my new home in upstate New York and I would be home most of the summer getting my new home ready. Her eyes lit up and this helped her from crying so much. I walked with her hand in hand to the bus circle, boarded the bus with her, placed her seatbelt on for her, and gently dried her tears as she realized it was truly time to go. I promised her that I would see her in September when she was a big girl in fourth grade. We could have lunch together. As I walked off the bus, I looked back at her, smiled, and waited outside the bus, waving to her outside with the biggest smile that I could muster. Seeing her cry truly broke my heart. I didn't walk away from that sidewalk until I couldn't see the bus anymore.

Twenty years later, that little angel, now a young woman, reminded me of that small act of empathy and compassion. She shared how at that moment she felt so loved. She shared that it was the moment she realized that she wanted to help others too. That day I remember seeing her beautiful face with the most beautiful chandelier earrings peeking through her long hair. I complimented her on her earrings, and she told me she got them from Colombia. Later on that day, Michelle came by again, handing me a little package wrapped in colored tissue paper. It was the earrings that she wore. With a grateful heart, six years later I still have those earrings. Every time I put them on, I think of Michelle, the walk to the school bus, and the moment that I shared that loving moment with little Michelle.

How many little Michelles are out there where a small act of kindness, a shared moment of comfort, and a gentle reminder that everything is going to be ok would touch a child forever? I love my teaching profession, and no matter how exhausting it can be, I realize how I must be entirely on and present all the time when I am with a student. They are watching, gathering moments of affirmation and encouragement with a smile, a wink, or a simple gesture. Whenever I feel overwhelmed as an educator, I think of Michelle. I am proud to share that today Michelle is a counselor at a local community college working with the next generation of Latino newcomer students striving to be future leaders in the midst of adversity.

Almost twenty years after I started teaching in White Plains, I taught the first Dual Language kindergarten class in the district with my Spanish zone partner Damari. I was the English zone teacher. I completed my doctoral prospectus. I was simply waiting for the institutional review board's approval to begin my study. I was conflicted about what my doctoral study would focus on, but I knew that a part had to explore math equity for English Language Learners.

Having this opportunity to teach dual language was mutually beneficial. I would sign up to do something that not too many people were excited about supporting the educational leadership, and this would offer me some fertile groundwork for action research. This was pretty groundbreaking considering that students were not learning Spanish until seventh grade. Our school district saw the importance of developing native language arts for our native Spanish speakers, and I saw the potential to explore how math equity can occur in a dual language classroom and possibly in other school programs in the school.

CHAPTER TWENTY-FIVE

PYRAMIDS AND TEMPLES

M y doctoral committee Chair Dr. Heather Miller was immense-ly proud of my efforts. She had recommended that I expand my work to examine math equity on an international level by joining her colleague and friend Dr. Johnny Lott who was the former president of the National Council of Teachers of Mathematics. He was traveling with a group of scholars from the People to People Ambassador Program around the world focusing on math equity which was an important tenet of the National Council of Teachers of Mathematics. At the time, he was the director of the Center for Excellence in Teaching and Learning at the University of Mississippi. This global mission with the People to People Ambassador Program was going to be his sunset tour before fully retiring in 2010. This opportunity fell on my lap from the heavens. Who would have thought this was possible?

I was able to travel with the People to People Ambassador Program with a team of national math educators and experts from different universities. I felt so honored to be a part of this cadre of inspirational education reformers and thought leaders. Within this international forum, I had the honor of engaging in bilateral, educational, and professional exchanges with international educational leaders and counterparts. This international congress offered a platform to examine effective pedagogy and educational reform. Being nominated to serve as a delegate in this international education mission was such a wild dream come true.

Concurrent with my research study, as a practitioner-researcher I was able to travel to Egypt, Cambodia, and Vietnam. With the full support of my district superintendent, I was able to produce with the White Plains Television Specialist a teacher training video that I co-produced in collaboration with teachers from my home school district—*Illuminating Effective Differentiated Instruction Classroom Practices for Math Learning*. The central aim of my professional work with the local teachers focused on developing collegial sharing environments that continually strived to differentiate math learning and meet the needs of diverse students. Many copies of this professional development resource were produced along with lesson descriptions of effective teaching practices.

As a gesture of professional exchange to the Cambodian, Egyptian, and Vietnamese educational leaders/dignitaries, I shared this professional development resource. Armed with this archive of best practices, I was asked to present at the Royal University in Phnom Penh, Cambodia; the Teacher Professional Center in Cairo, Egypt; and the Ho Chi Minh University in Vietnam. The challenge was presenting my preliminary findings on best teaching practices that had to be translated into Arabic, Cambodian, and Vietnamese. Dr. Lott had a lot of faith in me. He would smile every time I walked up to the podium in the lecture halls of these faraway places. Usually, the Minister of Educator or a dignitary was in the audience, and I just would do everything I could to not throw up. I would go back to my memories of teaching graduate school at Bank Street College as a young mom and remember that I have a larger mission in my heart. I had to boldly stand in my truth and this work was going to be necessary to further my doctoral research findings. We had a full itinerary visiting universities, schools, and government officials sharing best practices and research findings. Many times, I would pinch myself to see if this was a dream.

But there I was bracing myself at the podium in all of those venues and remembering what my core focus was. I wanted to make a larger contribution than the one I made in my home school district.

This Latina from the Bronx shed many tears of profound elation as I stood in the shadow of the Great Pyramids of Giza. It was a tremendous honor to be a part of the private night tour of the Cairo Museum of Antiquities with the famous Egyptian Archeologist and Minister of State for Antiquities Affairs, Zahi Hawass, who noted that my second long toe was like the toes of the Pharaohs...a symbol of Egyptian divinity. What?! All my life I rejected my feet and my ugly long toes. And now they were a sign of royalty and divinity? It was like I was transported to an alternate universe where a crown was placed on this poor little girl's head and she was magically beamed to stroll through the Siem Reap Temple in Cambodia or cry her eyes out while visiting the Killing Fields in Vietnam. How was this possible? How was it that they were no longer pages inside an encyclopedia? They were real. Like if I had stepped into the Magic Tree House landing into these past worlds. It was so surreal. Whenever I doubted my abilities, I just would pull up the courage from the depths of my soul just like I did when I prayed the Prayer of Jabez:

"And Jabez called on the God of Israel saying, 'Oh that You would bless me indeed, and enlarge my territory, that Your hand would be with me, and You would keep me from evil, that I might not cause pain!'"

I asked God to expand my territory...my platform for making a change.

Well, you know the saying, "Be careful what you ask for"? My loving God expanded my territory indeed! The humble prayer petitioning for help now opened a new world for this Bronx girl. Now with the heart of a teacher, my favorite part of these delegation trips was visiting the urban and rural schools throughout these countries. So many conversations, one-to-one interactions with students, and thrilling observations were made I still carry with me today. These first-hand experiences were invaluable. As much as I was there to share as a delegate expert, I walked away having learned from my international colleagues. I saw similarities in techniques and strategies as well as a stark contrast in teaching approaches. Ultimately the goal for all of us in that exchange was to learn what we might reasonably adapt from these cultures for use in the United States throughout our classroom. It was truly a professional and cultural interchange of educational theories, practices, ideas, and human connection.

My memories of visiting a girls' high school in Giza, Egypt. While touring the hallways before walking into a classroom with a member of the Minister of Education, I stopped to practice the very limited Arabic I learned to ask one of the girls if she could help me adjust my headscarf to look like her. She was so sweet to indulge me as she grabbed my hand to enter a nearby ladies' room. There she took off my poorly placed headscarf with strands of hair peeking out on the side of my face and she proceeded to wrap it beautifully around my face and using a small pin, tuck it into place. Securely placing it on my head. As I looked in the mirror, I smiled and said "shukran lakum." She received my thanks with a gorgeous smile. She shared that she had to go back to class "Wadaeaan." It was at that moment that I realized that my mission to find math equity was not only for the children in my home school district but that women needed math equity to open career pathways for a brighter future. Math education was a civil rights issue and it was a woman's right. I learned that math education is like a huge gateway to numerous career opportunities in science, medicine, engineering, and other technical careers where math was the language of that profession. Our girls needed us to tear away at that gate!

Visiting the classrooms in Siem Reap Cambodia in a modest little school, where they had no electricity, and cramming 50-60 students into a classroom, where I was most humbled. As I entered the classroom, and students jumped out of their seats to bow down in reverence, I cried. That they would receive this stranger with such hospitality and sheer respect made me see that the role of a teacher is truly extraordinary. As I looked at their beautiful brown eyes, tanned skin, their jet-black straight hair, their pearly white smiles, inside their crisp white and navy school uniforms I was in awe of how they all huddled up together.

I observed how they would look at their geometry lesson with such wonder, which consisted of a drawing on a dry-erase board with a few algorithms scribbled next to an Isosceles triangle. In his right hand, he had cut a triangle out of cardboard and used it as a visual prop to support his theorems and teachings. I witnessed how the teacher was very clever about encouraging his students to share their thinking with not only the teacher but with their fellow classmates. The classroom culture that this teacher created was truly the equalizer. It didn't matter what technology was at his fingertips, or what innovative teaching tools that he had at his disposal. It was about the connection he was making with his students one-on-one. He saw them, and they knew that they were seen. They felt present and cherished as his students. Something was being lost in our American schools. Content and rigor over relating and student-teacher connection. Cradling our nation's promise of prosperity involves a vested connection with our students. Math equity is not about not giving everyone the same thing. It is more about giving students what they need when they need it. This revelation was not trivial but more affirming. These young minds and hearts forever changed me and it was the fire that I needed as I was gearing up for the final phase of my dissertation writing.

After these math ambassador trips, my doctoral research took form and I chose to focus on math equity as it relates to the No Child Left Behind Act and funding used to offer supplemental educational services for economically disadvantaged students. In my preliminary studies and literature review, I discovered a strong correlation between disadvantaged youth and English language learners (ESL and newcomer students) and low performance on district math assessments and state assessments. Using Title 1 funding, schools were trying to close the achievement gap by offering after-school math tutorial support. However, there was very little guidance from the New York State Department of Education as well as the United States Department of Education. Traditionally this subgroup or marginalized group of students did not do well in mathematics and by the time they were in high school, they were not enrolled in the advanced placement math courses. Mathematics is the language of science and there is a natural link between math with chemistry, engineering, computer science, and advanced science courses. The demographics of students in advanced math and science were typically students who were not facing socio-economic hardships. They were mostly white Caucasian students and students who were not on the list for free or reduced-fee lunch.

This situation created the perfect storm to pursue an advocacy research study. I felt it was my civic responsibility to engage my local district and school leaders in a moral dialogue centered on the local implementation of a math supplemental educational service program. It was an impassioned concern for the inequity and needs of these students from the lower socio-economic classes. My goal was to bring forward research findings from this study that could bring about educational and professional change which could directly affect the nature of professional development for the teachers of these supplemental educational service math programs.

I spent many hours observing instruction in these after-school math programs, collecting data, recording field notes, and interviews with students and teachers. Ultimately, my findings from this research study revealed that not all of the students who were performing below grade-level math standards and expectations were receiving access to supplemental math services. With the use of a standards-based math program assessment that the district purchased, they were beginning to centralize student performance data that was helping them identify math progress in addition to what the state reported on the standardized math assessments. Prior to this, there was a huge vacuous space which I would personally call "the data black hole" where there was a limited scope on how our economically disadvantaged students were doing. With the support of this performance data hub, the teachers in the after-school math programs had a better sense of where the math deficits lay and how they could address it. Data from interviews revealed a significant level of frustration because teachers felt that they needed more professional development using a broader set of teaching strategies to support students with varying needs of instructional math support. The class grouping of these after-school math programs was smaller than the average class size. This fostered smaller cooperative learning groups and time for more one-on-one direct teacher support.

In my findings, I learned that the majority of the students in these after-school math programs were Latino or African-American students. The minority math achievement gap was very wide in our school district. There was also a large subgroup of English Language Learners that were mostly girls. Triangulating findings with interviews, field notes, and demographic data it was revealed that many of them were very quiet and did not actively engage in large group discussions. It was found that promoting dyadic partnerships or small groups would be more instrumental in supporting these students.

The use of instructional technology at the time was lacking, and it was not consistently used by all of the teachers. Using interactive and supportive visual technology was a way to pull students into the math tutorial lessons and small group work. Teachers noted a need for more professional collaboration and exchange to continue supporting each other creating a toolkit of instructional strategies. This would help inform their instructional planning and the need to differentiate learning opportunities for students.

One of the biggest gems discovered was the impressive impact that collaborative team teaching had on students. Whenever an ESOL teacher (English to Speakers of Other Languages) worked with a general education teacher or with a special education teacher, there was a significant increase in student performance on the math standardized tests. Their experiences and feedback were necessary to begin scaffolding a more efficient and supporting scope of sequence for lessons throughout the year.

There were three math topics or areas of study that students struggled with. They were multiplication, fractions, and data with line graphs and line plots. Once it was discovered what the potential pitfalls were, teachers could be better supported by professional development math coaches to augment or give more direct teacher support on these math topics. The main takeaway was that teachers expressed a strong need for a clear vision of the work that should take place across the upper elementary grades. The minority math achievement gap would begin to take shape in third grade and each year it would become progressively wider and wider so by the time they were in middle school, they had a slim chance to be in any accelerated or advanced math courses. This was disconcerting.

Math education for all is about leveling the playing field and offering access to future careers in technology and the sciences. Math is the gatekeeper to gaining access to more diverse career pathways. If we are essentially not offering quality math education, then we are not honoring the student's future. Math is a civil rights issue! We are denying them the full active citizenry of a student when we deny access to future income-earning potential. We delegate them to limited access to now lower paying jobs and limited opportunity to fully participate in a college-bound track. If students can't pass the basic algebra placement exam, they will not be able to earn college credits for their core coursework in the sciences. It is the building block of other science, technology, and engineering content.

Upon completing this intensive and arduous research journey, I was relieved to present my findings to the doctoral committee and gear up for my oral defense. It was such a daunting task. Just reading the word defense in oral defense sets you up for what to expect. It separates the boys from the men. It is the junction that many doctoral candidates do not even come to because life has thrown so many curve balls.

The professional and personal demands compete for your attention as you spend countless hours pouring over data, identifying themes, corroborating findings, pulling out your hair, crying over the drafts of writing, writing in your pajamas all weekend, forgetting to eat or wash your hair, and tuning out your family. All the while they simply see you as an inanimate and disconnected figure glued to a laptop. The oral defense is the space where you are presenting yourself as a scholar and as an authority in such a narrow spot of a wide discipline. It is the space where you are to cogently and clearly explain what you should see backward and forward. It is the place where you seal your fate by making a genuine contribution that fits with other research and scholarship in your field. What is supposed to be scholarly discourse feels more like a grilling session where you doubt if spending the past five years has truly prepared you. Unpacking educational research theories and doing it in a way that demonstrates the implication and significance of your findings.

The oral defense day was set for the middle of October, but life threw one huge curveball.

My stepfather was dying. He had cancer and was in hospice care in Fort Myers, Florida. My brother Rafy was close by and he was the main contact. However, my brothers and I in New York wanted to be there for these final moments. My doctoral journey was placed on pause and my doctoral chairperson totally understood. So I took a family leave and flew out on the first plane that I could. Standing by his side. Holding his hand. Crying and remembering the pain, but also making room for healing. My mother couldn't see him. She chose not to and I totally understood that. She carried over two decades of pain from the verbal, emotional, and physical abuse. She needed to set that boundary. I respected it and I felt it was my place as my brother's older sister to stand in the gap and be present. The love and support I received from James and our family was truly beautiful. He would fly to Florida on the weekends to be with us. We stayed vigilant in those final moments, bringing forth smiles, family memories, his favorite music, and suspending time so that he knew he was loved.

One of my final conversations with him was when he asked me to forgive him. I told him, *"Papi...esta bien. Tranquilo. Descansa."* He squeezed my hand. I shared with him that the next day I had to take a plane to fly back for my wedding anniversary. I got on that plane with a heavy heart. We had shared a moment of beautiful healing and my heart went out to him as he begged me for his forgiveness. In those moments I buried the antagonist of my childhood days. He was blind, suffering from the pain of the cancer, and the gangrene that took over both of his legs. The death of tissue in his body was creating sepsis and it was going to beat the cancer. It broke my heart to see him this way and to hear him speak in so much pain. It was so difficult to leave. I walked away with a heavy heart. But spiritually a huge load was lifted off of my spirit. I felt whole and at peace with the situation.

The next morning on October 31, 2010, I got the call. Papi had met his maker. He was at peace. I was at peace. Forgiveness filled the void in my heart. It was a gift to myself. My mother couldn't bear to see him in his final days. I had to be not only a math ambassador but also a love ambassador for my grieving brothers. Flying back to support my brother Rafy with funeral arrangements, prayer, encouragement, and grieving together was not easy. It was emotionally depleting. I had nothing else to give. I was tapped out. My doctoral chair rescheduled my oral defense and I had four weeks to prepare. Somehow I needed to make it happen.

I channeled into the peace that I received from forgiving my stepfather. That recharged my battery and imbued a strong sense of determination to finish and put this doctoral oral defense behind me. All the preparations were made for me to sit before the committee and present my case.

It is amazing how when you are faced with the insurmountable pressure of work, family life, and personal obligations you must tap into a reserve of fortitude and a bit of that numbing peace that will push you over the finish line. In retrospect, it is all a blur to me, but based on the feedback of the doctoral committee, I successfully defended my doctoral study findings. I was functioning on autopilot. My school principal Dr. Klemm was extremely proud and supportive of my accomplishments. In light of all of the obstacles and personal challenges I faced with a failing marriage and the loss of a parent, I persevered.

I was extremely touched that after I shared the news, she had a news correspondent from the local paper interview me. Little did I know the degree of the accomplishment I had just made. She reached out to the Pew Research Center and shared some stark statistics about the number of Latina women who earned a doctoral degree. *"Dr. Vilma Cabán-Vazquez is one of only about 46,000 Hispanic women in the nation to ever obtain a doctorate degree. According to the Pew Hispanic Research Center, Senior Research Associate Dr. Richard Fry reports that just .4 percent of Latina women ever reach that level of education, making her journey unique."*

Having the love and support of the people in my circle is what made me stronger, and I will forever be grateful for everything they did to help me grow. Crossing this threshold was not another checkbox, it was a major milestone on my way toward my future destiny of informing policy and advocating for the needs of children. Little did I know that completing this research would position me for the next humanitarian chapter of my life. A new world of postdoctoral research would open up to me with solicitations from various researchers and advocacy organizations. Now the math ambassador was becoming a global children's ambassador.

In the early part of 2011, I was asked to join my former doctoral Chair Dr. Miller, and my former research methodologist Dr. Cavanagh on a research study in Colorado centered on the lack of Latino representation in the environmental science fields. They had received a grant from my Alma Mata Walden University and all costs were covered for travel, boarding, and my peer review services. In April of 2011 after my mom's birthday, I had the great fortune of sharing our team's findings at the American Educational Research Association conference in New Orleans, Louisiana.

Attending research conferences as a doctoral student was thrilling, but now being on the podium sharing as a peer reviewer and a fellow researcher was truly leveling up my ability to conduct postdoctoral research. Dr. Miller was so encouraging. I will never forget how when I had hit a wall and thought of not proceeding forward to earning my doctorate, she invited me to stay with her in Colorado to support me in the summer of 2010. She encouraged me and implored me to push through because I was almost there. How was I able to walk away now? It was like deciding not to have a baby when the baby was already in the birth canal. I was ready to give birth to my doctoral baby. My educational journey was crowning and I was fully ready. She took me under her wing as a student, and at that educational conference, she supported me by sharing the world of future educational research with me. I will never ever be able to repay her for her profound belief in me. It goes without saying how I was struggling with imposter syndrome, but her encouraging words were always a sobering moment for me to snap out of it and trust in what Mother Destiny was setting before me.

STAGE V: HUMANITARIAN QUEST

CHAPTER TWENTY-SIX

KENYAN CHILD BRIDES

E arning my doctoral degree, opened a door to conduct post-doc-
toral research with a fledgling nonprofit, an African-centered
organization called Global Changers. The founder of the organization was a Nigerian woman and Public Health doctoral candidate
at Walden University. Linda was going to conduct a comprehensive
three-week research study in Kenya focused on female genital mutilation (FGM). Her doctoral research was centered on public health,
but she was going to need an educational researcher to conduct a
program evaluation on the educational program that was created by
a local Maasai woman leader. This indigenous leader opened a girls'
refuge center and learning center in a remote village in the Rift Valley
in Kenya. Linda invited me to join her and to consider joining her
nonprofit organization as an executive board member. After much
deliberation, I agreed to do it. I honestly did not feel qualified, but
I was pushing through the doubt and leaned in hard on my faith.
The executive board members included professors and other doctoral
students or graduates from Walden University. It felt like a natural next
step for me.

A part of the research journey involved raising funds. Each of the board members did a great job raising funds and awareness about this FGM research project. I did my part in pulling together a fundraiser. I was very grateful to my beloved circle of friends and colleagues for supporting my efforts. A remarkable group of teachers and teaching assistants did all they could to promote it and it was very well attended with over 100 guests in a local venue. Using a red carpet fundraiser theme, we were able to raise a few thousand dollars that we could use to help the girls get any materials that they needed to support their educational endeavors. The director Linda came down from Texas and shared her experience as a public health doctoral candidate and the importance of supporting this passion project.

Equality Now, Inc. which was based in Nairobi Kenya commissioned our research project and they were going to use our research findings to present to the Children's Human Rights Committee at the United Nations. A lot was at stake in pulling this off. At times, I felt like I was totally in over my head. The name of the Girls Refuge shelter I was evaluating was the Tasaru Ntomonok Initiative (TNI) which was a Kenyan community-based organization established in 1998 to raise community awareness on the issues of the traditional and cultural practice of FGM and child marriage within the local Maasai tribes.

As the lead educational researcher, I examined TNI's organizational structure, identified areas wherein TNI could further sharpen the infrastructural staff development of this grassroots organization, studied TNI's current and local child protection mechanism for girls suffering from or fleeing FGM, gained insight into TNI's community-based efforts, identified key community outreach components that were effective in helping to eliminate FGM and child marriage and identified integral areas and potential gaps that can be addressed and refined with future staff development and organizational capacity-building opportunities. This was quite a tall order!

Thankfully with the help of community leaders, local advocates, translators, and a team of supporters from the Equality Now organization, we were able to complete a report in a timely fashion. It was done in record time! Ultimately, the lessons learned from this program evaluation helped TNI refine existing strategies and structural approaches that were able to support them in acquiring vital international funding resources.

Conducting, recording, and transcribing 14 interviews, ranging from 45 minutes to 75 minutes, totaling approximately 1,000 minutes of interview data, helped Linda and I triangulate findings and corroborate data. Just coming out of my former doctoral research work had me primed to do this work smoothly. I learned how to maximize my field resources and acquired qualitative data from observation protocols, field notes, reflective notes, photographs, interview transcripts, electronic press releases, and other forms of unstructured text data found in newspaper articles, office memorandums, and formal and informal interoffice correspondence. The research findings revealed several themes. I was able to share with the founder as well as with Equality Now a SWOT (Strengths, Weaknesses, Opportunities, and Threats) analysis framework wherein I offered a narrative analysis of the results. I shared about inherent areas of study for future research which included examining and conducting a preliminary comparison of TNI's current efforts to eradicate FGM as they compared to another UN-recognized and US-founded approach of the Tostan model.

Conducting this research was extremely humbling due to my lack of knowledge about the indigenous culture of the Maasai tribe as well as conducting this research with a language barrier. The Maasai of Kenya are one of the indigenous tribes in Kenya. I was very grateful to have access to numerous books, articles, and ethnographic studies on the cultures of the Maasai. These indigenous people have remained one of the most insular identified original peoples of Africa. The Maasai have resisted indoctrination with external cultures and remain as true to their natural and cultural identity as possible under increasing socio-economic and political pressures to conform to globalization. To understand the Maasai, it is necessary to understand a little bit of their background, their cultural beliefs, and social patterns and systems.

They were reported to have migrated to East Africa around the 15th Century A.D. and remained a dominant nomadic and pastoralist people until the 19th Century and the coming of slave traders, missionar-

ies, and imperialist colonizers. The earliest European knowledge of the
Maasai was in accounts documented in 1850 by the missionary Krapf.
The Maasai were described as "Natural People" who were uncivilized
savages, fearless, and warlike. This early description of the Maasai—as
seeming warlike and possessing the peculiar culinary abhorrence for
cultivated food—is still prevalent. The distaste for cultivated food is
observed in the absence of agricultural activities, making the Maasai
pastoralists and herders.

Several factors negatively impacted the Maasai's way of life, most
importantly issues with land rights and ownership. Prior to the arrival
of explorers, missionaries, and colonizers, the Maasai through wars
captured large areas of land from their weaker neighbors for grazing
cattle. During colonization and post-independence, the Maasai have
been systematically moved and deprived of large tracts of land; making
it more difficult for them to migrate as freely as they once did.

In the case of how the Maasai culture related to Female Genital
Mutilation/Cutting it was important to understand the nature of this
global health risk. There was much I learned before I even hit the
field. Female Genital Mutilation (FGM) is a cultural practice found
in some African, Middle Eastern, and Southeastern countries. This
practice involves all procedures of the partial or total mutilation of
the female genitalia to different degrees of severity for non-medical
reasons. FGM is a man-made public health risk facing the four Maasai
tribes of Kenya. There are several root causes for the FGM cultural and
traditional practice among the Maasai with prevalence rates as high
as 93% to 96%. This cultural practice is predominantly carried out by
communities in about 28 African countries, some parts of the Middle
East and Southeast Asia.

There are essentially four distinct types of female genital mutilation,
from minor pricking of the clitoris to total removal of the labia minor
and labia majora. In extreme cuttings, the vaginal opening is sewn back
up with left-over flesh and this method is known as infibulation. Over
the years, over 100 to140 million women and girl-children worldwide
have been subjected to the harmful and health risks of FGM/C in any
of the four types of mutilation; and about three million girls yearly

undergo the procedure. FGM/C first came to world attention in the early 1960s, and at the time was relatively unknown and considered a culturally sensitive subject best left to the discretions of the practicing communities' governments. In practicing communities, the origins of the practice are never clear, and practitioners have given reasons based on cultural, spiritual, and religious bases.

The practice has been performed over generations and has become embedded in the sociocultural framework of those communities. The "cutters" are often the fervent defenders of the practice arguing the cultural significance of their identity. In some cases, women who have undergone the ritual do not consider themselves mutilated and take great objection to what they perceive as negative intrusions into private cultural issues.

Despite years of varying forms of intervention to promote the elimination of FGM in practicing communities, progress and success have been slow. The World Health Organization has also realized that the lack of adequate investment in programs directed at the elimination of FGM has not helped move the discussions or activities at an acceptable pace. Based on these reasons, the international agencies charged with coordinating efforts to ensure that FGM is eventually eliminated have increased their efforts. The greatest obstacle to the elimination of FGM practice is the lack of information on the harmful and risky health consequences of the practice. Ironically, the topic of FGM has culturally been regarded as a "women's issue", therefore causing men to try to avoid any discussions on it. However, this practice was a marriage preparation practice supported by the men to ensure the fidelity of women in their tribe. It was a common belief that if the woman didn't have the sexual organ of the clitoris then they wouldn't experience sexual arousal or temptation.

The Maasai indigenous people live in a predominantly male-dominated and patriarchal society engaging in polygamous marriages. Men own all the land and the main criteria for determining social status is the number of cows owned by the men as well as the number of children in their family. The more cows a Maasai man owns coupled with a higher number of children, the higher his social standing is in the eyes of his Maasai counterparts. Cows are neither raised for food consumption nor for sale. The mode of social exchange and payment is cows. Marriages involve dowries which are exchanged with cows. The marriage of a daughter brings wealth to a Maasai father. Consequently, daughters are seen and regarded as commodities of exchange for increased wealth. While there are laws in Kenya banning and outlawing the practice of FGM, the Maasai have continued to resist the elimination of the practice. Various health surveys by the Demographic and Health Survey (DHS) have shown increased awareness and slow declines of the practice overall in Kenya in other communities, but there have been no substantive studies to investigate the reasons for the apparent resistance of the Maasai to ending FGM.

Flying out to Kenya for this study required some extensive cultural research and organizational culture research. The girls' refuge shelter we visited had been established over 10 years before and it had received a lot of celebrity sponsorship and support from the United Nations and the writer of the controversial and high-profile play *The Vagina Monologues*. Organizations like V-Day were working hard to raise awareness. In fact, the Latina actress Rosario Dawson was an executive board member of that organization and she had coordinated several fundraisers to support the founder of this girls' refuge shelter named the Tasaru Ntomonok Initiative (TNI).

This center was located in the remote village of Narok about two hours from the capital Nairobi. It was established in 1998 to raise community awareness on the issues of the traditional and cultural practice of FGM and child marriage within the local Maasai culture. In 2000, TNI was registered as a community-based organization by the District of Social Development Office under the Ministry of Home Affairs in Kenya. TNI is located in the Narok District of the Rift Valley south of Nairobi, Kenya. This organization's close proximity to four local Maasai tribes (Purko, Keekonyokie, Moitanik, and Ildamat) advantageously positioned the organization to conduct local outreach community programs that help to raise awareness on women's health and rights issues which directly impact the health and education of local Maasai girls. Through its community-based efforts, TNI worked extensively to break the silence within the Maasai community about the traditional and cultural practice of Female Genital Mutilation. Through its collective efforts with community stakeholders, TNI has been able to work within a synergistic community child protection mechanism that works with local government officials to protect the rights of girls suffering from FGM and becoming victims of forced child marriage. TNI used the Children's Act—which serves as an anti-FGM legislative mandate—to protect the rights of the girls. TNI collaborates closely with local government officials such as children - officers, magistrates, and prosecutors to advocate for the girls' health and educational rights.

Throughout its work within the Maasai community, TNI offered a variety of awareness training opportunities that helped to raise community awareness of women's health issues and the educational issues impacting the Maasai community. The series of workshops are given to a breadth of community stakeholders located in school communities, churches, Maasai tribal leader meetings, local political organizational meetings, as well as a variety of Maasai village gatherings throughout the Rift Valley. Another facet of TNI's efforts is to offer safe refuge to girls fleeing from FGM and forced child marriage. With the support of international funding, the Tasaru Girls Rescue Center has offered a safe haven for girls. According to TNI's mission, the Tasaru Girls Rescue Center serves as an intermediate strategy for helping girls fleeing FGM and in need of reconciliation with their families. While the girls remain in the refuge center, they are safe from the threat of mutilation and forced child marriage. Quantitative findings from TNI rescue data spanning from 2003 to the present show that close to 1,000 girls have resided in the Tasaru Girls Rescue Center. At one point during this time span, the highest number of girls living in the rescue center was 185. At the time of my research, the number had significantly decreased and there were 73 girls residing there.

I was very impressed to learn that in 2003, with the help of a global advocate of women's issues, TNI was able to get funding support from Eve Ensler—a playwright of the internationally recognized play *The Vagina Monologues* that has been translated and performed in 130 languages. This passionate performer, feminist, and activist financially supported the founder's dream to develop a refuge shelter—where the Maasai girls have an interim safe haven while the TNI reconciliation team sought to reconcile the girls with their families.

It was great to learn that with the great success of this first center, TNI was able to expand. In the summer of 2009, with funding from V-Day (Eve Ensler's global activist and charitable organization), the founder of TNI opened the second refuge shelter called Sakutiek Rescue Center located in the Rift Valley. The center is strategically placed near two schools to help facilitate the placement of the girls in primary or secondary school. Global Changers program evaluators had the opportunity to meet with the master head teacher directing the Sakutiek Rescue Center. They learned that 50 girls reside at the second center.

The master head teacher described the challenges acclimating to their new home and the peer and family pressures the rescued girls face:

"But as you know an obstacle is that there is still pressure from outside, pressures from outside you know sometimes these girls are taken by force and the cutters will take them away. So even there was a problem when I first started. When I came to that school I learned that there were a lot of problems. Some people were even threatening the girls outside of the shelter near their school. And these poor girls were so scared. They would think that they saw something and they were scared, which did not help with their school because they were afraid to go to school. Yes, that was hard for the girls, but I think that has stopped. Now the girls are used to it. They know that the center is very safe. Now they don't have a problem."

As a strategy for empowering the girls to seek an education in lieu of the child marriage rites of passage of FGM, TNI has sponsored several Alternative Rites of Passage (ARP) ceremonies held at various local churches and the Tasaru Girls Rescue Center. Prior to the Maasai girls participating in this ritual attended a series of three-day workshops wherein TNI learning facilitators presented a variety of reproductive health topics that raised community awareness on the dangers of female genital mutilation. As a result of the organization's availability of alternative rites of passage ceremonies, the TNI staff observed an increased number of Maasai girls participating in the alternative marriage ceremony. More importantly, this signified that more community members recognized the importance of girls attending school and holding off on marriage and the traditional rite of passage—female genital mutilation. Currently, TNI received numerous requests from community leaders and members to facilitate more ARP ceremonies.

On the field, I was able to deduce that the lower number of girls currently residing in the Tasaru Girls Rescue Center correlates with the higher rate of community outreach efforts and ARP ceremonies in the area. TNI's increased community outreach efforts seem to have a direct impact on the number of girls fleeing from FGM. This grassroots organization strategized and facilitated women's health workshops in local schools within the Maasai district.

Being there for those three weeks was a life-changing experience. It reminded me so much about how men had the power and how this phenomenon crossed all cultural borders. Again women were working hard to get away from a hurtful and painful situation. So much of this triggered my suppressed memories of witnessing my battered mother. I was grateful for the time I was able to connect with the girls. I will treasure how they were able to create wonderful connections and conversations outside of the sterile conference room where I conducted my interviews. These beautiful Maasai girls showed me how to dance, speak Swahili, and laugh at some of my very odd questions. They loved touching my hair and one day the eldest girl pulled me out of my seat to walk over to a bulletin board that had clippings from visits of the V-Day organizers. She pointed to a picture of Rosario Dawson and she asked if that was my sister. I smiled. Looking at the actress' full lips in her smile made me feel beautiful. Just like these girls saw me. Different and beautiful. It was a true joy being with them and learning with them. Education was their equalizer to get away. Just like I was able to get away from my home turmoil as a teenager ready for college.

There were a few secrets from that trip that I kept close to my heart because I didn't want my husband to worry about me. One of them was that the location of the refuge shelter was in a remote part of the village where you had to go through a narrow road between steep hills where only one car could drive on it at a time. It was riddled with potholes and large rocks that could render a tire rim helpless. The driver was responsible for taking me and Linda to the different locations where we would conduct interviews. Visiting the local law enforcement wearing gold presidential Rolexes made me worry about local corruption and my safety. We were asking a lot of questions, and I was the only woman in our caravan of community liaisons and interpreters with light skin in the area which would easily make me a target. The locals would refer to me as a Mazungu which meant like a gringo. No matter how much I tried to explain that I wasn't white, that my family was from Puerto Rico, they would just give me a strange look of confusion.

One late afternoon near the last day of our visit, we noticed that the sign to the shelter was gone and in its place, there was a dead brown dog with a noose around its neck. You didn't have to tell me that was a coincidence. It was a message. Early the very next morning, we left and I couldn't help feeling paranoid so I kept a close eye observing my surroundings until we got back to a hotel in Nairobi. The long drive through the Rift Valley was a heavy quiet ride. I didn't speak of my fears to Linda for fear that my biggest fear would materialize. Our next stop was going to be Nigeria to visit her homeland and to present some support for a local water well project. Another goal she had was to visit a local wealthy Nigerian chief that she met in England when she lived there during her graduate studies. We were going to make two big stops in Nigeria...Lagos and the Federal Capital Territory which was where she originally was from.

I had another week to remain in Africa. I was feeling culturally exhausted from being the one that looked different and sounded different. Being around people and not understanding their dialect was exhausting. I longed to be home to hear my mother's native tongue–my Puerto Rican Spanish. I felt homesick. I was emotionally exhausted carrying all of those young girls' tragic stories in my heart. It stirred up so many memories of feeling unsafe as a child. Was it worth it? Would I even make a difference?

Conducting this summer research meant that I was not going to be able to attend my doctoral commencement. It was a big sacrifice, but a part of me was relieved that I didn't have to attend a large commencement ceremony that would make my mom feel nervous. She wouldn't be able to understand a word said by any of the speakers. However, sharing pictures of my travels and the girls' stories would be something Mami would understand.

During my travels, I was able to Skype with my former doctoral chair Dr. Miller to share some of the amazing things that I witnessed as a researcher. Having the nine-hour difference in time where I was ahead of her was challenging, but I would try to connect during her lunch hour while I was capping my evening. She loved when I would email her pictures of my travels. Dr. Miller was very excited for me. During one of those night calls, I was blessed to learn that former President Clinton, who was the keynote speaker at the graduation on July 30, 2011, highlighted a few graduates who were manifesting Walden University's mission to create positive social change. What I didn't know was that this Boricua was one of the doctoral graduates showcased. To my surprise, Dr. Miller shared that in an upcoming Walden Alumni magazine, there was going to be a feature article in the Walden Alumni magazine showcasing a picture of our time with the Kenyan girls at the refuge shelter and how we were helping to eradicate female genital mutilation through education, awareness, and informing policy! Hmmm....how did that happen? I was forever grateful for her faith in me. Having President Clinton speak about that was a moment that I was remiss not witnessing, but Dr. Miller shared how proud she was to hear those words. I was her student and now a fellow research colleague and she was beaming with pride. My decision to forgo attending my graduation placed me on a new path in postdoctoral research. In retrospect, the depth and range of my involvement with this humanitarian advocacy research were life-changing on so many levels.

A few months after submitting our final report to Equality Now, the director Efua Dorkensoo presented findings from our report at the United Nations Human Rights Council Sessions in Nairobi, Kenya

as well as in Geneva, Switzerland. It was quite an honor to learn that
UN delegates and international advocates were gleaning insight from
our work. Moreover, it was tremendously gratifying to know that
my fieldwork as a humanitarian researcher was going to make such
a public impact on public policy in countries fighting the war against
female genital mutilation.

This experience planted the seed of envisioning the possibility of
working for the United Nations. Would this be on my horizon? Would
my husband support me in these efforts? Many diplomatic lessons
would be learned and none in vain. I would need to make some humbling mistakes to see if this seed of hope would germinate.

CHAPTER TWENTY-SEVEN

CORNERED BY A CHIEF

E ven though I was traveling on the same continent of Africa from east to west, the trip from Nairobi, Kenya to Lagos, Nigeria was physically and emotionally taxing. African continental airline travel was haphazard and unreliable. After a huge layover on our connecting flight from Kenya to Ethiopia, we were on the plane stuck on the tarmac for four hours until the moment the flight passengers were escorted off the plane to a waiting tent outside the airport. How inhumane! It was utterly intolerable in that African heat. My Nigerian escort Linda had some choice words she yelled to the flight crew. I am certain that if we were in the United States, she would have been arrested for harassing the airport staff. Her words fell on deaf ears, and the complacent travelers were indifferent in their stares as if this was their normal. Get over it, lady. Why were we acting like spoiled brats? Just shut the hell up.

We finally arrived in the bustling capital city of Lagos, Nigeria. I learned that Lagos was one of the largest cities in Africa, beating Cairo, Egypt. It was a radically different experience than my former travels to Cairo. Egypt did not prepare me for what would lay ahead. In Egypt, I was traveling with a delegation that was well protected through the

People to People Ambassador program, a renowned organization that organized conferences and gatherings for dignitaries and scholars. This time, it was just two women figuring this out on their own. A Nigerian woman and a Puerto Rican woman who by all accounts looked like a "gringa" visitor and not a native Nigerian.

The moment we entered the taxi from the Lagos airport to the hotel, we were in another universe. Lagos was bustling with cars, scooters, motorcycles, and mopeds. With about 10 million people living in Lagos, traffic was brutal. I was encouraged not to be in the back passenger seat with the window open for fear of getting my purse snatched from my lap by a passing cyclist or person on a moped. Using my cell phone was highly discouraged because my skin color didn't help me blend in. I immediately would be spotted as a tourist. "Puuut a-waaaaay dat Black-berrrrrrry!" I was told with a heavy Nigerian accent. Traveling with a native Nigerian helped me feel more secure, and since we landed early in the morning, this was mostly commuter traffic. Hard-working people just trying to make a living and survive.

I tried my best to not let fear take over after reading the US travel advisory reports. Of course, I did not share those details with my husband. Kidnapping for ransom was on the list of concerns reported. When I read that it was recommended that I establish a "proof of life" protocol with my loved ones, I wasn't quite sure what they meant. Much later I learned that if I was taken hostage, my loved ones would know specific questions and answers to ask the hostage-takers to be certain that I was still alive and it was not a hoax. Instead, what did this stubborn woman do?! I left a colored copy of my passport with my husband and did not establish any protocol questions, because the only response he was going to firmly give me was that I was not going. Period. A part of me deeply regretted not having this discussion with him, but I was leaning on my faith and asking God for an extra measure of protection and favor.

We were staying at one of the best hotels in Nigeria where the frequent bomb inspections with police dogs and mirrors on a stick under the cars were a common sight for the locals. For me, it was terrifying but I tried to remain cool and not show any reaction. My face would just remain in a neutral "bitch face" stance and I would not show much effect–like I was walking where I "knew" I was going, so... move and get the hell out of my way. This was going to be my new normal. If there was a person who remained unhinged during a sight like this, it was me. In retrospect, I placed a lot of stock in the knowledge that I was traveling with a highly respected Ebu Nigerian woman. Frequently, she spoke about the Ebu's indigenous history. I believed that she was held in high esteem and that this offered her access to different social circles. We were safe because she was highly protected and revered. All I could do was walk in faith and trust that this final stop before coming back home would go smoothly.

We had several appointments with several of her supporters who wanted to learn about our work in Kenya and a local Nigerian water project that was going to develop access to clean water well projects for communities so that children didn't have to walk for hours in search of clean water for their families. Many times local water sources were contaminated and the young girls did not attend school because their family chore was to fetch cooking water and bathing water for their families. The walks to cleaner sources of water were further away, cutting into their school day. It required long walks to cleaner sources of water which were very limited in rural parts outside of Lagos. The boys would go to school, but not the girls.

This eco-problem presented socio-economic obstacles impeding girls' equitable access to consistent quality education. A culturally responsive solution was to set up water wells within markets near a church that would be considered a socially and politically neutral zone. Regrettably, in the past, there were some well projects placed outside of these aforementioned faith zones which fell into the hands of opportunists and swindlers that would charge girls money for access to their water well, or worse the girls would become prey to the advances of these predators seeking sexual favors in exchange for access to the water wells. This project was in line with our work in Kenya helping girls not become child brides but instead gain access to education. Both circumstances dealt with the power dynamics of men dictating the destiny of these young girls. I was looking forward to my time in Nigeria to be a time to contribute towards creating positive social change for these girls. As a woman, it would frustrate me to no end that the narrative of men controlling the outcome of girls' lives shaped by money, sex, and greed was just in every corner of our world. Something had to change.

Early in the afternoon in the hotel lobby, the executive director of Global Changers and I met an engineer who was highly recommended by her former neighbor in London–who was a Nigerian chief highly revered in socio-cultural circles. There we met with the engineers inside one of the hotel restaurants to review logistical information about the well project. Linda's organization had collected monies for the water well project through different fundraising projects. They were ready to break ground in a few weeks and they were finalizing the last few details. They spoke in English and in their native Ebu language. I was so used to tuning out the different languages that I heard in Kenya and now being in Nigeria it felt no different. Many of the gestures and languages registered as normal business banter and pleasantries. The chief was not able to join us because he resided outside of Lagos in the nation's financial hub, where the bulk of oil business transactions would occur with daily flights to Texas and the Middle East. Later in the day, we received a personal invitation to his estate outside in the Federal Territory where we would also meet Linda's former neighbor Toni.

The exemplary restaurants within this five-star hotel were a draw for us to receive our visitors. So many of her collaborators were more than pleased to come to us on that first day. I was relieved because I honestly didn't want to leave the hotel after the initial bomb inspection on our taxi ride to the hotel. I was so jet lagged from the travel, that I honestly didn't pay attention to the itinerary for this final leg of my African research journey. I was surprised to learn that we were not going to stay in Lagos for too long.

The next morning we got up very early and went to the market not too far from the hotel. It was a Sunday and she assured me that it would be less crowded than on a Saturday. I left my passport in the hotel safe and only traveled with a color copy for fear of losing my passport to a pickpocket. People were walking literally shoulder to shoulder like a teaming mass of salmon moving upstream. It was so tough moving around in the market. I kept a close eye on my purse that was on a shoulder strap.

Sustaining my seriousness and my *I am not scared of you* blank facial expression took some work to maintain. I am naturally so expressive, and I am certain that from time to time I wavered in my efforts. Peddlers had the bad habit of running up to you and waving their merchandise in your face to get you to react. I was forewarned to keep it moving. We slipped into a tent shop that sold scarves and I haggled with the merchant. I was happy to walk out with a few treasures and then we made it back to the hotel. My body was so tense. Finally, we went back to the hotel to retrieve our suitcases and personal valuables from the safe to then head over to the airport.

Our next Nigerian destination was the Federal Territory. It required that we go on a Nigerian domestic flight. This surprised me. I thought we would be able to drive there. Linda kept referring to it as an Airbus. I was puzzled by that. But the minute we arrived and purchased our air ticket, it made all the sense in the world. Can you believe the boarding pass didn't have a seat number on it and worse, there were no metal detectors or inspections of baggage prior to boarding the plane?! I was terrified that after the terrorist attacks of 9/11, their security protocols were not stringent. With the Muslim infighting in the northern part of Nigeria, how could this be possible?

It was an egregious disregard for public safety and that is when it hit me. In a country full of corruption, it would be in the best interests of crooked politicians to look the other way so that illegal activity would take place. Oil money would pay for the illegal and corrupt activity that was co-signed by not keeping track of or documenting cross-country travel. I tried to not look shocked by seeing this or to react. In retrospect, I was thoughtful enough to bring very long dresses with long sleeves, as well as a few scarves that I would be able to use as headdresses within a few upcoming political meetings, but nothing in a travel brochure would prepare me for the feeling of seeing that we were simply boarding this plane with our luggage and handing over our boarding passes to the flight attendant.

Our first appointment was with one of Linda's former Nigerian neighbors, Toni, who was hosting us for dinner. As we walked before dinner on the grounds I was so pleasantly surprised to see free-roaming peacocks all over his property. Prior to moving to London, Linda and her husband were neighbors with Toni. He was a very gracious host and it was such a joy learning more about their Ebu culture and customs. In my travels with Linda, I learned more about Ebu practices and beliefs. Watching her face beaming with joy at being home with a fellow friend was very nice to see. For weeks we had traveled together and I was longing to be back home. I was feeling homesick. Skype conversations and emails exchanged with my husband were short and few in between as we struggled at the time to gain access to quality internet service. I did not feel comfortable using internet cafes so I would try my best to remain centered and content. It was the first time I felt like I could let down my hair and breathe. I felt safe there.

I was pleasantly surprised that Toni had invited a few guests in honor of our visit and recent travels to Kenya. They had prepared a goat. I was shocked to see that as we approached the table, the goat head was still attached! As I stared at it, everyone at the table chuckled and looked at me. Toni declared, "Doctor this is for you! Our gift to you for your service here in Nigeria." He offered the delicacy of the goat brains as they lifted the top of the goat's cranium to reveal the cooked brains.

I gasped and asked... "For me? This is all for me? Oh my goodness you are all too kind. Allow me to enjoy your customs, if you will also be soooooooooo kind to consider indulging in my customs too. In Puerto Rico, it is my custom that the oldest person in the room enjoy our country's delicacy...pig feet. It is the ruuuuuuuule."(I said rule with a heavy Nigerian exaggerated accent). Then I gestured with a deep bow, "Please...I humbly ask. Whoooooooo is the eldest in the room?" To that end, the oldest in the room was Toni and he winked at me.

Toni, the eldest, took up the great "honor" of enjoying the delicacy...saying, "Thank you Doctor for the honor." Away he scooped at the goat brains and placed them on his plate. Whew! I dodged that bullet.

Linda smirked and whispered, "Woman, you are so clever." That is the moment, the universe gave me my cultural ambassador wings.

Over dinner, Linda and I took turns sharing with great enthusiasm details of our travels in Kenya and some of the most amazing things that we learned from the Maasai girls. We shared about the horrors that we heard from their interviews, and from the adult advocates that worked with the Kenyan girls. They were shocked to learn how cows were more revered than the girls in the family. I remember asking the host how women are treated in his country, and he chuckled, retorting, "Like a happy cow!" I smiled but was confused by that statement.

Prior to coming to Toni's house, I remember talking to Linda on the plane about her feelings about coming back to Nigeria. She mentioned that she had mixed emotions. In America, an overweight dark woman is considered to be a poor unhealthy woman. But when she was back home in Nigeria, she felt like she physically belonged and that she held a higher social status. Linda noted that obesity in Nigeria is considered to be a sign of wealth. So the happy cow statement is toting that the company I was keeping with Linda was with someone who is doing quite well and happy as a result of that status.

I recalled Linda mentioning on the plane that as a dark-skinned Nigerian woman she has to fight harder. A lighter complexion is viewed as more beautiful. There were several Nigerian tribes that held higher status because of their lighter skin like the Igbos and Ibibios. Unfortunately, in contemporary society, there is a lot of colorism throughout the continent of Africa– it is attributed to European colonization. I shared that in Latin America and in Asia the same level of discrimination exists. I shared how when I traveled to Vietnam, the women would ride on their scooters with gloves, scarves, and face shields so that they would not get too much sun and make their skin darker. The fairer you are, the higher social status you are perceived to have. So in the hospitality service, they only hire women with very fair skin color.

As a light-skinned Latina woman accompanying this dark-skinned and heavier Nigerian woman with a commanding presence, we would get a lot of attention and double takes. She whispered that perhaps some people in these affluent circles would assume that I was a celebrity or a rich Arabic woman based on how I was dressed. I remembered not to speak too much and looked coy when someone was speaking to Linda. Heck, I leaned hard into this new role and cultural perceptions. I was not responsible for their assumptions but instead considered using them to my advantage to get through this bureaucratic trip. I couldn't wait for it to be over!

After Toni's dinner, we arrived at our exclusive accommodations at the Transcorp Hilton Hotel where many Texan-American executives check in for their oil business dealings with local Nigerian executives. The familiar bomb checks were present and after coming from Lagos, I felt more secure being in the Federal Territory. It was quite apparent that there was more of a police and military presence. Many ambassadors and dignitaries lived in this area. Money talks.

As we came out of our taxi and stepped onto the valet curb, Linda noticed someone that she knew. It was the Nigerian chief that had invited us to see him when we were in Lagos. The chief was outside waiting dressed in a very fine tunic garment made of very luxurious traditional fabric otherwise known as a chieftaincy dress and a tightly woven cap on his head. He was waiting for the valet service to bring up his Bentley.

Linda called out to him and as she approached him she bowed her head. I was taken aback by this grand gesture, and then he placed his hand on her forehead. Linda bowed her head seeking to receive his blessing. As he touched her forehead, he said. "Hello, my daughter." At first, I was surprised by this statement, because I didn't realize they had that type of relationship. Apparently, their connection was more than just neighborly. She told me that they had been neighbors in London for a couple of years. Wow, this was quite an interesting opportunity to see a closer portrait of Ebu life. Linda motioned for me to come closer to them, as I was still standing further away on the curb. Reverting to my coy low gaze humble Princess Diana stance, I approached the chief and she introduced me to him. "This is the researcher I am working with from New York, Dr. Cabán-Vazquez." The chief did not give me any eye contact. When I extended my hand out for a handshake, he did not extend out his hand in turn but clasped his hands behind his back. Linda explained that he couldn't touch me because he is considered a holy man. We are out in public and must demonstrate proper respectful and professional decorum. I said. "I am so sorry. My sincerest apologies Chief. I was not aware of the protocol."

I experienced something similar in Cambodia at the Siem Reap temples upon meeting the monks in their orange traditional garb. I quickly said. "It is a great honor and pleasure to finally meet you." Hoping my comment would demonstrate some cultural sensitivity and responsiveness, I placed my hands behind my back and simply smiled.

Linda thanked the chief profusely for extending an invitation for us to visit him at his home for lunch and that we were truly looking forward to seeing him again.

He then asked her, "What color do you want?" Linda looked puzzled upon hearing his question. He clarified with, "What color Bentley should I send for you to visit me? I have a blue one, a white one, a red one, or a green one."

Linda quickly deferred to me to respond, and I immediately replied "White...the color of purity, because we come with the purest of intentions to ask for your support for the Kenyan child brides." At that moment, he looked at me, made eye contact, and he smiled replying "White it is. It will come and pick you up. Be ready at 10:30 a.m. My assistant will receive you in the drawing room and then we will be ready to share our meal."

Linda was beaming and again extended a deep bow wherein the chief placed his hand on her head and said goodbye. Suddenly, the green Bentley pulled up with a chauffeur coming out to open his passenger seat door and he disappeared into the night.

After a busy day traveling and making social calls, I was extremely tired and simply wanted to lie down in the hotel. As I lay in bed, I thought of how we ran into the chief and I was a little nervous. With

Toni, Linda's friend, it was so informal and laid back. Almost like coming home and meeting a childhood friend. However, with this Nigerian dignitary, it felt really official and political. In the morning, I asked Linda how long she had known him, and she said it had been about five years. "When my husband and I lived in London, we were neighbors in the same luxury building. I had called him prior to our trip to let him know that I was launching the well project in Lagos and about my public health research in Kenya. He was very proud of my efforts, and he told me whenever I come to Nigeria to come by and visit him. That he would love to hear more about it." This backstory put me at ease. Perhaps I was overanalyzing things. I deliberated over what I was going to wear. I was hoping I had something white to symbolically match the color of the car that was coming to get us. I wanted it to go with the theme that I had proposed regarding our intentions for the visit. But I only had a very long cotton black dress, and I wore a scarf over my shoulders and a peach-colored scarf around my hair. I didn't want to be overdressed like when we went to visit the dignitaries in Nairobi, Kenya. I didn't want to come across as pretentious.

We went down a little early sitting in the hotel lobby. Sure enough, at exactly 10:30 a.m., the car arrived to pick us up. To be honest I was quite nervous because I had never been inside a Bentley with a chauffeur. The fanciest car I had been in was a used Mercedes AMG sports car that my husband drove as our weekend car. Going inside the Bentley was like a scene from a movie. I felt like a princess. After a 20-minute drive through the city and moments outside the city, we were almost there. I assumed that it must have been in a more rural area. However, I am embarrassed to admit it, but I thought since he was an African chief, that he must have lived in a modest African hut. This didn't align with the moment that he presented the choice of colors from his fleet of Bentleys as he waited for valet service at the exclusive hotel! All of this had me quite puzzled.

When we finally arrived and pulled up to large palatial-style iron gates, I realized that we had not come to see a humble chief. After gaining access through the intercom, and driving along the long winding driveway, we captured a full view of the estate that was reminiscent of the White House. Okay, this was definitely not a village hut! I was blown away as the Chauffeur opened our back door and escorted us up the wide marble steps that led us to the front door. I felt like I was walking up the steps of the pyramids to meet the Pharaoh himself. It was unbelievable. I certainly was underdressed, but I held my head up high like I was wearing an invisible crown.

The chief's administrative assistant greeted us and brought Linda and me to one of the formal drawing rooms– which was more of a British style of receiving guests. We were in a narrow hallway passing by many closed doors. When he opened the double doors to our drawing room, it revealed gold gilded mirrors and antique furniture. We approached the opulent furniture and sat on the sofa. In came a South Asian house servant. The woman offered us some tea. As we waited, my heart was beating so fast. My stomach was feeling a little upset. I took deep breaths and just tried to relax. I asked Linda if she knew how long she thought we would have to wait, and she said, "Honestly, Vilma this can take hours. We are here for lunch, but we could end up waiting in this drawing room for a long time because if you recall we passed by a lot of rooms."

I couldn't believe it. Those were all waiting rooms?! She shared that people travel from all over the world to meet with him and when he is ready to see them, he'll see them. But in the meantime, they would serve drinks, meals, and whatever a guest might need right before the chief would come to meet with his guests. I was truly shocked to learn this. I guessed that there was no such thing as American military time here. Instead, it was a more relaxed timeline, an ebb and flow exchange that followed a totally different rhythm than I was accustomed to. It was like traveling to Puerto Rico when you visit your Tía (auntie) and she has you sitting at her kitchen table with a *cafecito* pretty much the whole day! Next thing you know, she is serving you lunch and dinner comes right around the bend and you are still talking. I realized that I had to go with the flow and just chill! When in Rome, do as the Romans do.

At that point, I figured out that this was serious business. After waiting for about half an hour, I started second-guessing what I chose to wear. Why did I choose to wear this long dress that looked like a sack?! I should have worn a business pantsuit! I was questioning all of my decisions, but I said to myself that in the end, I did the right thing. It's a modest dress and I thought I should be okay.

All of a sudden, the administrative assistant came in and announced that the chief was ready to see us. As he escorted us to the room where we were supposed to meet with the chief, I was feeling rather confused. I thought he was coming to our drawing room to meet with us. Where was he taking us? As we followed the assistant, we were taking a long walk to another section of the large estate. It was like we were walking to the West Wing of the White House. It didn't feel like the same formal business space that we were waiting in, these were more of his personal quarters in the home. As we were walking through a hallway, I saw pictures of Nelson Mandela with this gentleman and what I assumed was his beautiful Nigerian wife. She had a lovely large Gele swirling style headdress and very fair skin. A woman that looked at least 20 years younger than him and I guessed that the chief was in his mid-60s. She looked like a Nubian queen. A gorgeous Nigerian woman–a Nija (the Nigerian word for Nigerian woman). Immediately after seeing the picture of Nelson Mandela, I saw a prominent picture of the chief standing next to Prince Charles of Wales (who is now the King of England)! My stomach turned and I felt so ill-equipped to sit with this man. *What was I doing here?* I was not worthy to be in the audience of such a dignitary. I took a deep breath and reminded myself to find my center. The assistant sat us down at the extravagant dining room table holding a scrumptious lavish spread of food for lunch.

The chief stepped in and we immediately stood up and I bowed, as he sat at the head of the table. I was fidgeting under the table with my leg and feet shaking. Now the chief was smiling and giving us both eye contact and sharing pleasantries about his morning meetings. Oh wow, I couldn't believe I was in his home. What an honor!

He asked us to share details about our trip to Kenya. Linda did most of the talking and I simply nodded and smiled. When he would share a joke, I subtly laughed and regulated my otherwise loud voice and laughter. It felt so foreign. So repressed. But soon this would be over and I could breathe again. Linda asked me to share the details of how we were able to offer some scholarships to the older girls in the rescue shelter who were preparing to graduate high school and go to college. I shared how some of the girls wanted to become teachers and how truly inspiring it was to hear their stories of resilience and determination. I shared that the girls would graduate the following year and that there was a great need for them to get scholarships for books and living expenses away from the rescue shelter. Linda's nonprofit organization was able to organize a few fundraisers, but we are still in need of raising more funds to fully support the next generation of Maasai teachers in Narok. At that time, Linda boldly asked him for support in doing all that he could to sponsor them to go to college. He nodded his head and said that he would absolutely love to help. Perhaps the girls can consider going to college in Nigeria to give them a more global African experience. She smiled broadly and shared how much she loved the idea. The chief stated that he was going to call his administrative assistant over so he could assist in following through with the fiscal support of the scholarships.

The house servant came and cleared the table and brought us our coffee and small desserts to a smaller room off to the side. There were many family portraits in the space and it looked less formal than the dining space–more like a family room with large sofas and side tables. As we walk over, he tells the servant to get the assistant. At that point, I felt tremendously honored to have experienced the opportunity of breaking bread with this highly esteemed dignitary who has shared space and bread with the likes of Nelson Mandela! Oh my good-ness...what was I doing there?

The assistant came over and spoke on the side with Linda, as the chief and I spoke pleasantries over where I was from in New York. How long I had lived there and if I was married. I shared that I was happily married with a 19-year-old son in college. I discussed the nature of my doctoral studies and how I wanted to make a difference in offering quality education for underprivileged children around the world. He shared how pleased he was to hear this and to learn of our efforts in striving towards that goal. At that time, I heard the assistant tell Linda to follow him to his office so that he could prepare the check and offer some documentation regarding future housing for the sponsored students. I stopped talking and glanced towards her, and she looked at me and I wondered to myself...Do I get up? Do I stay? Is it rude to get up now and interrupt the conversation with the chief? Then I thought. No, I can't leave. So I stayed in my seat on the sofa sipping my coffee. The chief continued with his conversation and asked me if I enjoyed my trip to Kenya. "How do you like your stay in Nigeria?"

I shared that I truly had only been in Nigeria two days but it has been wonderful and Linda's friends have been so welcoming. The house servant came in and cleared the coffee cups and brought out some water and more desserts. When she walked out the door he said. "I am looking for a girlfriend in New York. I already have one in France. Would you like to be my girlfriend?

"I am confused. But you are married."

He looked sternly at me and declared "Yes...and I have a girlfriend in France. In fact, I have many girlfriends and I take very good care of them."

Then I tried to maneuver and said, "If you say you want to have a girlfriend in New York, where does she live?"

He said, "Wherever YOU live or you want to live."

I quickly responded, "I am sorry that is not possible, I am married and I can't have a boyfriend."

He looked perplexed, retorting, "You can do it."

I quickly thought on my feet and said. "No, No, No, not in my cultural circles or my status. I do not have the high standing as you to be able to have a boyfriend. I am a poor wife...highly educated but that is all I have. A humble poor wife and I can not have a boyfriend.

Then he stared hard at me and asked how was that possible, with someone so beautiful as you. "You must have many boyfriends." Then he gave me a hard dirty stare right at my breasts. Immediately, I covered myself more with the scarf that was on my shoulders declaring with a shaky voice that I was a devoted wife. "Well doctor, you are not so devoted if you are here."

I coyly responded. "My husband is very supportive of my altruistic efforts, and he knows that I am here on a welfare mission to support girls."

He spoke firmly and a little louder. "Well, your husband should be here with you."

Then I said, "Well maybe one day when you come to New York, you can meet my husband." I sarcastically responded.

"That would be a pleasure...are you sure you don't want to be my girlfriend. I would give you what you want because I LOVE THAT ASS!"

I nervously said. "Beg your pardon?"

He calmly responded. "I want you to beg me to fuck that ass."

Every cell in my body was on high alert and I immediately felt my body's soul lift off and hover over my body. In a spiritual bird's eye view, I saw myself in the room. Like a spirit lifting out of the house, I envisioned where I was in this place in the world. A speck of nothing, powerless, and defenseless. I had to find a way to maneuver out of this African chief's compound of hell. If I screamed, they would chase right after me and I would not be able to get past those iron gates. If I hit him with the heavy candle holder that was on the coffee table, I would rot inside a Nigerian jail. How was I going to get the hell out of this situation?

The chief stood up and walked past the coffee table and sat next to me on the sofa. I was silent with my eyes cast down and then I thought quickly.

"Please Father Chief...do not look at me with the eyes of a man. I am your Nija daughter. Your Nigerian honorary daughter. Please I beg you not to look at me as a woman. I am not worthy of being gazed upon as a woman, I am your daughter."

Then at that point, I bowed my head so he could bless me. He took the palm of his hand and shoved my forehead away. I remained centered, controlling myself with my legs so that I did not fall over.

Almost falling over, I recovered my footing and stood up, and looked down at him as he sat cockily on the sofa, "I'm sorry but I have to go."

"No, you can't go."

Then the Asian servant came in and read the room, rushing quickly to pick up the coffee tray, and slipped right out.

In my mind, I thought, Oh my God, this man is going to freaking violate me!

He stood up and I walked around the coffee table and sat down patting down on the sofa...saying, "Come sit down on the sofa." This sofa was facing the door, so anyone coming in would directly see what was happening.

"Let's talk a little bit more about how you are helping these girls who want to become teachers. Thank you so much for the great honor of seeing how you are willing to help them."

He walked over and said with the most perverted smile. "No, I want to still talk about your ass."

My body was shaking. "I am so sorry. I am so nervous. I just have never been approached by someone of your stature. I just don't know how to receive your attention. So please forgive me if I don't seem to know the value of what you bring to me. What you bring to me is with great value and I am not worthy. I am just a very humble servant here to help Linda. I can't pursue anything romantic with you because I am not a prepared woman for that."

He gave me a hard stare and approached. As he got closer and bent over to try to kiss me, placing his hand on my shoulders to keep me down, Linda walked in. I jumped out of my seat on the sofa and bowed down in front of the chief and Linda said, "What is going on here?"

I said. "Oh my goodness Linda, he just called me his Nija daughter, and I am just so humbled by this. Thank you so much, Chief." Bowing deeply with my head in utter humility. There was silence.

He looked at her and then at me and said, "Now I have two daughters here."

I then said, "Linda, the fact that you brought me here today I will never forget. What an honor it is to be here today." She smiled a great big smile and turned to the chief, extending copious amounts of praise and thanks. Inside I felt like I was going to faint, so I locked my knees so that I could stand up straighter. She shared that she just finalized the details with the assistant and that there were not enough words to share the level of gratitude that she had for his altruistic actions.

Surprisingly, moments later, the administrative assistant walked into the room with a tray of cell phones, sharing that the chief had another pressing appointment. But before he could meet with his next appointment, he should call the distinguished speaker of a conference to extend an invitation for dinner. In that instance, I seized the moment to ask Linda if we were going. She nodded, gesturing with her finger to wait a second. I leaned in and whispered, "Let's go and not be rude interrupting his important business."

As he saw us talking, he said "I would like for you both to come back this evening for dinner."

At that moment, I smiled and bowed and said. "I would love that very much."

We waved and rushed out of the room. I grabbed her hand and led her out as fast as I could and she looked very puzzled by my rushed reaction. We made it to the main door and I opened it. As we were walking down the marble stairs, the chief called out to Linda, pick the color you want my daughters. I kept walking toward the cars that were at the bottom of the steps, parked and ready for their passengers. Each one with a chauffeur in the vehicle waiting in that African heat. I firmly said, "Red," walking down faster to the car. The chief chuckled as he walked behind us going down the stairs and he said.

"Are you going to tell me what the color red symbolizes my daughter?"

And I said, "Yes, the blood of women, our dear women give life."

He smiled and said. "I like that. Yes women give life and I look forward to seeing you both for dinner tonight. I sped quickly to the red car and opened the back seat while the Chauffeur was still in the driver's seat. I left Linda many steps behind me as she was making her way down the steps.

Suddenly, I heard the chief scream, "You idiot, you are supposed to open that princess's door. Open that door!" Oh no, was he yelling at

Linda, or was he furious that I was getting away and yelling at me? Then yelling in his Ebu language, what I only can assume is profanity, I peered out the window to witness him pointing at the driver as he rushed up to him. Suddenly, the chief smacked the living shit out of the driver. The smack was clearly heard from inside the car. "You idiot, you are supposed to open the door for the lady!"

Linda kept on walking down the steps and finally reached the car, waiting for the driver to open the door for her. The driver opened the door and then went into the driver's seat. He started the car and drove down the long driveway, past the iron gates, and quietly through the back road that would lead us back to the hotel. Throughout the whole ride, I did not speak. Calm as a cucumber.

Linda asked. "So what do you think about that visit?"

All I said was, "Oh my goodness Linda, I can't believe that you have brought me to that place to meet such a great man. Wow!" She smiled. Then for what seemed like an eternity, we finally made it to the hotel, went past the sniffing dogs, and stepped out of the red Bentley. As I walked into the hotel, my blood was boiling. My mind was racing. I quickly turned to her as we entered the elevator and yelled. "We are not going anywhere. I am not ever stepping foot anywhere near that man. I am getting the fuck out of here!" Perplexed and befuddled, she wanted to know what I was talking about. That is when I proceeded to tell her everything I experienced while I was alone with him and she was away getting money for the girls' scholarship.

I was going to book the next flight the fuck out of there! She was doubtful that we would be able to get a last-minute ticket using the same airline that we arrived in. I told her that I needed to go and that I was not taking no for an answer. She called Toni and asked for advice, and he told her that the best thing to do was to leave that afternoon. He said that a man with that much power could stop a plane if he wanted to. While she was speaking with him, I was quickly packing up my bags and making sure I took my passport and money out of the hotel room safe.

Toni told her that we shouldn't even check out of the hotel to make it obvious. That he would do that for us. Thankfully, Toni sent a car for us and it took us to the airport. When we arrived at the airport, she implored me not to speak in English. That I must look like a hot distressed mess. Linda said, "Let me figure this out." I was puzzled by her request but knew that this woman had to make it right or else things could get ugly. It was not a good look for her if she indeed baited the chief with my presence. She then proceeded to tell the airport staff that the woman she was traveling with (me) was married to a powerful Muslim who had abandoned me in the city and that she didn't want to be responsible for me here with this white woman. If something happens to her, I am responsible. No, not on my head! I am taking her ass back to Lagos and putting her on the first flight back to her country. So you need to get me a ticket, right now!" Then pointing to each of the airport staff behind the ticket counter she yelled, "If you don't get me a ticket right now, it's going to be your head and your head! I don't care if you can't get me a ticket, but you must get her a ticket and you are going to put her on that plane!"

Well, that is exactly what they did. I sat in the first row next to her and all I did was cry asking God to remove any obstacles for my safe return. Ironically, the whole time she was yelling at the staff, her cell phone kept ringing and she didn't answer it. Finally, when we were in our seats ready for take-off, the chief called again and asked "How is the doctor?"

Her response was, "She is doing very well, she is taking a nap. She didn't feel too well. Maybe it was something she ate earlier in the day that didn't agree with her. She is just a little tired from all the traveling." He replied, "If you want, I can send my doctor over to the hotel." Linda paused and said that it would not be necessary. All I needed was some rest. She said that we looked forward to seeing him later on for dinner.

Seatbelts fastened. Engine started. Tightly folding my hands together and closing my eyes. I blocked out all of the sounds in the plane. I thanked God for delivering me safely back to this Airbus.

"Heavenly Father, I beg that you deliver your daughter safely back home. We have to take off. I want to see my Mami. I need my Mami."

Deep breaths.

I heard him say, "Hija, you are almost home."

CHAPTER TWENTY-EIGHT

DAUGHTER COMES HOME

A fter my trip from Nigeria, I spent some quality time with my mom as she was coping with the post-April birthday diagnosis of her twin sister who was battling Stage 3 Non-Hodgkin's Lymphoma. It seemed like this damn cancer was infiltrating the lives of our loved ones again.

We would visit my dear aunt Titi Lola throughout the remainder of the summer to pray. A few times my maternal uncle Maríano would come up from Newark, New Jersey, and lead us in prayer. He was an ordained 'fire and brimstone' minister as he would bible-thump his way through our conversations sternly preaching about hell and salvation. His pious nature ws so revolting and so holier than thou. This was very unsettling for my mother who was a devoted Catholic wherein the gospels were not shared in such an animated and threatening way. His objectionable demeanor was hard to tolerate, but I would grin and bear it for the sake of my dear aunt and mom. It felt more like I was watching theatrics. It reminded me of when I was a young girl in Puerto Rico observing my Tio Moncho who was very different about his faith. Aside from some peculiar subvocalization about how much he loved Jesus and an occasional hallelujah, he was more Christ-like and not as judgemental as this uncle. Now that I think about it, my mother was terrified. The same look would come over her face when my stepfather was in one of his tirades. She would put on that blank stare to not look afraid. After those visits, I would try everything I could to share positive thoughts and faith-filled messages as our beloved Titi Lola went through this trial.

My aunt was extremely spiritually centered so her faith did not waver and that was a big blessing to witness. Thankfully with intensive chemotherapy, radiation, and a positive mindset, my aunt's body reacted favorably to the treatments. Titi Lola was able to beat cancer. The love and support of her family meant so much to Titi Lola. It really made a huge difference. We believed that we were able to put cancer behind us.

Unfortunately, a few weeks after my aunt received the good news that she was cancer-free, on New Year's Eve, I got an abrupt call at 10:30 p.m. from my brother Nelson that my mother was in the emergency room. What was going on?! Customarily we knew that Mami wasn't into staying up late for New Year's Eve. So that was the night my brothers and I would celebrate with our spouses. Receiving that call made my heart stop.

A few days prior to receiving that call, my brothers and I had spent a beautiful Christmas day together in my home with our mom. It was such a joy to see her dancing in my kitchen with my brothers Rafy and Freddy. I had made some yummy pasteles, and she was helping me cook the *arroz con gandules.* She had stayed with us for a few days and I was so happy to have her with me. Mami had complained about some stomach discomfort, but since we had eaten so much food I was worried that I didn't cook the pasteles long enough. Now I will admit that mom was always complaining about intestinal issues, and it was such a common occurrence that we always felt that was her default excuse to not leave the house or when she didn't want to spend time in mixed company.

A few months before this incident, I implored her to go to the doctor, especially in light of her sister's most recent battle. My husband James had finally convinced her to go, and she shared that she was getting some medicine to help settle her stomach and that mostly she needed to change her diet.

So receiving this call as I was sitting in my mother-in-law Veronica's Spanish Harlem living room ready to bring in the New Year was deeply unsettling. When we raced to Westchester Square Hospital, my beloved mother was in emergency surgery. Was it my pasteles? I know the last time I cooked an undercooked chocolate cake was when my little brother Freddy, who was seven years old, landed in the hospital to get his appendix removed. Oh boy, my brothers were not going to let me hear the end of this.

We discovered that her appendix ruptured and that she had a perforated large intestine with sepsis which was that the infection in her intestinal cavity was now spreading around. They were dealing with that horrific procedure of removing a part of the large intestine that was perforated and placing a colostomy bag to reroute the waste that would need to leave her body after surgery. While doing this procedure, the emergency surgeons found massive amounts of cancer in Mami's intestinal area, stomach, and colon. I was devastated to learn that she had stage 4 stomach cancer and the cancer had spread and metastasized. Privately speaking with the surgeon, the oncologist, and my brothers, the doctors gave a poor prognosis. My beloved Mami had at best a minimum of three to six months of life. This news was like receiving a lightning bolt through my body. It was a short circuit to my soul. Mouths moved as the doctors spoke to me, but I was not present. I witnessed mouths making words without sound after that. Numbness covered my body like a weighted blanket. Heavy and overwhelming.

Mami had witnessed her sister go through the direst of circumstances of her cancer battle. My husband James was an anchor for me. He grounded me and encouraged me to talk with my brothers about a plan. Consequently, my brothers and I agreed that it was best that Mom not learn of her terminal diagnosis. We would keep it a secret. My mother understood how secrets helped to keep the peace. This secret that she was dying was important to keep her peace. We wanted her to have the best quality of life that those three to six months could offer. We felt that Mami had gone through so much trauma in her life that she didn't need this to be something that would rob her peace.

Our number one goal was to get her to recover from her emergency surgery and get her removed from the intubation that didn't allow our dear mother to speak with us. When she was off the intubator it was remarkable to hear Mami recanting what she experienced that evening. She was not able to move or get out of bed to call anyone. At that point, her appendix had ruptured causing a serious infection in her bloodstream and spreading around her body resulting in severe sepsis. Mami shared that she had come to terms with the notion that she was going to die. But then all of sudden she cried out and she saw an angel appear. She cried out saying that she had changed her mind. *–No me quiero morir sola. ¡Señor Dios mío ayúdame!–* That is when she heard the telephone ringing and ringing. It was my brother Nelson calling her to wish her a Happy New Year before she went to bed, but she couldn't pick up the phone. My brother later shared that he had the strangest feeling of urgency come upon him and he was compelled to go in his car from Queens and check up on Mami. I am so glad he did because that gave us the gift of time with our dear mother.

My siblings, in-laws, and close friends would take turns visiting Mom after work and keep her company. She enjoyed it when we would bring her the special treats that she craved. Our time together as a family was so special as she would hear about our days and how the kids were doing. At that time her grandson Christopher was 20 years old and her only niece Carolyn was nine years old. When she would see their faces, she would light up. My sister-in-laws and I would work together to wash Mami's hair, and do her nail polish. My devoted sister-friends Rae, Lela, and Sandy would come by with flowers, share prayers, and help me pour love on my beloved mother. Mami loved her pedicures and foot massages. She would complain that she didn't like the hospital rule that she couldn't wear any earrings. How was a woman supposed to look good in these horrible circumstances?

When they moved Mami to a rehabilitation center, so that she could work on walking again, she was worried that her children had shipped her off to a nursing home. It was at that point that I felt that I needed to go on family leave to alleviate Mami's fears about being abandoned. It was not easy taking time off, because prior to that I had taken time off to go to Florida to be by my step-father's side. At that time, I had a former Board of Education member's child in my class. That individual did not make it easy and complained to my school principal about my frequent absences. Now the same board member had their youngest child in my class, and the complaining continued.

It was at this moment that I realized that family truly comes first. It didn't matter how many degrees I had earned or how many years I had dedicated to my profession, it all was distilled to the crystalized notion that ONLY family can fulfill you. Only family can be by your side in your most life-challenging moments. When I wasn't at work, there were going to be only two primary questions posed at my job. 1. What was happening when the teacher was absent? 2. Who was going to be her substitute? The rest didn't matter to them. Every day that I would go to work knowing Mami was in a hospital bed and that I was losing precious time with her was unbearable. So I took my family medical leave. I was going to be there for my dying mother. Everyone else was simply going to have to wait and they were just going to have to deal with it.

In retrospect, I am so grateful to God that I was able to take time off from work to be by my mami's side. It gave us such tender moments of daughter-mother time. The embraces were a healing balm to my grieving spirit. Here I was grieving my mother, and she was still alive with us. I remember the social worker sharing that we should enjoy the present time we had with her. That she would sense our fear. So I made it a point to initiate happy conversations where I would ask her to tell me how it felt when she first arrived in New York from Puerto Rico. I chuckled as I learned about her curiosity and her wonder as she rode the subway and figured out how to travel around Manhattan. She would smile when she painted childhood memories through her narratives growing up in Toa Alta, Puerto Rico. Those were heartfelt words exchanged between a daughter who knew her mom was dying, and a mother who thought she was going to go back home and resume her ordinary life.

It felt like we were filling in the space of a lifetime in those few weeks to make up for the time I had not seen her by chasing my dreams and ambitious educational and professional goals. I would cry apologizing for not spending more time with her. She would ask me to stop and remind me that I was doing an important job. I was a mother, a wife, and a dedicated teacher. All those things were things that she was so proud to write about in her letters to her family in Puerto Rico. –*Vilma Luz Cabán es maestra. Vilmita es doctora. Vilma Luz se fue a África. ¿Sabías que ella estaba en una revista con el Presidente Clinton?*–

While I would walk Mami around in her wheelchair so that we could get out of that depressing hospital bed, my beloved mother had many conversations about going back to Puerto Rico. I told her that I would help her fix her *casita en Toa Alta*. Telling her that the first thing we needed to do was pick the color of the tile she wanted in the house that her brother Nolin built. Her eyes would light up and I said that I would spend my summer months doing what I could to fix her house. She would tell me to not forget that the house needs to get painted. She loved the idea. –*A mi me gusta mucho el color aqua que parece como el mar.*– Mami would ask me every day to inquire when she was finally going home. With the help of her physical therapists, physicians, and nurses after three months of hospital and rehabilitation center stays, we were able to bring my mom to her Bronx apartment on March 23, 2012.

Mami enjoyed *sancochito, pollo guisado, arroz dulce, viendo su novelas y Caso Cerrado con Dra. Ana María Polo*. We would laugh at some of the absurd cases that Dra. Polo deliberated over as she banged her gavel on the court bench and yelled –¡*Caso Cerrado!*– She enjoyed morning masses on the television where we would both pray to Mary thanking her for bringing Mami home. I learned how to work with the visiting nurse to administer her pain medication intravenously and handle her wound care. She was able to sit in a wheelchair, but moving her from the bed to the chair was tricky. My brothers and I would take turns taking care of Mom while she was home. They were dedicated husbands and coaches, but they were remarkable sons. Rafy had moved from Florida to Pennsylvania so he was a few short hours away. We were all together just like growing up in that small apartment on Stratford Avenue. Mami had her *pollitos juntitos*. Mami's blessing lasted a week, and then she had to be rushed by ambulance back to where it all started at Westchester Square Hospital. The cancer had spread to her lung and she was having trouble breathing. My brothers and I came together at Mami's bed and held a vigil throughout the night taking turns being by her side while we would take turns sleeping in the family room next door. We played music, had loving conversations, took turns holding her hand and talking to her as we leaned in close, comforting her...telling her that we knew she was tired and that we were all here together with her. In the early afternoon of April 2, 2012, our beloved mother took her last breath. It was during the Easter Holy Week...*Semana Santa*. Mami had her homecoming in one of the holiest weeks for Christians.

A few days later, we held a lovely memorial in the Woolworth Chapel on the grounds of the historic Woodlawn Cemetery. It was a gift from Fred and Velma Woolworth. Wow, the woman Velma sounds like Vilma. I took it as a sign that the universe was speaking to me. I remember as a child going to Woolworths with my dear mother and we would go window shopping because we couldn't afford to buy anything. I told her that one day when I would save some money from my tutoring job, we would come and drink coffee at the lunch counter. She would tell me –*Hija, guarda tu dinero.*

This was the place I would celebrate my mother's life. Beautiful and strong just like her spirit. Built of stone, with a gorgeous tower, this historic chapel had golden yellow walls, high ceilings, and the piercing glow of sunlight streaming through the antique stained glass windows. It made me feel like Mami was closer to God. Her body in the closed white and gold casket covered with flowers was merely an offering to our grieving family and friends that filled every corner of that chapel. Seeing my brother Freddy's softball team in their uniforms sharing their respects as they all stood on the top balcony had me break into tears. I had to regroup to find the words to speak that day. This was so different from a cold impersonal funeral parlor where you feel that only a few corners of the formaldehyde-smelling room are a reminder of the deceased. Having Mami's images projected onto a large screen at the altar brought me closer to her. We had a guitarist play "Ave María" as he sang while different images cycled through on the screen of our beloved mother. It captured moments of her life as a devoted mother, loving sister, dutiful wife, caring friend, and big-hearted volunteer who served at her church and neighborhood food pantry. During the eulogy, several family members spoke about loving memories with our dear María Concepción Cores-Ayala.

La hija de María put on her pearls, her black/white dress, and a stylish large-brim hat befitting for a royal funeral. My mother was a Queen. She deserved a regal memorial. The sight from the podium took my breath away with over 100 guests in attendance as family, friends, and colleagues supported my brothers and me as we coped with this tragic loss. Mami was laid to rest in the beautiful mausoleum in front of a giant white stone statue of a beautiful angel surrounded by an indoor fountain. It looked like a scene from a movie when we continued to play music and hear the priest pray over her coffin for the final entombment.

Walking in grace, I channeled the strength that I had witnessed as a daughter of a battered woman. My heart ushered the best instructions as I planned the memorial and confronted different heartbreaking moments for preparing her body. Standing tall with quiet dignity, I kept it together stoically. Just like she would. Enduring and not folding. Standing like a marble statue unphased. No matter the cosmic loss, this statue had to keep it together because I feared that if I didn't, I would lose my mind.

CHAPTER TWENTY-NINE

LATINA PROJECT- BREAK THE SILENCE

After my beloved mother lost her battle with cancer, I didn't allow myself time to grieve properly. I dove right into work and lost myself in the inner workings of teaching. I just wanted to numb the pain and the tremendous loss that I was feeling. One day while showering a huge weight of sadness came upon me that literally knocked me to the ground as I lay in the fetal position while the shower water washed over me. I was in utter despair. Prior to this moment, I remained stoic and moved forward with such poise that the facade cracked and I came to the end of myself. I needed to find a way to process this grief. I needed a way to metabolize this hurt. I had gained so much weight that I was literally carrying the sadness in my body. It was on that shower tile floor that I decided something had to change.

As I dried off and looked at my body, I made a decision to change this state of living. I decided I had to get healthy again. I had to release this grief. I had to release these pounds. Running was always my default strategy for coping with stress and shedding extra weight. I lived in such a beautiful mountainous area with the perfect Bear Mountain trails to run, and now it was time to use them. A few years prior, in preparation for my milestone 40th birthday and to be able to look fabulous in a black cocktail dress, I was able to lose 40 pounds. My muscle memory would kick in. I had to believe that. I had to find a way to shed my sadness. The endorphins that rushed through my body after each run would help me conquer this grief. My goal was to get strong again and work on preparing for a November half-marathon in San Juan, Puerto Rico. It was called the Diva's Half-Marathon. The capital city of my mother's homeland where I could pay homage to her life's race. I registered and started to train. It was like a fog was lifted from my brain. I was moving forward with laser beam clarity.

One day while having a Sunday dinner with my dear "sister from another mister" Lela and her husband, we spoke about how I wanted to do something to honor my mother's memory. I confided how my mom was a survivor of domestic violence and how much I regretted that it took her over 25 years to break free. I wanted to break the silence around domestic violence. This former neighbor and now Dominican soul sister spoke about how domestic violence was a huge problem in the Dominican Republic. So much so that the First Lady of the Dominican Republic was working to raise more awareness about its prevalence in the country.

My dear friend Lela who served as a United Nations consulate gave me such insight into this problem. I was surprised to learn that her husband witnessed his mother go through the same thing. However, he was so loving, supportive, and caring to my dear friend. How was that possible? Can the children of batters break the cycle too? In speaking with them, we brainstormed about a way they could help me gain access to a small town where I could interview women to learn more about their struggles. As a family, they were going to travel to the Dominican Republic in August with her 85-year-old mother who was a retired teacher and women's advocate. The fact that they were willing to fold me into their trip and make this happen for me was such an enormous offering to my spirit. Her husband was more than willing to reach out to some community advocates and activists in his childhood town of Bonao in the Sonador province of the Dominican Republic. He mentioned the possibility of speaking in a few small community events to raise awareness. They would reach out to a few journalists to cover the events and perhaps give me a few interviews to talk about this topic. I was floored to think about how quickly they were so willing to help me follow this research dream.

I decided to call the research project The Latina Project: Breaking the Silence, Breaking the Cycle of Domestic Violence. Everything I had learned in Kenya working with child victims would help me face domestic violence head-on so that I could somehow wrap my brain around this phenomenon that left us with more questions than answers. Perhaps questions could lead the way to creating a stronger understanding of domestic violence.

Therefore, I framed my inquiry with the following research questions:

1. Is there anything you would like to share regarding your experiences with domestic violence?

2. What are some of the obstacles that women face as they try to break the cycle of domestic violence in their lives?

3. What would you suggest is a way to take care of the problem of domestic violence?

4. How can the community help women who are victims of domestic violence?

5. What are the necessary resources that help to address this problem?

6. What role do men play in breaking the cycle of domestic violence?

The goal was to launch my advocacy research study on domestic violence in the Dominican Republic in the summer of 2012. This Latina researcher would examine how the epidemic of domestic violence follows many of the immigrant Dominican women who settle in the Washington Heights and Dyckman areas in New York City. Regrettably, many women's shelters and community outreach groups in Manhattan are not able to be culturally responsive to the unique and complex needs of this particular immigrant population. As a result, many of these battered women eventually go back to their abusers and face insurmountable obstacles to break the cycle of domestic violence in their lives. The goal of this research project was to collaborate with a local grassroots organization in the Washington Heights area, and offer research findings that can steer and shape their organization's action plans to better serve this population of battered women. Ultimately, a program evaluation can demonstrate how this grassroots organization is effectively meeting the needs of Dominican women and making a noteworthy impact.

In preparation of this advocacy report, a great deal of coordination and international collaboration was necessary to make the following Latina domestic violence research study a reality. In June of 2012 with the help of my friend Lela, I was able to reach out to former president Hipolito Mejia who endorsed my project. This helped to open doors for a future sit down with the Senator of the province where I was conducting the research. Senator Aristi-Castro of the Altagracia Province had a daughter in another town that was the mayor of a town close to Bonao and perhaps my research work could extend into that region.

During this trip, I had the honor of meeting with the aforementioned dignitaries to discuss public policy and potential channels for raising awareness to ratify the change. With the help of several Dominican local community advocates such as former Councilman Victor Manuel Batista and Mr. Pena, I conducted focus groups and individual interviews with battered women in the town of Bonao. This field study helped me to better understand the multi-faceted phenomena of domestic violence in the Latino community.

A close childhood friend of my dear friend's husband connected me with former Councilman Victor Manuel Bastista. He played a pivotal and instrumental community role in serving both as a representative of this initiative in his small rural town of Bonao, as well as one of our strongest rallying supporters. In solidarity and support of this domestic violence cause, community advocates Mr. Pena and Mr. Batista locked arms to serve as advocates and shared voices for community change by coordinating various domestic violence conferences in numerous faith-based and educational venues.

They were quite resourceful in their outreach and traveled across different towns and villages to network with various community stakeholders. They submitted press releases to various regional news media. As a result, news coverage about the domestic research project was shared with *Hortensia Magazine*, which was based out of the capital of Santo Domingo. They reached out to Mery De La Rosa at the local television program *En Familia* and fortunately, they gained a community news slot wherein they reported news of the upcoming events on Bonao Television, Channel 12. Their outreach efforts encouraged local women to attend the domestic violence conference as well as extended an invitation to consider being a part of the research study. Thanks to their noble efforts, over 50 participants attended the domestic violence awareness conferences and educational workshops. Eventually, the editor of the *Hortensia Magazine* traveled from the capital Santo Domingo to observe the research discussions. As a way to demonstrate her support, she wrote a feature article about the merit of my study.

Using various informational platforms, Mr. Pena and Mr. Batista helped to raise community awareness about the prolific rate of domestic violence in the Dominican Republic. I was immensely grateful for all of their outreach. I was inspired by their natural leadership abilities to tenaciously mobilize a much-needed service to their community. Their campaign action plan was to bring the issue of domestic violence to the forefront of Bonao's community economic agenda. This was an extremely viable outreach strategy. The ultimate goal of involving several philanthropic community agents, faith-based organizations, educational institutions, telecommunication organizations, as well as town and provincial legislative leaders would help pave the way. In due course, their proactive stance could help the victims of domestic violence by opening potential lines of future funding and community support. In addition, the lead researcher particularly extended her greatest appreciation to Senator Amable of the Altagracia Province in the Dominican Republic. This distinguished public servant welcomed the research team's arrival in the midst of his personal holiday with genuine warmth and enthusiasm. Senator Amable's willingness to assist the team in any way possible to achieve a successful preliminary research study indicated his level of commitment to his battered constituents of Bonao, Dominican Republic.

After completing the field research, I was inclined to reach out to my mom's hometown in Puerto Rico, but after much introspection, I realized that personally, it was too soon to examine this challenging topic—so painfully close to home. At this juncture, it was best to continue examining the broader issues of domestic violence. I recognized that it was important to widen the aperture of this obscure topic and gain a stronger understanding of the issues related to domestic violence in many Latino communities.

Ultimately, as a qualitative researcher, I elected to pursue a replicable course of study that could help me examine the underlying universal themes that are evident in domestic violence in Latino communities. I selected the Caribbean sister community that received me so well the summer prior. It was not far away from Puerto Rico, it was Columbus' first discovery, and symbolically it would serve as this researcher's first discovery of the deeper roots of domestic violence. It was the captivating country of the Dominican Republic, my prima-hermana island. There I would muster the courage to ask some tough questions, tougher than the questions I had posed the year before. My goal was to get candid responses from participants across different socio-economic strata. The comfort was that I was getting by in my mother's native tongue. Perhaps those victims could speak the truth that my mother just couldn't formulate the words to give me. To give the big reason why she stayed so long.

With the joint and dynamic efforts of this initial team that supported me on my first visit to the Dominican Republic, we tapped a larger
compassionate international team of community advocates willing to
help me bring the epidemic community issue of domestic violence
to light. The collective endeavors of current and former United Nations staff, political figures, physicians, prosecutors, legal advocates,
media correspondents, and community volunteers were effective in
creating a larger impact. Over time the Latina Project: Breaking the
Cycle...Breaking the Silence research project became noteworthy news
outside the small town of Bonao. As such, another project was set in
motion and I would need to go back in the summer of 2013.

My goal after launching this economic empowerment project was
to travel to Geneva, Switzerland to confer with the United Nations
Dominican Republic Ambassador as well as meet with the United Nations Dominican Republic Ambassador stationed in Santo Domingo.
As the advocacy researcher, I wanted to apprise the UN dignitaries
of the status of the research project. My ultimate goal was to present
research findings and the implications of this research at the 2014
World Humanitarian Conference in Geneva, Switzerland. I wanted
to reach out to the Equality Now Organization that I worked with
in Nairobi and see if their support would help me present at the
New York United Nations in New York. I was grateful to my fellow
executive board members of the humanitarian research organization
Global Changers.

Global Changers' belief in my humanitarian research capabilities
and their support nurtured my idea to bring my research findings to
inform policy. I was immensely proud to be an active member of this
outstanding organization and I was hoping that having the support
of this non-profit organization would position me to get a seat with
policymakers.

Throughout all of this fluid research momentum, I sought to bridge
the creative world with the research world. After attending a few Latino cultural events sponsored by my friend with her organization in
the Bronx, I purchased a painting of a beautiful image of the Taina
Goddess. I reached out to a talented Latina artist Tanya Torres to

thank her for her artistic contribution and to see if she would consider extending me permission to use her inspirational and cultural iconic figure—Cacibayagua: Taina Goddess— in any promotional literature and research reports sharing the worked centered on the Latina Domestic Violence Research Project. I wanted this image to catch the attention of the UN dignitaries. It would be the cultural seal of our Latina/Taina women suffering from domestic abuse. Tanya Torres was very excited about that collaboration and exposure and she generously agreed to use her image as the cover of my report. She also had another beautiful idea/gift that we could offer some of the survivors in my study.

In August 2013, I traveled back to Bonao, wherein I delivered a special inspirational gift specially designed to inspire the 10 domestic violence victims. The artist Mrs. Torres lovingly handcrafted unique wearable art necklaces with the inspirational image of Cacibayagua— the mythical Taina Goddess. Traditional Dominican folklore describes how Cacibayagua is the original life source of the indigenous Taino Indians that emerged from her beautiful cave. The inspirational intention behind sharing this gift was to encourage women. In the face of adversity and their personal decision to renounce the economic stranglehold of their abusers, these empowered women can recall the legend of Cacibayagua. The necklace signifies their promise and legacy as Latina women and descendants of the rich Taino culture. It is a symbolic reminder to tap into the spiritual strength of their inner Taina goddess. This artistic gift serves as a beautiful and concrete reminder of their legacy and the promise of their destiny as empowered women and not beaten women.

I was eternally grateful for the generous support I received from a loving circle of intimate family and friends. After I did an extensive literature review of viable empowerment strategies for battered women, I recognized the strong potential for making the greatest impact in the lives of these abused women. Subsequently, I rallied for financial support through crowdfunding and mutual aid with the Friends Against Domestic Violence fundraising website with Go Fund Me. This community grassroots initiative helped to secure a modest portion of funds. As a result, with the additional financial support of my husband and my dear friends, I was able to purchase 10 sewing machines and secure the safe shipment of those machines. In addition, money raised helped to purchase the bulk of the essential seamstress tools needed to economically empower domestic violence survivors.

A compassionate circle of friends saw the collective power of this economic empowerment vision and they worked together to establish a toolkit for the success of this school uniform cooperative. I kept my dedicated group of supporters updated on the latest developments of this work using my research blog on www.doctoravazquez.com and on social media. Throughout these fundraising and campaigning moments, I was grateful to my husband for his support. He showed interest in coming with me on the second trip to the Dominican Republic and he collaborated with my dear friend's husband who was joining us as well.

On the second trip, my husband was able to witness the degree of community outreach as I presented at a large local university in Bonao and met with different regional leaders like Congresswoman Dra. Fernandez. She invited us to her home, and we were able to strategize how we were going to present at the university together. She was going to share her story as a physician witnessing the effects of domestic abuse when her patients would see her. She linked me with a local prosecutor who was going to speak after I presented my findings to the women and how as a community we could lock arms to support our battered victims.

I shared my story as the only daughter of a battered Latina immigrant from Puerto Rico. I told anecdotes of how I witnessed my mother María suffer as a victim of domestic violence. When I was young, my mother would urge me not to say anything and to keep family problems PRIVATE. She would advise me that it's best not to get other people involved in marital problems. As a result, María dealt with the conflicting pain of staying in an abusive relationship for the sake of her family and children. She carried this pain for over 25 years. I shared stories of how I was my mother's accomplice in her efforts of trying to get away when I was a child. I shared stories of false starts and false getaways and the mistakes that she had made. All in all, it was important for these women to learn that on average it takes about seven to nine attempts for battered women to finally break free from their abusers. At the time, there were horrific stories of women getting stabbed or shot in front of their families when the abuser was finally able to find them. I wanted to equip the women with the foresight to see that the pattern of domestic abuse runs complicated and deep. It was important to learn about the profile of the abuser and how the victim can transform into a free survivor.

After the speeches, the workshops, and more interviews with survivors, I was astounded to learn that our efforts had reached close to 700 women. Seeing their smiles as we raffled sewing machines at different speaking venues, lit a fire in my spirit. They were going to embark on working collaboratively with a team of women on different economic empowerment initiatives. Many of the women were excited about sewing school uniforms for their children and selling school uniforms to the children of the community. Later I would learn that the women were extremely resourceful in making money renting out the sewing machines to private seamstresses that needed the machines to sew and sell women's dresses for birthday and wedding events. The women had entrepreneurial spirits and I was so proud to hear about those stories.

All of this compelling research gave me a path to examine how this would affect Puerto Rican women on the island as well as in the United States. It was a brave choice that was not supported by my husband. When we were in the Dominican Republic I started to sense a bit of resentment from my husband as all of these speaking arrangements were happening so close to his birthday. He communicated that he just wanted to be at a resort. He was frustrated with the crowds and the endless traveling to different venues as I spoke and interfaced with the different community leaders. I felt torn, but I tried my best to make it special as we went to a resort in between public speaking events. In retrospect, I should have planned our resort visit after all of the traveling. Believe me, he was not a happy camper complaining that as a diabetic these were very long days and that he was frustrated with the food because they didn't have very appetizing snacks. Where were the good restaurants? We were visiting very humble and economically depressed communities and the local women received us with such love, offering what they could to host us at different community centers. I felt like I was responsible for his well-being and he reminded me every day about it.

My husband was not happy about my idea of presenting or even thinking about working with the United Nations. On our flight back, he said that he didn't think it was a good idea. That my place was to be home with my family and not with all of these crooked politicians who just want to get in my pants. Meanwhile, there was not one inappropriate interaction with a crooked politician. They were all so welcoming and supportive of this cause. I felt that he felt threatened seeing these men buttress my efforts. In fact, it was quite evident that the only reason why he decided to come was to get a better sense of the landscape his wife was walking through, vetting possible threats to his home balance and lifestyle with me.

This was the pivotal moment when I knew something was going to have to change. He wanted me to stop doing the research. He felt that all this work would make me decide to leave my pension job and his dream to retire in Florida would be thwarted by my ambitious desire to do work that really wasn't going to make a difference in corrupt countries. Every time we were with family, he would raise this point and use it as his platform to rally his family or my family to concur with him. I completed my mission by dedicating a project to my mother. Now it was time to let it go. My husband offered an ultimatum and in a nutshell, I refused. I saw it as a way for him to try to control me and I wasn't going to tolerate it.

We agreed to separate and we parted ways. It was a painstaking decision, but I wanted his full support and I wanted to follow my dreams. Now I was not only grieving the loss of my mother, but the loss of my marriage. Diving into my research was going to be my place of refuge. A place to process the grief just like I did in lifting the memory of my mother. Now I was going to lift the memory of every woman who felt trapped in an overbearing relationship where she did not have full agency to speak her mind and speak her truth.

My dear son encouraged me to pursue my research dreams. He was a junior in college and after his abuela's death, he knew how much this really meant to me. I valued his support so much because my husband's support was starting to wane. In the fall of 2013, Chris served as the editor-in-chief of his college newspaper, and he invited his mother to write an informational article about this topic. This proud moment meant the world to me. Chris used this journalistic platform to share what I had discovered. After sharing my article, I received a call from a correspondent from the Research Institute of International Journalism. He cited me as an expert in the field and wanted some direct quotes shedding key lessons learned on my domestic violence research trip. I was honored and quite humbled by their interest. I shared how this research was a way to honor my mother's legacy as a victim of domestic violence. In her final days fighting cancer, we processed so many experiences and moments that she wished she had broken free much sooner.

In the article, "Ending the Silence: Domestic Violence in the Dominican Republic" the correspondent cited quotes from our article interview.

"It wasn't until she was on her deathbed that she finally opened up to Vilma about the abuse she endured. 'I just felt like there were moments where we weren't allowed to talk about it,' Dr. Cabán-Vazquez said. 'But in those final moments, my mom spoke freely, candidly about her struggles, and I just promised her that I would go on to use her story to be able to help other women break the silence early and break the cycle. After realizing there were many stories similar to her mother's out there, Cabán-Vazquez then put it upon herself to study the women of the Dominican Republic to better understand the issue of domestic violence."

Reading those words in print crystallized my efforts into a tangible gift that I could offer to my mother in heaven.

Perhaps this is where I began fine-tuning my advocacy lens. It was in the midst of these turbulent moments that sparks took the form of my heart's desire to share the urgent call for helping battered women.

Regrettably, there are unsettling memories that at times tend to resurface and they activate this researcher's desire to examine the extent of how my mother María suffered. I had a tough secret to keep. I wondered how many other women and children actually walk around with domestic violence problems weighing down their heavy hearts. How many of those children who witness the abuse attract overbearing partners and domineering partners that nullify their voice? Was this the norm that they witnessed as children and now seek in a future partner? My goal was to leave a research footprint on an elusive phenomenon that maintains an emotional, spiritual, physical, and economic stranglehold on many Latino communities.

CHAPTER THIRTY

EXPERT WITNESS

After these two trips and different interviews wherein I shared my constructivist grounded research findings, I shared various theories on how battered women can ultimately break free from their abusers. I received emails and phone calls from different advocacy centers helping immigrant women seek political asylum from their abusers. I was surprised to learn that I truly was leaving a research footprint in the Google search engine.

I had a student from Columbia University who was a Human Rights major reach out to me because she wanted to get more information about domestic violence in the Dominican Republic. Her name was Carla Marie. She was a young Latina scholar who had earned a full scholarship to Columbia University and here was this young woman asking me for help. I was so honored that I could be of service. Carla Marie was a young first-generation Dominican woman who lived in New York City. She was the proud daughter of a single mother who came to the United States for the American dream. Carla Marie was truly grateful that I had dedicated so much time to this topic. This was something she was examining for a research paper she was working on. I responded to her email and offered to meet for coffee so that I could talk to her more about the topic. At the time, a student from the E.W. Scripps School of Journalism wrote an informational article about domestic violence in the Dominican Republic and he directly quoted my research data within the article. Carla Marie had run across that article as well as my research website and she wanted to learn more about what I had discovered on this topic in her mother's homeland of the Dominican Republic. I am glad to say that after meeting this young lady, I became her Latina scholar mentor and we still remain in contact to this day. What an honor to see the power of education in our Latino community. For this young woman, education was her pathway to a better tomorrow. It brought me back to my early undergraduate days of feeling empowered by a circle of Latina young women lighting that fire for change in our community.

My research website helped me weave my field experiences and first-hand accounts with others seeking to find information on this topic. My original goal was to share my work to help support those who were in need of empirical research findings, up close and personal narratives of domestic violence survivors, and information from an expert that could help make a difference for other advocates trying to help these women. One of those advocacy organizations was the PAIR (Political Asylum Immigration Representation) Project. These organizations would link me up with law firms that had pro-bono cases supporting Dominican women successfully attaining political asylum to remain in the United States after fleeing from their abusers. I would write and personally present court affidavits centered on domestic violence in the Dominican Republic and how it directly impacted a client seeking political asylum.

Some of the victims were battered women and domestic violence survivors who fled from batterers who were law enforcement officials in local enforcement for the capital (Santo Domingo) or even the national police. In one case, I presented findings that would help a victim escape from a political figure who was using his resources with the national police. In doing this work, I would consult with the human rights and immigration defense lawyers representing the clients. All of the cases were helping women who lived in different cities in Massachusetts. Here I was launching this work to try and offer findings to support programs in different neighborhoods with a large population of Dominican residents, and now the network to support battered women was impacting a larger region. There were many lessons learned from my field research and advocacy work with the victims of domestic violence in the Dominican Republic and with the women who were seeking refuge.

I had to make a compelling case that domestic violence is a form of torture therefore an international crime. Under international human rights law, torture is an action against a person that causes both severe physical and psychological pain. It is inflicted intentionally for a spe-cific purpose—control over the victim. Domestic violence is a result of gender inequality and unequal power relations between men and women. There are several abusive power dynamics displayed by the batterer that instill an overwhelming level of fear and present a real physical and emotional threat to the victim. Through male privilege, the abuser dictates and defines the gender roles wherein the man is the dominant figure in the home. Machismo is a phenomenon within the Dominican culture and many Latino cultures that perpetuate the man maintaining power in his home. This can involve preventing the victim from participating in educational opportunities or seeking employ-ment for professional advancement. If the victim resists or defies the abuser's forceful objections to her personal freedom, the abuser will use physical and mental coercion and threats to hurt the victim.

Intimidation through the use of physical gestures, and actions, de-stroying the victims' property, displaying weapons, and using weapons around the victim is the abuser's tactic to keep the victim in a constant state of paralyzing fear. Emotional abuse through public humiliation and loud public arguments creates an intense level of shame for the victim. Over time, the abuser will socially isolate his victim by limiting her outside involvement in the community using jealousy as the means to justify the ends. Dominican women within an abusive domestic relationship are viewed as property by their domestic partners and by their immediate and extended family. My research findings revealed that this gender-inequitable social norm is highly connected to the

Dominican societal view of manhood and male dominance. By virtue of their subservient status, battered Dominican women must acquiesce to their abusive partners.

Frequently, the abuser will use the victim's children as a tool to create leverage by threatening to take the children away from the mother. The abuser will use manipulative language, and covert tactics to use immediate family members as tools in maintaining steady intimidation pressure and unrelenting surveillance techniques to control the victim. Guilt and shame are at the core of the manipulation.

There are limited social support structures for abused women in the Dominican Republic. Within Dominican culture and many Latin countries, there is a commonly held belief that people should not get involved in other people's relationships. Many times neighbors witness or hear a domestic violence altercation, and they do not intervene. It is a commonly held belief that it is a personal fight between husband and wife. They believe it is an intra-family matter. Victims of domestic violence struggle to escape from their abusers without family, friends, and community support. Research findings prove that, over time, the violence displayed by the abusers will increase in intensity and frequency. In the majority of the most tragic domestic violence cases, the victims were killed after fleeing their abusers and returning back to the abusers by force or through the use of emotional and mental manipulation.

Economic disparity places an abused woman in a very vulnerable and compromising position with very limited options. Without the support of an immediate family member or friend, it renders the woman powerless. With limited education and no workforce experience, the majority of abused women are in desperate circumstances where they must remain with their abuser. It becomes a "do or die" hopeless situation.

In trying to legitimize the victims in the United States seeking political asylum through immigration law services, I had to paint a picture of the political scene in the Dominican Republic. It was a complex political landscape to explain, but I did my best to show the different tiers of entanglement for victims and the legal system that was not supporting them. Many American judges were surprised that in the Dominican Republic in 1997, the National Congress of the Dominican Republic approved Law 24-97 Against Domestic Violence. It took that long to legally set in motion domestic violence laws in the Dominican Republic. Our US system was a few decades ahead of the game. At the time that Law 24-97 was ratified, about 80 percent of the women seeking medical care were victims of domestic violence. In 1997, data findings showed that one in six women were victims of domestic violence. When the law was introduced, many women's advocacy groups were hopeful that this new law would ratify much-needed change. However, there were political and cultural challenges that limited the effectiveness of this law to protect victims of domestic violence.

Today domestic violence in the Dominican Republic is at an epidemic rate, and worse than it was 25 years ago. Law 24-97 has not been effective. The Center for Social and Demographic Studies (*El Centro de Estudios Sociales y Demográficos*) reports that one in every three women in the Dominican Republic becomes a victim of some form of domestic violence. Based on my research findings with survivors from different parts of the country, many of the domestic violence victims did not only have limited financial means. Domestic violence is a reality for many women across different socio-economic strata According to official statistics gathered from reports filed with the National Police, in the first half of the year of 2017 there was a 21% increase in the number of killings of women and girls compared to the same period in 2016. From 2011 to 2015, over 100,000 complaints of violence against women were reported across 23 different towns and cities.

Many Dominican women face this lonely battle and are often victimized twice, first by their abusers and second by the judicial system created to protect them. Official statistics from the capital's Santo Domingo Public Prosecutor's Office confirm that the alarming level of domestic violence continues. It was shared that approximately only four percent of the charges brought up against the perpetrators actually attended legal trials. In an interview with the Office of the

Prosecutor General, it was reported that the office was not able to offer full protection to all victims and witnesses except in the most extreme cases such as in international drug trafficking. It was surprising to learn that a date for a preliminary hearing typically takes three months to one year and the defendant may request bail at the time.

The National Police have dedicated units to respond to violence against women contained in Law 24-97. For example, Law 86-99 (199) created the *Secretaria de Estado de la Mujer* (State Secretary for Women's Rights). It is a government ministry dedicated to protecting and promoting women's rights. Special police departments were established to deal with violent cases against women. However, they are only located in major cities like Santo Domingo, Villa Altagracia, and Santiago that can be as far as a three to four-hour drive depending on where a victim is located in the country.

This lack of accessibility is not centered on addressing the immediate threat to the victim. Victims have to contend with the economic hardship of finding long-distance transportation in an impoverished nation that has a weak transportation infrastructure. It is not safe to travel throughout the country at night. The United States Department of State Bureau of Diplomatic Security produced a 2018 crime and safety report for US diplomats traveling in the Dominican Republic, warning that traveling at night on intercity highways and in rural areas can be highly dangerous. It can be a perilous journey for a battered woman. The establishment of these special police departments has also created the perception that domestic violence is a policing situation that must be dealt with by these special departments and not by the local police. They do not view it as a regular police matter. Many police officers are functionally illiterate or have not completed elementary and high school. Police training does not include an in-depth analysis of existing laws and criminal procedures.

Unfortunately, the re-victimization process in the Dominican Republic continues to occur for battered women and sexually abused victims seeking justice and counseling in Santo Domingo. The same location where domestic violence victims can receive their counseling is also the same location where an office established by the Commission for the Support of the Reform and Modernization of Justice provides legal aid services, public defenders, and counseling for accused batterers and offenders. There is a strong likelihood that women who are receiving counseling are in the very same place where their assailants are preparing their defenses. Within such a small city, it would not be difficult for a batterer to find his victim.

It was frustrating to learn that the Inter-American Commission on Human Rights reported that although the 24-97 law was intended to promote major advances in the protection of women's rights in this nation, many Dominican judges do not apply and enforce the law. This commission investigated the knowledge base of many judges and Public Ministry representatives and they were completely unaware of the extensive content of Law 24-97.

Research findings from my 2012-2015 field study showed that only 12 percent of the women who were in an abusive relationship were able to remain free from their abusers. As I conducted field research in various provinces in the northern and southern regions of the Dominican Republic, I met with various prosecutors and gathered data that is quite compelling. The existing institutional protocols hinder the judicial process. The ineffectual policies do not protect the lives of battered women and instead place those women in danger.

As a researcher, I witnessed how many of the victims I interviewed made numerous references related to a local and tragic domestic violence case. It had many of the research study participants petrified. The domestic violence case in Santiago, Dominican Republic involved a man who stabbed his 33-year-old wife fifty-two times in a beauty salon. Prior to this heinous crime, the victim Ms. Martinez went to the district attorney's office 18 times in two weeks to report her husband's violent threats. The victim had no choice but to leave her home. As a result, Jonathan Torres killed Miguelina Martinez because she no longer wanted to be with him. The knife he used to kill the battered woman was hidden in a bouquet of roses. It was in plain sight of numerous witnesses.

A few towns away from Santiago, I corroborated findings gathered from the Dominican Republic investigators Casado and Skewes

wherein data was obtained from record books of the Provincial Prosecutor and institutions that provided assistance to domestic violence
victims. I analyzed epidemiological variables within the municipality
of San José de Ocoa. Close to 79% of the affected women were between
the ages of 15-49 years and 82% of the attacks came from partners or
husbands.

More than half of my research participants wished they had a
women's community center where they could attend more *chalas* or
educational workshops. They believe that this community strategy
would increase the awareness level about domestic violence in their
community. Prior to attending my informational sessions about domestic violence laws with the participants, the majority of the battered
women communicated in their interviews that they were not familiar
with Domestic Violence Law No. 24:97. Some women shared that if
they knew where to go and get a legal advocate, they would feel more
comfortable trying to leave their abusive partner.

Many of the women felt it was necessary to involve the men in the
community awareness initiatives centered on domestic violence. The
men in their communities need to be aware of the ineffective systems
and measures that are in place hindering victims of domestic violence.
Some of the women suggested a faith-based counseling group for
abusers with a local spiritual leader, pastor, or priest. They expressed
that it was part of the church's responsibility to address the issue of
how the church congregants were also abusers of their wives.

Regardless of my ex-husband's words that my efforts would not
make a difference, I believed in my heart that they did. Change was in
motion and it was the community's responsibility to move it forward.
I had done my part in creating the change I wanted to see. Even if I
was just the stone that was cast in the water creating the first ripple of
change, over time that contribution could ripple out and continue to
grow. Perhaps a few more ripples occurred when I went to court as an
expert witness on domestic violence in the Dominican Republic.

Now it was time for me to spread my research wings and soar above
my personal adversity of divorce. It was time to see where I was going
to land in my new life as a humanitarian researcher and educator.

CHAPTER THIRTY-ONE

MOROCCO'S FORGOTTEN CHILDREN

A few months after my marital separation, I literally wanted to break free and get away from it all. Did running away from the heartbreak and disappointment mean I was resilient or in true denial like Nefertiti the queen of the Nile? Staying 20 years in a relationship and married for 10 showed that I was committed. Was I in denial that the person who was my husband really loved me? Was he just looking at the end game (retirement) and not wanting me to change the game plan?

After finding evidence that he was having a marital affair a few years prior, I tolerated it, and "I" worked on my marriage. But it had to be on his terms. I had to come home early from work, cook, and just do whatever he felt like doing on the weekends. He did not want me stuck on the laptop like I was when I was working on my doctoral dissertation. I played by his rules, and still, he was not happy. We were at an impasse. In order to overcome a marital impasse, you must make a commitment to remain connected. I had no desire to do that and neither did my husband.

He told me he wasn't happy and he wanted a divorce. I was relieved, but heartbroken. Seeing that we came to this junction prompted me to take deep stock of the future. I was 44 years old and if my life were on a clock, I was hitting the mid-afternoon of my life. I didn't want to waste the prime years of my life fighting to do the things that truly made me happy. I wanted to continue dreaming and not hear the same record over and over again. It was time to play the Gloria Gaynor hit "I Will Survive" and Chaka Khan's "I'm Every Woman." I had to keep moving forward.

Sometimes I felt broken. Would I be able to recover from this? In my headspace, I kept going back to the definition of resilience. It was the ability of a substance or an object to spring back into shape. It is meant to be elastic. Separating from my husband was not easy. The adage of getting married is very easy, but getting a divorce is very hard. How do you bounce back from such a tough challenge? I thought that I was capable of springing back from this heartache, but first I needed space and time to reflect as I sought to recover. Having a deep font of soul resilience is necessary. It is the quality that I witnessed in my mother as she lived and talked about the adversity she experienced in her life. A few years after her death, I learned from my aunt that there was so much more that Mami didn't share from her childhood experiences of witnessing her mother Juana battered by her father Evaristo. She slipped into that cycle again in seeking a life partner. However, I was going to break that cycle. My husband never laid his hands on me, but his domineering self-centered ways had the same stranglehold on my dreams. I broke free.

As a way of coping with the lonely evenings of not having a life partner in my life, I dove into different books that would take me away. I read Paulo Coelho's book, *The Alchemist*. I was inspired by the setting of the story from Spain to Morocco, as this guy is traveling to Egypt. Egypt is a place where I traveled when I was doing some international doctoral research work. I wanted to go back to that museum of antiquities.

Was this God telling me to literally go back to the Nile as I did in 2007? Was this about going back to that place where I was learning, professionally growing, and being a part of a network of researchers that stretched me? Perhaps I was just going to tear a page from the book *Eat Pray Love,* where a woman leaves behind all of the soul-crushing traps of modern society. Professionally I was fulfilled, and my service to others was so gratifying. Maybe I could merge the two?

I did a Google search with the words 'international service' and sure enough there it was the organization Cross-Cultural Solutions. I read more about how this volunteer/traveling organization connects international volunteers with different community volunteer initiatives. They had a program in the capital of Morocco and it sounded wonderful. In the morning you serve, and in the afternoon you get this great opportunity to engage in awesome cultural activity. So I signed up and I booked my flight during my academic holiday break. Most people would not consider volunteering during a vacation as an attractive option, but for me at this stage in my life it was perfect. There was a spiritual call for service that I needed to answer.

Morocco is a monarchy. It's simply beautiful and actually one of the safest Islamic or Arabic-speaking countries in the world. Based on what I had read, the King of Morocco was considered a great model for Arab nations in terms of humanitarianism. After his father's passing, he was leading this nation toward more progressive policies. When I was in Egypt, I loved the culture and the language. Morocco was going to be the place where I would tap into my spiritual self, learn, and serve.

When I got there, it was like a dream come true. The other people who signed up to do the same thing all shared this beautiful sprawling Moroccan estate that once served as a former United Nations Ambassador's headquarters. There were different wings and courtyards so that the volunteers would feel right at home. Even though this was a vacation, we had a very full itinerary. For my volunteering assignment, I ended up being placed in a children's hospital. Many of the children either had cancer or were struggling with lung issues. It was heartbreaking seeing these children struggle and hearing their parents' stories of how they traveled across different parts of Morocco to receive the treatments that they needed. Having time with them practicing the basic Arabic I learned with the CSS house staff, and doing artwork with the children was a healing reprieve for both of us. It united hearts and gave us a space to forget reality. Looking into their beautiful eyes offered mirrors reflecting the woman that was reaching out to them. Who was she now? A kind stranger seeking to heal herself and perhaps others?

In the afternoon, we would have different excursions that took us to beautiful and historic spaces in Rabat. I loved learning about Moroccan culture. We were able to have Arabic classes and cultural classes to learn more about the country's customs. It reminded me so much of my friend Oulea. She was a teaching assistant in my school. Oulea spoke English, French, and Arabic. She was so helpful when I traveled to Egypt in 2007. She helped me prepare a note with a professional development gift that I presented to the minister of education at the Education Conference in Cairo, Egypt. Having her help with the Arabic note gave it a special personal touch. I remember looking at the Arabic writing and feeling like it looked like musical notes. It flowed and looked so elegant. When I was in Morocco, I loved hearing the Arabic language. We went to different mosques and art museums. I loved looking at all of the vibrant colors in Islamic art and architecture. It was a dream come true to me and I could see the confluence of events and the tugging cultural soul ties that were leading me into a new direction in international volunteerism.

In the evenings, all of the CCS volunteers would share a communal meal, break bread, and share our experiences of the different assignments. Many of them worked in the orphanage and talked about the different narratives they heard about children struggling in the streets. The issue of street children captivated my curiosity. My heart just kept leaning toward this topic. The issue of street children first came to my attention when I traveled as an educational reform delegate with the People to People Ambassador Program.

It became quite apparent when I traveled to different parts of Egypt that there were many children in the streets either working or begging from tourists. My observations helped me conclude that Egyptian street children were generally viewed as delinquents, feral children, and a plague that should be treated with detention or jailing. Further examination revealed that Egyptian government legislation and policy towards street children was primarily punitive. After witnessing a child getting physically abused in a market in Giza, I was emotionally drawn to this societal issue. I wondered why these children were unseen and did not have a voice. I wondered why it seemed like these forgotten souls were not valued and were viewed as illegitimate members of their local society. After witnessing this unsettling experience, it made me curious to understand why.

After hearing the volunteers speak about the Moroccan street children, I had the same curious spark ignited in my spirit. Perhaps this could be the next topic I could explore as a humanitarian advocacy researcher. I wanted to understand the idea that many of the children were described as illegitimate. The whole notion of being illegitimate, not belonging, and how it's wrapped in shame resonated in my spirit. Many of the children were conceived out of wedlock and placed in orphanages. When the children would be of a certain age, they would end up on the streets creating. Living together on the streets offered a network strategy to survive. Perhaps if I pursued examining the issues surrounding the lives of street children or abandoned children, I could better understand the resilient spirit of these young people. What were some bigger lessons we can learn as a global community?

Before the end of my volunteering trip, I spoke with the CCS country director of this organization and shared my interest in coming back in February 2014 (which was my academic winter break). With this remarkable person's support, I was able to connect with several directors of NGOs (nongovernmental organizations) that would be willing for me to conduct site visits to further explore some research themes on the topic of street children and abandoned children, otherwise known as the forgotten children. These organizations offered educational and social service support to smaller grassroots organizations directly helping orphans and street children. I couldn't believe that it was this easy! All I had to share was my business card from

Global Changers, and say that my name was Dr. Cabán-Vázquez from New York. It was like I was given a great privilege and cultural pass to research any city in Morocco. Lord, could this be possible?

After completing my Cross-Cultural Solutions volunteering assignment in Rabat, Oulea was so gracious to connect with me in Casablanca. It was during Ramadan and she wanted to meet me at the famous restaurant Ricky's Cafe, with the art deco nostalgic look of the Casablanca movie with the legendary Humphrey Bogart and Ingrid Bergman. Even though she was fasting for her holiday, she came out to see me. Afterward, we were able to enjoy the large mall in Casablanca. Receiving this support from a friend and dear colleague meant so much to me!

What made it even more special was when my dear sister from another Mister Lela flew out to meet me in Morocco on the last day of my volunteer assignment. Having her there with me helped me unpack some possible research ideas. It gave me the opportunity to share some of the language and Moroccan customs that I learned during my volunteer trip. We stayed in Rabat for two more days, took a train to Tangier, then flew out to Spain for a quick hop to Barcelona. What an adventure! We almost missed our train because my dear friend was still chatting with other locals about the train accommodations and how she was enjoying her trip. We were free-spirit soul twins. Adventurers. Kindred spirits that loved humanity. What a remarkable partner to travel through Morocco with. All of this before we made our way to Geneva to meet with some of her former colleagues at the United Nations. It was such a quest! I didn't have to worry about anyone complaining that I was traveling and following my heart.

I knew I was going to be back in Morocco. It was just a matter of time. When I made up my mind to make this sacrifice, it sparked a form of inner transformation. Why is service such a part of the process of inner transformation? It's because every time you stretch yourself, and you pull yourself out of that comfort zone, you are forming yourself into a different configured being that you never could have imagined being in a particular place or being with a set of individuals that are like-minded in serving other beings for the greater good.

Upon completing the preliminary research and getting a stronger sense of the socio-political and cultural backdrop, I felt more confident about heading out to Morocco again. I followed up with the NGO Cross-Cultural Solutions country director on Skype. Mohammed shared that he and his fiance would be very eager to support my efforts. In preparation for my future trip, they would reach out and coordinate various visits around Morocco to conduct my interviews. I was offering them a modest research honorarium by US money standards, but it was very generous in their eyes. They were truly excited about helping me.

Preparing for this next trip to do research in Morocco would require that I immerse myself in learning more about the language and cultural norms that I would encounter. This would aid me in being culturally responsive in my visits to the different NGO locations. As a researcher, I wanted to be the light that could inspire a positive change or to serve as a mirror that would reflect and further transcend light, so folks can continue to be inspired and have that reflect forward into the universe.

When I was a young college student attending a rally against the persecution of Puerto Rican activists, I remember hearing the phrase ...the personal is the political. At that time, I didn't fully comprehend that statement. But after going through some personal experiences that resonated for me, it became more apparent that the personal is certainly more political. Many times it is something that we lose sight of because if we hear about an injustice, that is not directly affecting us in our comfort zone, we just choose not to mentally go there. It's a coping mechanism as well as a way to channel our emotions from not getting too emotionally vested. Someone else will take care of it. Someone else will address it. Hey, it is not happening to me right now. It is occurring in another country, another continent, and another hemisphere.

It all came full circle for me. It helped me examine my spiritual belief system of "giving can equal to sacrifice." Giving = Sacrifice. That is the balanced scale of a fulfilled life. I know it sounds radical, but sacrifice should not be comfortable. So when you choose to give to your immediate circle, that's comfortable. When you choose to step out of that comfort zone, that's sacrifice. Personally, the sacrifice was to save money to be able to serve in this capacity and to deny me anything lofty. As long as I could pay my son's tuition for college, and pare down living expenses to the simplest form, I could pull off doing this research in Morocco.

Again the universe sent me a sign that I was on the right track and that I should not be dissuaded. I found an Arabic tutor to help me learn more common phrases. His name was Mohammed just like the program coordinator in Rabat! My future tutor was a kind, social barista that I had met at a local Dunkin Donuts in one of my afternoon runs for a very necessary cold brew of sustenance. It was like God was placing the right people in my path to reassure me that I was moving in the right direction. One day while working late and deciding to get a pick-me-up coffee, I heard Moroccan music playing while this young man was preparing my cold brew. I asked him if he was Moroccan, and he smiled. When I told him I was going to visit his childhood town, he was thrilled. I told him that I needed to learn more Arabic, and then he offered to tutor me. I learned that he immigrated to New York, from Salé, Morocco. Salé was one of the cities I was scheduled to visit in February 2014. How awesome was that?! I offered to bring anything to his mother on my next trip on his behalf and he was so grateful for that gesture.

Just like my friend Oulea, Mohammed was multilingual. He spoke English, French, Arabic, and Spanish. I was so impressed. We met every week to review "survival Arabic" and conversational vocabulary to navigate introductions and small talk. He was such a helpful soul. I will be forever grateful for the way our paths crossed so that I would be better prepared to do my best research. When you wholeheartedly seek to do good, and you want to make that your life's mission, the universe will conspire to help you achieve this. It will pull on the heartstrings of those instrumental souls that can aid you in your mission.

In learning with Mohammed, I discovered that he was a devoted man to his Muslim faith. There were times he had to stop and pray. We would never be alone and always met in a public place. We always met at a local Au Bon Pain bakery where we could literally break bread and have soup while I learned. Some of the phrases he taught me were greetings that were also Muslim greetings like *As-salaam alaikum* (peace be with you) or a quick hello like *Salam*. However, he taught me certain Moroccan dialect phrases that would communicate my cultural interest to the NGOs that I was a culturally responsive and vested researcher.

After several tutorial sessions, Mohammed was abbreviated to Mo and I felt like I found a little brother from a Moroccan mother. Mo would always say "inshallah" (if Allah wills it) every time I told him that I would see him next week. I realized that working in an Arabic-speaking country would require me to also be mindful of the religious norms. So I went to the local Barnes & Noble and purchased the Quran in English. This would help me understand some cultural and Islamic faith-based references that I had first learned about in my former volunteer trip in Rabat. In addition, I visited an Islamic center to witness a lovely moment of families coming together in their Islamic faith. I read Moroccan traveling guides to give me a better sense of the lay of the land. The best part that helped me prepare for my final weeks was meeting with my friend Oulea to give me insight into more cultural dress norms for women as I traveled across the country. As a native Moroccan, she had insight into gender norms and regional norms. It seemed that everything was aligning perfectly and no matter how much I wanted this to happen, the universe was truly conspiring to give this girl a hand, and it came in so many forms of altruistic gestures from so many unexpected places.

Before I was ready to leave on my February trip, I had an extraordinary circle of friends organize a heartwarming send-off surprise bon voyage party. Seeing how they all planned to make this special evening come together was one of the most humbling experiences. The theme of the night had many hashtag themes, but the focus was #ShineBrightLightADiamond! I couldn't stop crying! They presented me with a T-shirt with those words that had a word splash with all of the adjectives my circle of friends used to describe me. Kayleen Lugo was so clever in putting the T-Shirt logo together. Leanne, Gwen, and Bonnie all led the charge in getting many of the women guests to come earlier to create personalized sashes. They made designer beauty pageant sashes with glitter choosing a word that would best describe me. Each woman took their turn sharing their word at a microphone as they proudly described their love offering for what I was doing, then removed the sash they made from their body to place it over me! Leanne Santo Denato (may she rest in peace) was such a cheerleader on the microphone! The tears flowed like a river of love. Their choice words like "Inspiration", "Compassionate", "Brave", and "Generous" all were written on their sashes. It was the quintessential embodiment of love, encouragement, and devotion to this personal cause.

As much as I was deeply grateful for this surprise send-off, it terrified me to my core! I didn't want to let down this loving circle of extended family and friends. In the past, having all these devoted and supportive friends and colleagues come together to support the girls in Kenya was such a great honor. I felt so confident having my program evaluation research commissioned by a UK-based advocacy organization because they gave me the language resources, the traveling resources, and the financial resources to navigate in Kenya.

With this Moroccan trip, none of these traveling infrastructures would be there. It was a solo trip! No one from Equality Now was sending me a language interpreter. No one was sending a cultural liaison to help me connect with the program directors so it could facilitate interviews with the study participants. Then to top it off, I was feeling the strain of not getting the full support of Global Changers because the founder was moving to Nigeria and she wanted to do more Nigerian-based initiatives. All I had was my Global Changers business card, my passport, and some funds to personally finance this trip. Knowing that my support circle had so much faith in me, was like receiving oxygen to my soul. It fueled my boldness and all I could do was move forward!

Like an eagle on the edge of a cliff, I threw myself off and let the wind of encouragement lift me up toward my research destination. After a long connecting flight from Paris, I finally landed in Rabat. The sounds of the Arabic and French languages swirling around me felt so familiar. During this trip, I made it a point to bring more neutral-colored clothes and amp up my headscarf game to blend in more with the local women. It would really help as I traveled on public transit and asked local women questions if I felt lost or needed help finding a location. Approaching a Moroccan man was discouraged because it would single me out as a tourist. The local women would ask another woman for help. It was the way things were done, so I was going to follow that norm.

Upon arriving again in Rabat, Morocco I fell in love with the country again. I fell in love with the language. I loved the way the sound of Arabic fell on my ear. It is a beautiful language. It reminded me of how I would hear women speak super-fast in Spanish in the Dominican Republic, and it flowed. I felt that listening to Arabic was awakening a part of my spirit that was dormant my whole life. Like I was supposed to be there listening to this awesome language. I was mesmerized and captivated by the structure of the language.

My body was shaking as I took a taxi to the hotel. I quickly showered and rushed to get dressed to make it in time for my appointment with the Country Director of the Cross-Cultural Solutions organization. I frantically reconfigured my suitcases to leave some of my things at the Cross-Cultural Solutions headquarters so I wasn't traveling with too many items. I didn't want to look like a character in one of Erykah Badu's songs. Woman, I was going to hurt myself carrying all those damn bags!

The first thing I did when I arrived at the Cross-Cultural Solutions main headquarters was offer the director and his cultural liaison a beautiful glass award from Global Changers as a token of appreciation and recognition for their efforts. It was an award very similar to the awards I presented in the Dominican Republic to several dignitaries and senators. What they didn't realize was that the true person receiving the ultimate gift was me! I was so grateful for their participation in extending me this research opportunity—to a novice Latina researcher with a North American lens on this issue. They were surprised by my gesture, but I wanted them to know how even more grateful I was for their support in helping me coordinate such a long trip.

The call for prayer five times was beautiful to listen to. I heard it many times on my former trip as a CSS volunteer. Now as the researcher, I found it to be grounding. I was realigning my internal clock to the call for prayer. It was a reminder to be still, a call for everybody to suspend life right now! Stop and connect, really connect, with your God. That struck me so much. The chance to witness the personal sacrifices people made for their faith. The way people suspended their carnal desire on some level, whether it be in terms of what they eat or don't eat (during Ramadan) or in terms of what they acquaint themselves with, really made me stronger in my own faith journey. It was a reflective moment that spoke to my soul saying... "Vilma you do the same, it just looks a little different." I have to say, that was fascinating.

Prior to finalizing my research itinerary, I was able to confer with my country contact about the very tight timeline. I was only off for about ten days during my school winter break, so time was of the essence. All I was absolutely certain about was that first I was going to take a train with Mohammed and Kahdija to Fez from Rabat where we would visit an orphanage that served infants up to toddlers. Fez was the furthest city on a train. My intention was to work my way back down to Casa lanca, Rabat, and Salé, and then take the trek across the country on a bus to a little Oasis in Errachidia. All the wheels were in full motion and the moment I arrived, it all fell together seamlessly.

With the support of several Moroccan NGOs in Salé, Rabat, Casablanca, Fez, and Errachidia, I was going to get a broader scope of the complex issues related to the abuse and tragic circumstances that Moroccan street children face as victims of child labor and sex trafficking. The first leg of the journey involved taking the same train with Mohammed and Khadija. I was familiar with the train system that I took to Tangier. However, the trip to Fez was not as far.

Fez is the second largest city in Morocco. It is a university city, known for its elaborate and ornate doors, and its large Medina (outdoor market) similar to the one I visited in Rabat. All of these conditions were prime for street children to beg and sell their bodies to sexual predators and tourists.

The irony is that in the face of this reality, there are such strict social and faith-based protocols for the men and women in this society. I was surprised to learn that it was frowned upon for a Muslim man to travel with a woman alone if he was not married to her. Thus the reason Mohamed brought Khadija. Believe me, I truly appreciated that gesture. Not that I was worried about any impropriety, but it was an extra measure for my security. It was a long day trip, wherein we woke up before the crack of dawn to take the long trek to this metropolitan city. We were able to conduct an interview with the program director of an orphanage and they were kind enough to give me a tour. They shared that they received government support as well as support from private donors. I was not allowed to take pictures and as a researcher working with vulnerable populations, I truly understood and respected their policy. In the grand scheme of things, I was just getting my toes wet as I started to dive into the abyss of this social epidemic.

The next day I had the great pleasure of collaborating with two other Moroccan humanitarians. Fatima and Leila who were friends with the program director whom I visited in Rabat were going to join me in my travels to Casablanca. Then we would work our way back up to Rabat and Salé before I would head across the country, through the desert to Errachidia. I was relieved that I was not doing this on my own.

After our site visits, we would debrief enjoying some yummy Moroccan tea and breaking bread together in different small cafés. My attempts to use the little Arabic I had learned from my tutor were truly paying off. They were impressed with my efforts and showed me a few more words and phrases that I could use within various exchanges of greetings and pleasantries. They would compliment me on my headscarves, and outfits, and say that I was very stylish. Here I was trying to tone down the outfits, and they thought I was hip. The biggest compliment was when I was online waiting for my tea in one of the cafés and a local woman tried to strike up a conversation with me in Arabic. I smiled and shared my favorite go-to phrase "I speak a little Arabic (ana atakallam al khalil min alerabia)." She smiled and I would look at the girls to help me fill in the gaps. The interviews and site visits went rather smoothly, smoother than the site visits I had conducted in Kenya. Blending in and looking like a local Moroccan woman truly helped. I was not considered a novelty, and that helped me navigate through the awkward pleasantries and abrupt interruptions that I experienced in Kenya.

Another time we were waiting for the tram (which is a kind of trolley system in Rabat) and I spotted two girls signing in American Sign Language. I was stunned! Quickly, I excused myself from my Fatima and Leila and I immediately walked up to the Deaf girls. I began to sign with them. I apologized for interrupting their conversation, and I shared that I was curious about the fact that they were using the same sign language that I learned in the United States. They used the 'world' hand sign and I smiled. Yes, the deaf language is universal. Silly me...hadn't I learned that or did I forget that ASL was really a mixture of old French sign language signs? Morocco at one time was colonized by the French and to this day, they have French as their business language. It all came together for me. I smiled, thanked them, and apologized for that abrupt conversation. Then I proceeded to meet my language interpreters back at the tram station by the sidewalk.

A part of me felt so good to see and recognize a language that I felt more comfortable with than Arabic. Sign language is such a conceptual, gestural, and visceral language It was at that moment that it all came full circle for me. I realized just what I did in that Lexington School of The Deaf internship experience that I was in over my head. But I was not going to quit like I did when I walked away from teaching Deaf students. I always regretted that decision as an expecting mother. But now I was alone. My adult son was so proud of me. I could do this if I really tried.

I longed to communicate more effectively and comprehensively with the ladies helping me. When I would chat with Fatima and Leila, I would get frustrated by the language barrier and I would tell them to try to speak with me in French if their English was hard to retrieve. We were operating within four languages–the Moroccan dialect of Arabic, French, English, and some Spanish. As I listened to the women converse between themselves I would feel relieved and just mentally retreat to my goals and vision for this research. My frustration was trying to communicate such complex notions and theories with my limited Arabic. I realized that I was really stretching myself as a researcher. I could come up short being a Christian woman and living in a sheltered world here in the Northeastern part of the United States. Once again I was going to an Arabic-speaking Muslim community in North Africa. I was grateful for the experiences I had presenting in Egypt, but similar to Nigeria I was trailblazing this journey not with a prestigious or esteemed delegation. There were moments where healthy paranoia would creep in and I said to myself... What would happen if these women set you up? Woman...they can place you in a room with a dirty old man and take your money belt. How would you get out of that one? Huh? When that would happen, I would emotionally regroup and remind myself that I can always lean on my sixth sense. Trust in the journey! It is NOT a fool's journey!

Even though I was challenged to communicate my research vision with my collaborators, I knew what I wanted. My vision was to further explore the international phenomena of the invisible and forgotten children of the world—abandoned orphans and street children. But first I needed to dig deep into the mire of the topic of 'illegitimate children' otherwise known as "atfal ghayr shareiiyn." This topic was not commonly spoken about in this mostly Muslim and Arabic-speaking nation.

I looked up policy documents, United Nations research findings, and other information from a hub of international advocacy centers. I learned that in 2011, the Child Rights Governance Programme offered statistical findings that shed some light on the plight of Moroccan orphans and street children. Moreover, it captured the limited impact that recent initiatives were having on this marginalized population. Despite Morocco's implementation of the UN Convention on the Rights of Children in 1993 and the New Code of Criminal Procedure in 2002, there was an astounding number of over 46,000 Moroccan children deprived of a home environment. I can only imagine that the true number of orphans is not fully and/or publicly disclosed. The World Health Organization reported that in various regional and national news press articles, the numbers are quoted as lower and closer to an estimated 30,000 abandoned children registered as orphans in the Kingdom of Morocco. Likewise, it was quite challenging to find the exact figure of Moroccan street children as documented by local and government officials. The State Secretariat for Children, Women, and Family acknowledged the difficulty of reporting the exact figures and attributes it to the children's mobility as they travel within a city and/or region. According to the Moroccan American Center for Policy, despite several Moroccan initiatives to address this issue through public policy, the high rate of increased numbers of orphans and street children is a symptom of underlying societal issues related to this phenomenon.

During the time of my research there, the issue of Moroccan orphans and street children had grown exponentially. It was negatively impacting not only the lives of those forgotten children but also the economic prosperity of this nation. A country's future lies in its next generation of citizens. If a large portion of the citizenry is not positively active and serves as contributing members of that nation, the trajectory of that nation's promise is highly compromised. Recent research findings by worldwide advocacy organizations reported that the significant level of apathy and indifference directed towards street children and orphans, coupled with the sexual predatory and child labor risks that these children face, can further compromise the economic vitality of this nation. There was a statistical trend and a strong correlation between the poverty level of a community with the high rate of abandoned orphans and street children in urban settings. Although protection laws have been slowly introduced to protect the rights of children, the process of enforcing these legal sanctions has been an arduous and quite complicated journey for NGOs seeking to advocate and intervene to improve the quality of life for thousands of Moroccan orphans and street children. A rigorous review of research studies revealed two complex themes. The societal factors and stigmas that shape the course for the increased rate of abandoned children by single mothers. As well as several pressures for older children to flee from their families and face life in the streets of Moroccan urban centers.

Through my interviews with orphanage directors and field advocates throughout different cities in the country, I was able to gain a deeper understanding of the scale of this societal phenomenon. It was difficult to walk into some of those orphanages that were in my opinion subpar in offering safe and clean living spaces for the children. I didn't see too many books or toys for the children. Many of the building facilities looked a bit dilapidated with chipping paint and older furniture. However, there was one place in Rabat that looked like a country club compared to the other orphanages in Fez, Casablanca, and Salé. This orphanage was one that worked with various international NGOs and received traveling volunteers, mission trips, and other aid from Christian organizations that wanted to offer support.

Here I was thinking I was alone in seeking to learn more about this issue and lend support to this cause. Everyone was playing their small part in helping work on this journey. Having Fatima and Leila join me in my visits to the orphanage sites helped me understand that these women were also curious to know what helped to perpetuate this huge form of dejection for these poor children who fell into the system and eventually would end up on the streets.

I can loosely frame that my 'research team' was able to help me gain access to personal accounts of situations wherein children were left abandoned in front of mosques or orphanages in the hopes that compassionate souls would be guided by a moral compass to care for them. All of this helped to corroborate some of the things that I read within research findings related to human rights, international human rights initiatives, and Moroccan policy and mandates. However, there were a few policies that were written in Arabic and they required that I receive translations of what they shared. I was at the mercy of their best form of translations and at times I worried about the validity of my findings based on these translations. But I was operating in faith and that is what kept me moving forward asking questions and following my hunches.

Prior to my trip, I did a literature review of primary sources that were available from various United Nations published reports across a broad span of human rights commissions and committees which included the United Nations International Emergency Fund (UNICEF), United Nations Development Project (UNDP), United Nations Human Rights Council (UNHRC) and other vital documents and publications from the United Nations Office of the High Commission of Human Rights (OHCHR). I also found secondary resources were used to further gauge general public opinions and perceptions regarding the status of Moroccan orphans and street children.

I doubted my true capability to shed light on what other Arabic-speaking researchers were examining. At times, I felt like I was truly out of my league. When this happened, I remembered what I was able to accomplish in Kenya. The greatest asset of my work there was that I was an outside evaluator and foreign researcher suspending subjectivity on this topic because I was not enmeshed in the cultural or spiritual beliefs. This would, in turn, serve me well as I would pose questions that I thought were a bit basic, but they would get raised eyebrows and a look of revelation when I would offer follow-up questions about the potential fathers of these illegitimate children and how they would be viewed by their fellow Moroccans. In preparation for the interviews with the NGO staff and directors, I was able to review numerous NGO executive reports that helped me assess the public face of this phenomenon and compare it to the anecdotal stories of the children who were in these facilities. It offered a broader aperture and depth of current intervention practices. It helped me gain insight into the implications for further research.

One of the things that I noticed as I was doing the research in Morocco that really kind of struck me was this idea of Moroccan child maids. Imagine this! You have an eight-year-old or a seven-year-old in your house as a maid. They obviously had less education than other girls. One-fourth of the child maids are less than 10 years old, if you can believe it. They are pretty much babies. I asked if the girls came

from the orphanages. They shook their heads with disdain saying
"Absolutely not!"

I learned from my interviews that the families of these girls were
seeking appointments for these girls as young as four or five years of
age. Any prospective employer that would come into the rural area,
and was actively seeking a child maid, was considered to be such a
blessing. They were offering great favor to this family. The families
really relied on the girl's income. They needed it.

What were the tasks that I thought of when it came to child maids?
When they moved to these urban centers, as children they became
surrogate mothers of children like themselves. They would run the
errands that the housewives would do such as bringing the children to
and from school, washing clothes, ironing, and scrubbing floors. They
handled all of the small domestic chores. Their work day could start at
8:00 in the morning and last until about 11:00 p.m.

As I looked more into this topic, a large majority of the child maids
did not get the money. How interesting? Since they are minors they
couldn't handle their own finances, so clearly their families would get
it. How much would they earn? It could end up being about 300
Dirhams per month, which is about $35 American dollars. About 25%
of the girls that were appointed to this child maid role, did not visit
their parents. Unless there was a death in the family or a parent was ill.
Many of the girls reported some abuse such as verbal abuse or worse
corporal punishment.

There was a lot of social isolation among these young girls. For
example, if you have five well-to-do families and they have child maids,
they don't want them to associate, because they don't want them to
compare notes. They also isolate them from their own families. They
wouldn't bring them back unless the employer was present. Why?
Sadly, in many of these assignments, these child maids have to contend
with physical abuse or 'training' with slapping, kicking, yelling, and
punching. All of these things shaped the child maid to conform to
the new role. Now I can't say that this was the case for everyone. In
my interviews, there were cases in which employers had taken on these
girls almost as extended family. Somehow these families would make

sure that their child maid would attend in the evening when they have literacy classes for the girls. In the evening classes, the girls would get about two hours daily, learn some Arabic, and some math, and will have the Quran to study. Unfortunately, there are not too many of these literacy centers in Morocco. That was considered a luxury for th ese girls.

Many of the child maids stayed in these assignments until they were about 15 years old. Some of them did not even know their exact age. That blew me away. They were estimating their age by the way their bodies were developing. There were some girls who had started working as young as seven years old, and then they lost their connection with their families.

The correlation with my research with street children was that many of the child maids that got older were asked to leave their assignments because now they posed a threat to the housewife as a beautiful young lady around the house. So the wife would send the older child maid back home because they feared that the husband would consider her as an option to take on another wife. Many times, these young ladies went back and they struggled to adjust to life in their rural home settings. Now back in their rural homes, they didn't have electricity or running water. They had been estranged from their family. There was limited communal connection in a community structure that was pretty insulated. As a result, some girls came back to Casablanca, Marrakesh, Fez, Meknes, Rabat, or Tangier. They went back to the main objective to find employment. But these sheltered and naive girls ended up falling prey to the opportunists. They ended up becoming child trafficking victims. Many of them landed in Casablanca because they got caught up in the glamor of the city.

Sadly the same tragedy happened to young boys living on the street. For boys, the cultural norm was that the guys were stronger. They were resilient, and they would figure it out. One of the issues that forced these boys to live on the street was a broken home. Maybe the father was not acknowledging the child. Many times, the woman that had this illegitimate child was shunned by her family and she did not receive any social and emotional support.

There are also street children who actually have families. They are just absent working families. They are just searching for that financial resource. So the young people are peddling. They are selling tissues and shining shoes. Often, the young outcasts seek to serve as city tour guides. They live in overcrowded housing situations, and they are not in a very stable family connection.

Sadly, many times there is also sexual abuse among themselves. The older children abuse the younger children. Perhaps this is attributed to the fact they were sexual victims themselves perpetuating the cycle of abuse. They connect to the friendships they create on the street and the ties that they have with gangs. Horrifically the glue sniffing that they use to self-medicate kind of suspends their reality. They are dejected, and not received and loved by their community. They are numbing the trauma of sexual abuse, and how they have been exploited.

I got to have a very unique perspective on this topic from the field. I took a very close look at what were the push factors that have children living on the streets. What were their pathways and what were the cofactors of having them not be able to stay? In spite of the fact that there are services and orphanages, many of the boys were compelled to still live on the street. They gravitated to the street like a moth to a flame. This placed them in a position where they were going to be victims of sex trafficking. The deep pit of being exploited. Hearing about their stories was quite challenging. I had to dig deep to remain neutral and not offer any kind of reaction to these stories. Suspending all subjectivity!

When we concluded all of our interviews on the west coast of Morocco, the hardest part of the journey was on the horizon. Our next stop was the Province of Errachidia and we were passing through Merzouga –the gateway to the Sahara Desert. Errachidia was an oasis a couple of hours into the Sahara Desert traveling by camel. Yes, by camel! In total, it was 10 hours away from Rabat. Mohammed and Khadija accompanied me on this part of the trip because we were going to Mohammed's hometown.

First, we would travel on a charter bus for seven hours through the Middle Atlas Mountains! I made the huge mistake of sitting in the first row with a full view of the front windshield. Getting past the anxiety of what lay ahead, I felt that we had seen every type of landscape imaginable. From low beautiful valleys, through what felt like the Rocky Mountains. How these roads were carved within such hazardous terrain was truly a miracle! There was no way I was going to sleep through that! It was like I was on a cross-country trip in the middle of the United States. It was breathtaking, but also very stressful as I would look over the edge of the narrow precarious winding roads that felt more like mountain goat trails than roads!

Finally, we came to the edge of the Sahara Desert in Merzouga, known for its marvelous desert tours. There we hired a guide to take a caravan of camels to a campsite. There were other tourists who joined us. When we mounted the camels and proceeded to walk towards the sand dunes, the town disappeared from view. All I could see were gorgeous reddish sand dunes past more majestic sand dunes. I prayed for God to lead the way. In retrospect, I believe I had a mini-panic attack, but I kept it together. I wore layers of clothing and scarves over my brown leather jacket and boots. As we were getting closer to the campsite, it was getting chillier. I focused on filming the camel trip on top of my camel Sharif using my mini-iPad and being of course first on the caravan of camels helped me focus on where the young man was leading us. I wanted to rename my camel Moses for obvious reasons in the hopes this camel would get me through the desert!

The guide shared that the sand dunes are like a highway and he knew where to turn. I had no choice but to trust him. I tried to make light of the situation by sharing with the young man that I was confused. He looked at me perplexed. I asked him. "Where can I find the camel's gps?" He giggled. By the time we got there, it was early evening and the young teen guide brought us to a campsite with very large tents. One tent was the designated women's tent and on the other side of the campfire, was the male tent. When we arrived at the campsite, I did the same thing and asked where to plug in the hair dryer. He let out a cute laugh. Mohammed and Khadija smiled. I couldn't believe I was doing this! The guide prepared a delicious meal and serenaded us with musical instruments that he had on the campsite. He shared that at sunrise, we would move again and head towards Errachidia arriving in about two hours. If you can believe it I slept like a queen. No worries. I simply trusted that I was safe. I reminded myself that I was not in Nigeria. I was in excellent hands.

Right before sunrise, I slipped out of the tent, placing a pink scarf over my head to keep any sand from blowing into my eyes. I headed towards the top of one of the sand dunes by the campsite. From the top, I could see the humble campsite. The camels resting facing each other. My heart was stirring and I cried a good cry, thanking God for the safe journey and how much I believed in him. I begged God to forgive me for doubting that he had me cradled in the palm of His hand. He was taking care of His daughter!

At that moment, I sensed someone coming up next to me and it was Khadija. She said... "My sister, you look so beautiful, just like a desert queen!" I smiled. She said, "I must take a picture of this moment. Please." Thankfully I had my iPhone in my pocket and she took pictures of me and of the campsite. I am so grateful she did that! What a memory! A few moments later just like clockwork, we gathered our things, mounted the camels, and again went on a caravan trail towards Errachidia. The first sight of the palm trees and what seemed like a little bustling city was truly surprising. This was in the middle of the desert?

Mohammed looked so proud to show us around his childhood town. He took us to the medina, purchased different cultural artifacts, and bought a few treats to bring to his mother. Visiting his family, and interviewing a small NGO that serviced orphans was truly wonderful. They were extremely accommodating and it was so well worth the desert trek!

The next day a lot of what I uncovered in the interviews corroborated my findings from the larger cities. Many of the cultural norms and commentary echoed what was shared in my interviews with advocates and other community organizers. I felt that this trip was a way for me to witness one of Morocco's jewels. I wish that I had visited Agadir, the town where my friend Oulea was from the coast and the home of Argan oil, but perhaps on another trip, I would be fortunate to see this other Moroccan jewel. We visited with some of Mohammed's friends and he shared proudly about the work that I was doing. They were curious about my life and I would answer some of the bold and direct questions about being separated from my husband and doing this work alone. That was quite radical for them. I was a cultural anomaly for them.

The best part of that trip to Errachidia was doing it all again. But this time, I had to complete the journey on my own! Khadija developed a fever and she was not feeling well enough to travel. I had a very tight timeline in which I had to travel and I couldn't miss my flight back home. So this gypsy did exactly just that. I traveled across Morocco by myself. It was reassuring to see that I had the same guide with his blue turban, I slept in the same tent with a group of different women, I woke up in the morning beating the sun for that sensational sunrise, and I boldly traveled forward on my camel ready to meet my bus back to Rabat. The whole time I thought how much more spiritually centered I was than when I first arrived. It felt like my new superpower–riding on a camel in the middle of the desert.

My mission on this journey was to pen the stories of these forgotten children. With a grateful heart and the rhythmic bumpy ride of the camel, I would fall into a reflective trance, mentally teleporting myself throughout different junctions in my research journey. I reflected on how I met up with some remarkable advocates of women and children. I was in awe of how we joined our public-spirited gifts to collaboratively research and share effective community-based and international humanitarian strategies. I was humbled by God's love to touch the hearts of so many people who were willing to help me.

Little did I know that after my trip, there would be a huge spotlight illuminating several highlights of my travels. I was interviewed by a reporter from the *Global Woman Magazine* based in the United Kingdom. A former colleague, Tammi who still remained connected on social media, saw my posts and asked this correspondent to write an article about me! So the writer Rezarta Mataj did a feature article about how this teacher blended traveling and volunteerism.

In addition, I was able to tell about my Morocco research journey on a popular international podcast called *Awakin Calls* with Servicespace. The founder Nipun Mehta of this organization was recently called a modern-day Gandhi by the Dalai Lama! This platform allowed me to talk about my journey to Morocco for close to an hour. It was titled "How Morocco Changed My Life!" Boy did it change my life and my research trajectory! The universe was flexing and truly showing off! I took it as a sign like the north star that I was heading in the right direction. Everything was lining up in the constellations.

CHAPTER THIRTY-TWO

GUATEMALAN ORPHANS

A fter my arduous research trip spanning one corner of the Moroccan coast past the interior Saharan desert lands of Merzouga back to my little haven cottage in Connecticut, I had my hands quite full of rich data. I spent the whole spring pulling together themes and drafting research findings. After a full day of teaching and commuting to and fro from Silvermine, Connecticut, I would dive into my writing. It was my new haven. After my separation, it was my way of escaping from the reality that I attended divorce mediation sessions, conferred with my lawyer, and eventually signed divorce papers. Were these my freedom papers? What I didn't realize was that the Universe was still conspiring to continue making a few more alignments and adjustments on my research path. The constellation path was set and I had to reach it.

I received an enthusiastic call from a long-lost high school friend Miriam. About four years earlier, she found me on Facebook and we hadn't connected in almost 20 years. In essence, we were strangers but worked on reconnecting our friendship. She was eager to learn about the details of my most recent trip. Moreover, she wanted to share some other compelling news about an organization that she learned about which was helping orphans and street children...but it was in Guatemala. When I heard her say that, I halfheartedly sighed and took a deep breath. I quietly asked God for strength to respond to my friend's request. I wasn't even done putting together the research narrative of my time in Morocco. Was this woman crazy?! She obviously had no clue what all of this work entailed. But then I felt bad that here she was trying to support me in my work and I was acting like such an ingrate. So I listened.

Moments after receiving that predestined call, I did my due diligence research about the organization that she mentioned. I learned about the grassroots organization *Proyecto Mi Hogar, Inc.* and the organization's founder Joe Negrón. *Proyecto Mi Hogar, Inc.* was an international non-profit organization working to provide long-term care, education, and housing for orphaned and abandoned children in the country of Guatemala. They offer community-based services through assistance, donations, support, and awareness to other non-profit institutions helping needy children and troubled teens in Guatemala.

This NGO's mission statement and program goals and objectives were closely aligned with many of the guidelines outlined by the United Nations Department of Economic and Social Affairs, Population Division (2009): "We believe in creating opportunities for growth and advancement, with the goal of positioning our children to succeed in every future endeavor, and to be beacons of hope for future orphan generations. It is our goal that each child we care for will grow to be wholly integrated, independent, and productive members of society that will teach the same principles that are taught to them. Therefore we expect a decrease in the percentage of children and youth placing their lives at risk by immigrating to the United States in search of a better future, like the teens Proyecto Mi Hogar visits at His House Children's Home in Miami, Florida." (*Proyecto Mi Hogar, Inc.* Non Profit Business Plan)

As I watched a YouTube video that was forwarded during the call, I was moved to tears. My heart was awakened by the urgent call to serve displaced orphans and street children in Guatemala. The rest as they say is history. Little did I know that I was on the brink of a blessed humanitarian quest to support this NGO that works tirelessly to serve these forgotten children.

I asked Miriam to be a liaison for me in connecting with Joe Negron because he had spoken at one of her church events about his mission trips to Guatemala. She had connected with him via Facebook and she made the first contact. We arranged to do a Skype call with Joe at her house to explore ways that I could support his work by following with a program evaluation similar to the one I did in Kenya.

I humbly approached the founder with a proposal. I said, "This is selfish in some respects, but I also want to serve selflessly. Mr. Negron, I can do a pro bono program evaluation for your NGO, which if you were to commission the service would command about $30,000.00. Just because of the amount of work and detail doing a SWOT analysis (Strengths, Weaknesses, Opportunities, and Threats) can take quite some time." I explained that if he allowed me the opportunity to lean in closer to some of the issues that affect this type of community outreach. Ultimately, this could help me with my personal research. I would treat the findings regarding his organization confidential, but many of the broader themes and some of the details from my interviews could be used in my research. We would sign a confidentiality agreement and I could present my findings to his executive board so that they can consider some strategic planning steps for future work.

I shared, "At the end of the Guatemalan research journey, I could evaluate the remarkable impact you are making with your grassroots organization. I offer you feedback, in terms of what you can do to take the next steps to grow because I had done something similar in Kenya." I was floored by how confidently I shared those words. Ultimately, my program evaluation could yield more research data that could help me identify areas for a preliminary review of PMH's preventive and response services within their future home facility (orphanage). Research implications existed for a structured comparative analysis of PMH's research-proven field site strategies with other international NGOs program sites endorsed by the United Nations and other international advocacy NGOs seeking to offer family-strengthening services for refugees and *los niños de la frontera*"—otherwise known as the influx of unaccompanied children crossing into the United States creating a humanitarian situation along the southwest U.S. border. There were many reports shared from the Department of Homeland Security documenting this influx in the number of children unsafely crossing the border, serving as mules for drug trafficking, and becoming victims of sexual abuse and sexual human trafficking.

After some further discussion, Joe shared that he would confer with his team and let me know if this would be possible. They deliberated for some time. A few weeks later, he reached out to me and said that he got the green light from his executive board. I was going to Guatemala to explore the difficult and heart-wrenching reality of street children and orphans in Guatemala. My goal was to lean on what I understood about the Latino culture to bridge some of the gaps that I had in my former research.

I reached out to my Global Changers director and shared my interest in continuing to expand my research footprint into Central America. She was excited for me but mentioned that I would have to raise my own funds for this project. At that moment I asked myself, why am I still a part of this organization? Clearly, my vision and my intention to work globally were no longer aligned with the mission of this organization that had the words global in its name. I felt I still needed the legitimacy of being a Global Changers researcher to be able to conduct this research in Guatemala. But afterward, I was going to reassess how long I wanted to continue serving with this organization.

My intention was to conduct the program evaluation in two weeks. I predicted that this was all that I could afford in terms of travel costs. So this researcher put on her fundraiser hat and did just that. I actively worked hard to raise funds for this research trip. I was able to raffle luxury tickets to breakfast cruises for World Yacht (that I purchased on a credit card). I received a donation from the Service Space organization which helped me with the technical costs. I was able to rally support from a close circle of friends to help me raise the money for my trip. Finally, I packed my lunch every day and saved every penny I could to be able to have the money to travel to Guatemala with my new research assistant Miriam. I was more realistic about this trip. I knew I couldn't do this work alone, and who else would be more helpful being that she brought my attention to this organization? The exchange rate for the American dollar was similar to the exchange rate in Morocco. So that was very reassuring.

Prior to arriving in Guatemala, I did an intensive literature review. Studies and anecdotal findings report that the issue of street children and orphans is a worldwide phenomenon as well as a prevalent problem in Latin America. Empirical findings gathered by qualitative ethnographers studying this social phenomenon have noted that there are mixed public views on the issue of street children and orphans. Globally there exists a very vague definition of street children, whereby there are many assumptions regarding the notion that children who are seen on the streets are homeless, abandoned, and/or orphans. Moreover, recent findings can offer a heuristic analysis of the central issues related to displaced street children and orphans as well as a societal landscape of the cross-cultural themes that shape the tragic plight of this marginalized population of at-risk children.

In 2007, the Guatemalan congress banned international adoptions in response to research findings cited by the United Nations that Guatemala was plagued with allegations of corruption in the adoption process of thousands of Guatemalan orphans. The pace of adoption was extremely high. Baby brokers solicited an exorbitant amount of mothers and the desperate women were paid for their babies. Many high-profile investigative reports by international advocacy agencies raised the level of awareness within the global community reaching human rights commissions in the United Nations. The astronomical number of children leaving Guatemala for the United States (18,298 Guatemalan babies between 1995 and 2005) as well as the obscene amount of money profited through the system (as much as $200 million US annually) were at the heart of the belief that adoptions through Guatemala were solely a business. This swift legislative sanction to block international adoptions actually sealed off the viable option of so many children to receive an opportunity to get adopted by many families in the US—which is the leading nation in the number of international adoptions.

This new law assumed that many Guatemalan citizens would domestically adopt their nation's orphans and abandoned children. However, in the past 10 years, this country has experienced inconsistent economic trends that still place many of its citizens in economic depressive plights—consequently, this stagnate fiscal climate is not conducive to promoting domestic Guatemalan adoptions. Many families are struggling to survive and many desperate parents or single mothers in dire circumstances have turned to what they believe is their only life-saving option...child abandonment at a local orphanage, church, or outside a police station. Many of these children live in extremely crowded orphanages with many children living in poor living conditions with limited resources and access to a quality education and healthcare.

I was truly looking forward to visiting the capital city as well as the smaller town where I was conducting most of my research. The locals referred to the Guatemalan town we were going to visit as 'Xela'. I was grateful because the spelling and pronunciation of this town were quite a mouthful. Travel expenses were not high because we would use public transportation. We would arrive at the capital Guatemala City and take the long trek to Xela. I was grateful that Mr. Negron met us at the airport and we prepared for the long journey to the town he was working to make a great difference in. Although it was extremely congested, it was very economical.

When we arrived at Xela, Mr. Negron made boarding arrangements with a local non-profit orphanage in Quetzaltenango, Guatemala for us to stay on the premises during our program evaluation process. The leaders of this nonprofit organization were community stakeholders who worked closely with *Proyecto Mi Hogar*. They placed us in a small suite available for volunteers. They mentioned that when the nuns and priests who would visit the older section of the orphanage would come, they would stay in that suite. It had a very retro fifties vibe and the room where I was staying had a desk. I was a very happy lady. Thankfully, no one else was there visiting the orphanage during our visit so we had the whole place to ourselves. I extended a very modest stipend to the director of this orphanage for our stay. It helped us save a lot of money because if we stayed in a hotel, our housing costs would have been ten times more. Our humble accommodations felt like home and we made the best of our arrangement. Personally, I was used to the humble stay in Kenya, but Miriam on the other hand was a bit surprised that getting hot water required seeing a heating contraption attached to a shower head. She feared we would be electrocuted! Was I traveling with a diva? Time would tell.

In my time conducting the program evaluation, conducting interviews, taking field notes, taking pictures and videos, and debriefing with the PMH founder, I discovered that he collaborated with a dynamic team of generous hearts and compassionate guardian angels that made his work possible in Guatemala.

Upon learning about his church-sponsored mission trips, the steps he took to launch Proyecto Mi Hogar's nonprofit organization, and the personal sacrifices he made to make that mission I felt that it was short of a miracle how he was able to sustain this work with very limited resources. I was quite impressed by how this grassroots organization mobilized, rallied, and leaned on a core group of volunteers, sponsors, and a diverse body of supporters.

While doing the first preliminary phases of assessing strengths and opportunities that Joe capitalized on, I made the profound research connection that many of the effective and research-based strategies that Mr. Negrón employed actually aligned quite well with the research-proven strategies that I witnessed and evaluated in the UN-endorsed and sponsored Kenyan organization. Both NGOs showed great promise, but more importantly, they demonstrated evidence that they directly impacted the lives of vulnerable children. The fundamental bottom line was that both of these aforesaid NGOs helped to promote sustainable positive change that significantly impacted the lives of so many at-risk and vulnerable children. The only difference between these two notable organizations was that one was in Africa with a sustainable stream of UN-endorsed grants and sponsorship, and Proyecto Mi Hogar was on the field in Guatemala creating a wider range of impacting programs with extremely limited funding and regrettably without a large UN or international endorsed financial or technical support.

I wondered if given a program evaluation measuring this new grass-roots organization's operational and program effectiveness, would the SWOT data matrix look similar? Does Proyecto Mi Hogar's NGO leadership have great promise for replicating their efforts to a larger frontier in Guatemala? What would be the largest impact that this organization can make on the current plight of Guatemalan street children and orphans? How could their effective and research-proven organizational practices help to inform Guatemalan public policy that could ratify positive social change? How could Proyecto Mi Hogar's efforts help inform empirical research on a global phenomenon that unfortunately is endangering the lives of so many disadvantaged children around the world? The only way to fully examine and reach a conclusion on these aforementioned questions would be to further investigate all the steps that this PMH used to make the magic happen.

We were able to visit the orphanages that Mr. Negron collaborated with. He coordinated outreach projects with volunteers serving single mothers and displaced families living in crowded living quarters. Recently, he created a Guatemalan-based executive advisory board with the hopes of getting recognized as an international nonprofit organization. When I learned that his formal education did not include any background in nonprofit management, I was truly stunned and quite frankly impressed by all that he was able to accomplish!

We did interviews with single mothers who had children working on the streets peddling or doing any type of side work to bring money home. We interviewed several teens in the center of town in their local central park and interviewed them about their experiences living in a local orphanage. They shared their tragic stories of living on the streets and how they found some haven in the orphanage. I was stunned when they confided in me about issues related to physical and sexual abuse by the older orphans living there when they were young. They candidly shared their fears about "aging out" of their facility. Once they turned 18, they were discharged from the orphanage and they had to figure out a way to survive. Some of them described very loose plans of going to Guatemala City and finding jobs there. In my heart of hearts, it reminded me of some of the stories I heard about in Casablanca, Morocco. So many common themes came across in my interviews and conversations with community stakeholders.

Within my two weeks, I examined Proyecto Mi Hogar's organizational structure. I was able to identify areas wherein PMH can further sharpen the infrastructural staff development and capacity of this grassroots organization. I assessed PMH's current and local child protection mechanism for displaced children living in Guatemalan streets or orphanages. More importantly, I gained insight into PMH's community-based efforts as well as identified key community outreach components that were effective in helping to impact the quality of life for displaced children. I was able to pinpoint integral areas and potential gaps that can be addressed and refined through the use of future staff development, technical support, and organizational capacity-building opportunities. Ultimately, lessons learned from this program evaluation would further assist PMH in refining existing program strategies and structural approaches that can attract vital and substantial international funding resources.

The plethora of qualitative data from my observation protocols, field notes, reflective notes, photographs, interview transcripts, electronic press releases, social media, and other forms of unstructured text data found in newspaper articles, office memorandums, formal and informal interoffice correspondence gave me a treasure trove of data. In addition to the field site data collected from interviews, field notes, and other forms of qualitative data acquired from the US-based and Guatemalan program-based locales, Mr. Negron invited me to view, as well as to have direct access to, various forms of accountable NGO qualitative and quantitative data that was transparently shared with PMHs' community stakeholders and fundraising sponsors via postal correspondence, social media updates and postings, as well internal PDF files and formal documents submitted in password-protected storage portals such as Dropbox and email. The organizational communiqué updates were delivered in various forms of social media, pro-

motional videos, as well as recent regional and international press rele
ases.

The amount of transparency and the strong willingness to learn
helped me assess that Mr. Negron and his team were light years ahead
of so many other larger international NGOs. I highly encouraged
him to seek governmental funding because this program evaluation
would demonstrate that they were properly vetted and positioned to
function as a higher-impact-making organization.

There are many international organizations working to serve needy
children. However, many times they function as isolated sources of
relief without research-proven methodology or community outreach
systems for creating sustainable and lasting impact in the lives of those
at-risk youth. The community-based efforts and effective practices of
Proyecto Mi Hogar can serve not only as a noteworthy and replicable
example for the larger global community, but this stellar and effective
organization can continue to shed light on the plight of the forgotten
and displaced Guatemalan street children and orphans. Moreover, this
program structure assessment and refinement process can favorably
position this new international NGO to effectively and efficiently
compete and obtain sizable grants from diverse international foundations and United Nations grant funds.

Due to the nature of our confidentiality agreement, I will honor
that by not sharing specific outcomes of the SWOT analysis. But
overall, I will share that if I could extend this nonprofit a final grade
for its mission-centered fieldwork, organizational infrastructure, and
level of impact in this community, I would give them an A!

After returning from my trip to Xela, I got busy typing and pulling
together the program evaluation. Prior to the November Thanksgiv-
ing break, I was able to meet up again with Joe Negron in New York
City and share my final report. Joe came with his vice president of
PMH. They were so grateful for my time and attention to helping their
organization grow.

A few months later, I got a call from Joe that he had acquired major
funding. It turns out that the core group of Guatemalan volunteers
that he mobilized were architects. This altruistic circle of volunteers

mobilized their social circle to develop a fundraiser. This helped to support the larger mission of building a children's learning center in Xela. He was excited to share that PMH had acquired a piece of land in Xela. With these funds, they felt fortunate to begin construction work of a symbolic perimeter wall on the property until they were able to raise more funding for the full construction of the center. Furthermore, he was happy to report that he was working on a few fundraisers for the continued construction of the future PMH Children's Learning Center. He invited me to join them, but I said that unfortunately, I was not able to go. He totally understood but insisted that after this experience together, he had found a new friend. I was honored and from that point on, Mr. Negron became my humanitarian friend and *mi amigo* Joe!

The universe conspired once again, taking the risk to approach Joe about doing research in Guatemala truly paid off. I was feeling more confident about taking these leaps of faith. My faith in humanity was restored. There are great people out there in all corners of the world who believe in the power of service. Not all men were sneaky chiefs lurking in higher influential circles. There were good men out there like Mohammed and Joe who wanted to make a difference too. They believed in my work and ultimately they took a chance on me. For this, I will forever be grateful.

CHAPTER THIRTY-THREE

LA CASA DE MARÍA EN PUERTO RICO

I t was time to get centered. I needed to immerse myself and make sense of all of the findings I had gathered from Morocco and Guatemala. I was extremely grateful that I could use my December holiday break and my February winter break to sort through mounds of field notes, photos, interviews, and reflection journals. Little by little, it began to come together. I wanted to write a narrative that compelled readers to see the epidemic nature of what I had witnessed. My podcast interview on *Awakin Calls* helped me to begin processing my experiences. I was able to get a transcript of that podcast interview and that was so instrumental in framing my thinking. I wanted to share the story of the forgotten children that spanned across different continents and not just a fact sheet of findings. After all that effort, I needed to make a name for myself as a global humanitarian researcher.

My intention and my reality were not aligned. Unfortunately, I was struggling with writer's block and feeling very lonesome. I was struggling with the reality of this newfound freedom. I didn't have someone in my corner. In the past, I had a life companion. Someone to cook for. Someone to say goodnight to. However, that someone was the same person that I had to constantly argue with to do the things that were personally fulfilling. Did I really get my freedom papers or was this the harsh stark reality of my choice...desolation?

One day, my son encouraged me to try to go out into the dating world. Chris suggested that I try online dating. I was terrified about that techy option. He helped me pull together a profile on a dating website. Chris was my number one cheerleader, telling me what an amazing woman I was and that I was a great catch. "Mom, you've got this!" He strongly encouraged me to put myself out there just like I did when I took chances going out on the field to conduct research.

Oh my goodness, I was a sack of nerves! It was tremendously anxiety-producing to take those dating risks. I was working on reducing my weight and I had lost over 40 pounds, but I was still not at my ideal weight. At first, I thought that I needed to lose all the weight to feel ready to date. Why did I have to look perfect? The perfect guy will love me just as I am. If he can't love me at my worst, then he doesn't deserve me at my best. I knew that I couldn't give up.

Ultimately, one of those dates became a second and a third date with the same charming guy. He was a carpenter by trade. This new beau was artsy. A man after my own heart. In the past, he attended Parsons School of Design. But when I met him, this fine carpenter was working on a construction project at the Whitney Museum in New York City. He worked with a very exclusive construction company that had just completed Ryan Seacrest's huge brownstone in Manhattan. On top of this, he was a very talented portrait artist with oils. His technique for creating texture, and depth within portraits was stellar. Through studying several of his portraits, I learned that working with oil paint was a very challenging art medium. This guy seemed absolutely different from anyone I had dated. Weeks after learning more about each other, it got very serious. The relationship moved very fast. In fact, it felt like it was moving at warp speed. I enjoyed the exhilarating ride and I held on tight!

This chica believed that I had met my prince charming on an iron horse. He was a motorcyclist. By the time I met him, I had ridden motorcycles for about seven years. First I rode a Ninja Kawasaki, and the year prior to meeting him, I had acquired my Yamaha YZF. Both of them were sexy sport bikes. But this guy rode a Harley-Davidson. I thought he was the ultimate badass! He loved that I was a motorcyclist. He confessed that he thought that seeing me on my sports motorcycle was so sexy, but seeing me straddling his Harley would be another kind of epic sexy! He signed me up for the challenge, and I was game. I knew we were serious when he let me borrow his Harley for a week to try it on for size. Who does that?! A guy who is seriously trying to woo you and bring you over to the Harley-Davidson side of motorcycle joy.

Well I was hooked, and I got very distracted from my research work. My desire to write about my research waned. I didn't want to try to pick up the writing again. Who was I kidding? I didn't have what it took to make a dent in this global issue of street children and orphans. I needed to wake up and stay grounded. Humble myself. Meeting this somewhat grounded and humble guy living a simple life was going to be my wake-up call. It was time to establish some roots. Did I lose my husband because I was too damn ambitious? My dreams were too big! My dreams were too lofty. It was time to work on my personal life. It was time to nurture love and to keep it small and simple...*estupida*!

As crazy as it sounds, that was how much I wanted to have love in my life. I was willing to shrink myself. Not take up too much space. I was in love with the notion of being in love. Soon he introduced me to his family who lived in Connecticut. I fell in love with this tight-knit family. They were all such talented musicians and artists. More importantly, they shared such pride in our Puerto Rican heritage. I felt like the old me had died, and I had gone to heaven. Puerto Rico reminded me so much of my mother. I was going to do something to show my mother that I was happy. That I found true love. I found a Puerto Rican man that I was going to keep! This Puerto Rican man was going to keep me. I was not going to scare him away.

Later in the Spring of 2015, Joe from Guatemala called me. Again he asked me how he could ever pay me back for everything I did for his nonprofit organization. He shared how everything was going so smoothly with his nonprofit work. He was taking the necessary steps outlined in my program evaluation to centralize systems for the nonprofit organization, its management, and how it could run seamlessly. This allowed him to take the important and vital steps to step back and work on his health. It meant he was going to be in the United States more frequently and he was taking care of himself. The missionary life was truly taking a toll on his body. Joe was working on being the best version of himself. His steps were very inspirational, and I vowed to do the same.

I told Joe that it was my great honor to support his organization. I shared that at this point, I was brave enough to work on a passion project in Puerto Rico to honor a promise I made to my mother. I was going to fix her house. Since the guy I was dating was a construction worker, he encouraged me to really dive into fixing my mother's home in Toa Alta, Puerto Rico. I explained that it was my time to fix the house that my mother was never able to finish building. The house that was going to be her safe haven from the abuse she received from my stepfather. Sadly, it was *la casita* that she never got to live in because she died too young from cancer. In her final moments of life, my mother and I discussed how I would help her accomplish her dream of fixing up her home in Puerto Rico. Mami shared how she would love to paint the house a beautiful Caribbean ocean blue. She longed to have a garden planted in the back of the house that would include *yuca* (cassava), *yautía o malanga* (cocoyam), *guineos verdes* (green bananas), *platanos* (plantains) *aguacate* (avocado), *gandules* (pigeon peas) and *mangos*. My goal was to film that journey and develop a chronicle of how this daughter completed one final wish for her mother.

Joe jumped at the chance to help. "Vilma, I could help you film your journey." He was thrilled about the prospect of creating a commemorative project TOGETHER. He offered to do this filmmaking service *gratis*! Just like I did for him with that extensive program evaluation in Guatemala. All I would need to cover were his traveling costs, and later in the editorial process help with acquiring some software or hardware to make the process move smoother. I knew what a tremendous gift that Joe was offering. It would take some time to complete this work together as we collaborated intercontinentally and from different cities in the United States. Joe was willing to do that with me, and I felt so honored!

In the past, Joe was able to make a living as a wedding and portrait photographer as well as a videographer. Joe would be in his element. Seasonally, he would fly to New York and back to Florida for different weddings and promotional gigs to sustain him as he worked remotely towards his Guatemala dream. I considered ways that I would be able to financially sustain such a project. Should I apply for a grant? Should I do crowdfunding like I did for the work in the Dominican Republic and Guatemala? I told Joe that I needed some time to think about this. But I really needed to run it by my boyfriend.

I was terrified of the notion that my boyfriend might become jealous about the fact that I was working with another Puerto Rican man on this project. Would the Boricua *machismo* that was so prevalent in our culture rear its ugly head now? How would I tell him? Would this push my boyfriend away? Could I afford this? At first, I was hesitant to share the documentary idea with my boyfriend thinking he would probably shape-shift and that his potential nice guy mask would fall off. Was this really him or was he just sending his best dating representative? Was there a jealous and self-centered man at the core of this person I was dating? Would he slip into the expected Latino jealousy role just like my ex-husband and become that needy man whining that I wasn't paying attention to my man? I had to be true to myself, but I was going to be careful. I was going to plot my way through this labyrinth. Step by step, feeling my way through this maze, because I was terrified of losing him.

However, I had to be true to the promise I made to my mother on her deathbed. *Vilmita* was going to fix her mom's *casita*. My ultimate vision was to have my little brothers and I walk in the footsteps of her dreams. We would enjoy the house she made so many sacrifices to secretly build. Built with her sweat and tears, in the face of being discovered and facing a terrible fate by the stranglehold of my stepfather.

One day after a beautiful motorcycle ride down the Merritt Parkway, I nervously shared with my boyfriend the documentary idea that Joe offered. I explained how Joe was willing to be the director of my documentary as a way to demonstrate his gratitude for the pro bono program evaluation I did for his nonprofit organization. To my surprise, my boyfriend told me to go for it. I couldn't believe it! He reacted positively to the news sharing that this was a wonderful opportunity to share my mother's story and to reach my dreams. I almost fainted! As I placed all the wheels in motion to sock away some funding for this documentary, I felt more confident knowing that I had the full support of my boyfriend.

Happily, I reached out to Joe and said that I would take him up on his offer. I proposed that we could begin the documentary in July 2015. We were not going to waste time. We had to strike while the iron was hot! What if my boyfriend changed his mind? I wasn't going to take any chances. After a few conversations with Joe, the idea developed of creating a commemorative documentary project called *La Casa de María Contra la Violencia Doméstica*. That vision evolved into chronicling the narrative of this first-generation Puerto Rican daughter working against several social, emotional, and financial obstacles to create a future space for the local community of Toa Alta, Puerto Rico to visit my mother's dream home. The preliminary vision for fixing up my mother's house was to seasonally host cafe-style events in the living room and the open layout of the kitchen of this humble space in Toa Alta, Puerto Rico. I would offer different cultural events, literary writing events, and book readings, as well as invite guest speakers to discuss ways to support our Puerto Rican community in addressing the tragic statistics of domestic violence in our Latino community. I could tap into the gifts of local artists and artisans to help me with this new vision. I could reach out to Puerto Rican advocates on the island to help me develop workshop series and events for the local residents. Joe as the director would use his gifts to help record that journey. I was so excited about capturing these moments. One final gift for my beloved mother.

This was such an exciting venture. At the time, the place that I was renting was a guest house cottage in the artsy and progressive hamlet of Silvermine, Connecticut. The owner of the property had a sick mother who was going to move in with them. They needed the cottage space for the caregiver. So that meant my lease would be up soon. My boyfriend at the time strongly encouraged me to get a place together with him, but I was very hesitant to move that quickly. So I downsized and coordinated a move into a smaller apartment that was constructed in a former red barn within the small hamlet of North Salem, New York. It was only a 25-minute commute from work and it was located near an equestrian ranch. It was a little slice of heaven. This frugal chica knew how to make things happen. Making this move helped me save a lot of money!

The next step was reaching out to family so that I could get a stronger sense of what I was walking into as I landed with the film crew on the island of Puerto Rico. All I had were my childhood memories of my grandparents' farm and some memories of traveling around Toa Alta during my teenage visits to the island. So I spoke to my mother's twin sister who is also my dear godmother Titi Lola. I was so grateful that she survived cancer before my mother passed away. Titi Lola was a living walking and talking reminder of my mother's memory. Through her, Mami's soul was still present. Whenever I was with Titi Lola, Mami was with me here on Earth as well as in the celestial realm. How fortunate was I to have someone who shared my mother's DNA very much alive to consult with in terms of fixing my mother's house? Titi Lola was so excited about the fact that I wanted to fix the house that her sister never had the chance to live in.

Years earlier she had purchased the house that her brother owned right next to my mother's home. Tio Ismael had passed away from liver cancer and his daughters sold the property to my Titi Lola. Both houses were right next to the main house where my grandparents once lived and now where my Tio Nolin lived. He was the patriarch of the family and the only surviving son who still lived on the island. At the time, my mother's youngest sister Titi Teresa lived in a bright yellow house right on the property right next to my mother's house. This meant that now my Titi Lola could visit her youngest sister Teresa and that her niece and Goddaughter (me) were going to continue fixing her sister's legacy on the island. She suggested that I reach out to Chino who lived in the same neighborhood where my mother's incomplete home was situated. She gave me his telephone number. I felt like I was on my way!

I had no clue about the condition of the cement house that stood on that Toa Alta property. All I saw was a picture of a gray cement house that was never painted with white rusty metal jalousie louver aluminum windows which are very common on the island. The metal windows didn't have any screens and they were extremely rusty. In order to close them, you would need to turn a lever that would simultaneously close the panel of aluminum window shades. The house didn't have any doors whatsoever! So I was curious to see what I was going to find inside. I spoke with Chino and he shared honestly that the house was quite run down and truly an abandoned lot. There was a ton of garbage inside the home from different squatters frequenting the location. He mentioned that before my uncle Moncho passed away, he would spend time there reading his bible in the back room of the house. He was taking care of some chickens that were in a chicken coop in another back room of the house. Chino asked me if he wanted me to clean it up before I got there. I asked him to wait until I arrived with my friend Joe. I knew that this was going to take a lot of time and effort. My friend Miriam, who had introduced me to Joe and traveled with me to Guatemala, offered to help me but she didn't have any money to travel. She earned a low wage as a teaching assistant in the city. I told her that I would take care of the costs just to have the extra help and moral support. I was grateful for her willingness to come with me. I was going to be able to use all the help I could get. Perhaps we could all roll up our sleeves and Joe could record us doing the work.

Our plan took flight as I took care of the travel and boarding costs. As promised, I helped Joe upgrade any videography equipment that he needed to complete this project. I wanted Joe to keep the equipment and use it for future work with his nonprofit. I wanted our efforts to continue paying forward to help others in need and chronicle the work of other organizations collaborating with Joe. Ultimately, the objective was that we could do this project in about three years.

The documentary crew flew out the last week of June–a few days before my 46th birthday. Joe was able to make arrangements with his friend Carmencita to join our team. She was a family friend living in Puerto Rico. She was only 45 minutes away from my mother's hometown. Carmencita was a social worker, and she was a dear long-time friend from Joe's family church in Florida. She reached out to a colleague that on occasion would rent her three-bedroom house when she was traveling in the summer. Thankfully, my documentary trip coincided with her friend being away, so I was able to get a great deal renting a home for the documentary crew. Miriam and I would stay together in one room, Carmencita had a smaller room, while Joe had his own room in the larger suite. The director needed to be comfortable and rested after these compressed nine days of running around the island capturing footage. It was so awesome getting everyone together for the first time. We all had outgoing personalities and there were so many laughs as we would talk and get to know one another. It was like lifelong friends coming back together for a reunion. It was truly special!

The documentary team worked so seamlessly together. I truly couldn't comprehend how we almost completed each other's sentences and laughed our way through the awesome moments of capturing my interviews and worrying about the best angle. Even though I was training for a half marathon in Puerto Rico in November, I had gained a significant amount of weight. No matter how much I exercised, I was not losing any weight. I think a lot of it had to do with intestinal discomfort, higher levels of stress, and sleep deprivation. So I was extremely self-conscious about looking overweight on camera.

It was so helpful having Carmencita and my friend there helping us with the equipment, the sound checks, and kicking ideas off each other. It was instrumental in setting up the filming scenes and checking the quality of the recordings. Moreover, I was extremely grateful for the support that Carmencita coordinated before I even arrived on the island. She was able to arrange some interviews with a few of her friends who were social workers helping battered women gain access to community services and community resources. We were excited about conducting some interviews to help shed light on the issue of domestic violence in Puerto Rico.

Once again, the universe rewarded my bravery and boldness in pursuing what I wanted to do. On the second day of filming, I took the scary drive to Toa Alta. I was using the GPS to get to Toa Alta's town hall, but after that I was going to have to figure out how to get there using my gut instincts and very faint memories. I was driving around in circles until I decided to stop and ask a local police officer for help. My cousin David still lived in Toa Alta and was a retired San Juan police officer. I was hoping that by mentioning that David was in law enforcement, I could activate some kind of *policia* fraternal code of professional courtesy and that perhaps this police officer on a motorcycle would help me get there. Well to my surprise, the police officer mounted his motorcycle and he offered to escort me to *El Barrio Ortiz*. I took it as a positive sign that since he was riding a motorcycle, the universe was confirming that I was on the right path.

My mother's home was located in the smaller sector of Toa Alta which was high up in the mountains. *Alta* means higher ground. The town of Toa Alta has ten small hamlets that fall under the jurisdiction of the larger province of Bayamón. I was deeply grateful that he was willing to go out of his way to help this Nuyorican *gringa* from *Nueva York*. Finally, we passed by a large reservoir on the right side of the road, and that is when it all came back to me! This was the same reservoir I would take long walks to after my grandmother would cook lunch and I would go on my exploration expeditions. Alone and sometimes carrying a stray puppy or kitten. Now this little girl was back, but I was not lost. I knew exactly where I was and what I wanted to do.

When I arrived, Chino was standing in front of the house. He invited me to follow him, and sure enough what I saw was truly a scene out of a horror movie. The house was an absolute disaster. Every corner of that house and most of the floor was covered with garbage, old appliances, and even a weight-lifting set in the area that would be a kitchen. Graffiti-riddled walls and dirty chicken coops were in each room. It turns out that someone was using this space to raise roosters for cock fights. Apparently, Chino told the guy that was squatting in the house to leave the premises with the roosters before I arrived.

The first order of business was to close up this house. I still couldn't believe that Tio Nolin did not place any doors within this structure. My mother would send a little bit of money at a time, and his main priority was building the cement house section by section. A large ticket item was the windows and I guess by the time they were ready for the doors, that is when my mom couldn't work and send any more money. María's daughter had to reclaim this space.

While running to the local hardware store in Bayamon, a dear friend Jacquie Zenon called me from New York. I cried on the phone with her sharing the news about the present condition of the house. I was overwhelmed. I truly felt that I was in over my head. This dear friend was a strong faith warrior and we prayed together on the phone. Then to my surprise moments later, she wired me the money to cover the cost of the front door of the house. Jacquie wanted to bless me with a symbolic gift. She declared that there would be many women and children walking through that donated door of *La Casa de María* to be blessed with the work that I had planned for that local community. It was her prayer seed for my work. It was the door that was going to open to reveal my dreams! Those words lit a fire in my heart. I got spiritually stronger and I kept it moving inside the hardware store. In addition, I purchased the side door to the kitchen. There was a window missing from the bathroom. We made arrangements for that afternoon to have Chino install the missing window and the two new white doors. I was grateful to Yaya for suggesting that I reach out to her family friend to help with the installation. Both men were very knowledgeable and quite reasonable with their pricing compared to New York construction prices. I felt very grateful to have all hands on deck to seal up the house.

In the middle of the afternoon, I spotted my Tio Nolin as he came around to the side of the house to watch as the men installed the doors. Prior to my visit, I had sent word to Yaya to tell him that I was going to come by and begin working on the house. My aunt Titi Teresa was very vocal in sharing that I didn't have to tell anyone or ask permission from anyone since that was my mother's house and clearly that was my house now. Titi Teresa was known for her boisterous personality and for saying what was on her mind.

I didn't want to be disrespectful coming there and not letting my uncle know. Tio Nolin didn't have a phone so there was no way to communicate, so I had to do it the old-fashioned way, by word of mouth. Tio Nolin, otherwise known as Manuel, was the brother that did the construction for my mom. During this 2015 visit, he was 87 years old and I was very impressed by how strong he looked for his age. He had a beautiful tan and the most gorgeous head of dark hair. I couldn't believe it. He only had a few gray hairs on his head. I remember as a child seeing my grandfather and thinking the same thing about how much stronger and healthier he looked compared to my grandmother. Working the fields with a machete had its benefits. A true workout indeed!

Tio Nolin lived in the house in front of my mother's home. It was my grandparents' original home. At one time it was a wooden shack but then in the 1950s they converted it into a cement house with the help of my Tio Nolin who did construction work in his earlier years. On that plot of land, the children set up a few homes. Titi Teresa, Titi Lola, and the house that belonged to my other aunt Guillin who passed away when I was in college. Now it was just my uncle Nolin and my Titi Teresa who were living now on the Core Ayala family plot. My cousin David (who was Titi Teresa's only surviving son) lived nearby on a parcel of land that my uncle gave him as a part of Tio Nolin's inheritance. Tio never had any children and he had a very close relationship with my cousin David. I was told by Yaya that David and Tio built a large home. Every morning with great pride, Tio Nolin would tend to the property clearing the land and taking care of a donkey that was on David's property. Just like a proud father, he would come by and check up on his beloved David. As a child, I had a lovely relationship with David when he would visit New York from living in California with Titi Teresa. They relocated to New York for a while and we would celebrate a few holidays together. When

David was a young teen, the family moved back to Puerto Rico, and he pursued a life there.

By the time I came back to Puerto Rico in the Summer of 2015, David was a proud military veteran and he was very close to retiring from the police force. I wanted to visit David, and I tried to reach out to my cousin. But he was working and he was not available. I figured that I was there for such a short visit, that maybe I could stop by quickly. But I didn't dare just show up. The last time I saw David was in Puerto Rico. It was November 2012 after my mother passed away. He had come by to share his condolences and to congratulate me on my San Juan Half Marathon race efforts. He worked in San Juan at the time so it was convenient for him to swing by. He was quite proud that I dedicated my race to my mother. I hoped that the next time I would come back to Puerto Rico that I would be able to see him.

While the men worked to put up the doors and window, Tio Nolin was outside talking with a few men that were visiting him. I wondered if these were the same friends that my mother had spoken about that would make moonshine rum with Tio and once got arrested with him for making illegal rum on the premises. My mother had a newspaper clipping from the local newspaper *El Vocero* that she received from her sister sharing the news. Were these the guys that had all that crap in the house? Were they encroaching on my mother's property with their dirty roosters and cock fights?

After all of that, it was surreal to witness my dear uncle standing there watching the installation of the doors placed on the house he built with his own blood and sweat. I stepped away from the installation of the door and I walked up to my uncle. I noticed that as I approached him, he was a bit distant. When I told him that I was Conchita's daughter, *la hija de María*, he said "*Oh, Vilmita...la hija de Concha.*" Joking immediately, he shared that he didn't recognize me. It had been so many years since he last saw me as a young teenager. He reminded me that I was "*gorda*" (fat) and that I looked so different. He totally changed his tone and his demeanor with me. His voice and facial expressions were softer. He was less serious and tried to strike up more conversations with me. He was always a serious man so that didn't surprise me. He was just like I remembered him as a child. Seeing this gentler side of him was so endearing.

At that moment, an ice cream truck passed by and he asked me if I wanted an ice cream treat from the truck. I immediately accepted his offer and we walked up to the ice cream truck. At that moment, I was magically transported to that time and space as a little girl who didn't speak Spanish too well where he asked me if I wanted to eat *un mantecado.* This word sounded too much like *manteca* (butter) so I declined the offer. Immediately to my surprise, I saw my uncle walking back with just one ice cream cone. He was enjoying his ice cream. I started to cry saying that I wanted one too. He laughed loudly and teased me that I didn't know the Spanish word for ice cream. "Every kid should know that!" That is when I learned the word *mantecado* means ice cream! On this trip, I was not going to make the same mistake. I gladly enjoyed my ice cream treat on the front lawn with him as we stood in front of my former grandparents' house. To think that I was going to fix Mami's house and enjoy some of the same tender moments of being a child here. But now I would experience them as an adult. I couldn't wait!

Yaya was my mother's cousin and she lived about 100 meters from my grandparents' home. I remember as a child walking over to her property. She was one of the key persons that I was truly looking forward to talking with. My Titi Lola gave me her number and I was able to chat briefly with her telling her that I was coming to check in on my mom's house. She sounded very happy and said that it was important to keep that property in the family's hands. My uncle Nolin was renting a house on the property to a man named Angel. She wasn't too fond of him. As a Christian woman, she highly disapproved of their distillery antics. Yaya was the woman who helped my mother learn how to sew and prepared her for getting a job in New York City. This was the lady who always received me as a child when I would go on my strolls and offer to give me food or coffee. Yaya was going to help me with my mother's house.

The first visit to begin filming the documentary was extremely important in establishing a baseline of the conditions of the house.

It was truly a cement shell of a house. I paid Chino money to clean out the house. In addition, I paid him to repair the roof which was leaking in the kitchen. There was also flooding in the front of the house because the ground had to be leveled so that the water would move away from the house and not collect in the front cement porch. We made several trips to the hardware store to get the cement and tools to get the work done on the roof. We seized the remainder of our time there to celebrate my birthday as well as do some interviews about my experiences as a child in Puerto Rico. We recorded interviews of my childhood memories with my mother and some tough moments near the end of her life.

I will admit that seeing the house in those conditions was very disheartening, but I was not going to be discouraged. When I was married, I was fortunate to witness the construction of our ranch home and our larger townhouse. I trusted in the process of seeing cement blocks, perimeter walls, and the process of laying down cement foundations. So this was actually somewhat of a blessing. I had a clean slate to work with. It would happen slowly and with the resources that I could collect and save to get the work done.

For the next two years, I worked very hard to save as much money as I could to continue with the repairs of the house in Puerto Rico. Then to make life more interesting, I experienced some major health setbacks, and that made it very hard to try to plan a trip to Puerto Rico. I was focusing on my health. But aside from this curveball, things were moving along quite well.

I was also focusing on the new relationship that I had established with the guy I met online. In fact, I had fallen in love with an artist. A creative. After two years of dating, I took a huge leap of faith. We moved in together with his son who was a very talented bassist attending music school. We rented a beautiful home in the northern part of the Bronx by Van Cortlandt Park and Riverdale. It was a thrilling moment in my life. I was pursuing all the things that brought me joy and love. We threw a huge housewarming party with our family and friends. We had over 100 guests. They were all there to celebrate this new milestone as a couple. I was truly on top of the world. It was all coming together for me.

The best part is that this new love supported my dream to write. We would go to different cultural events and art exhibits in the Bronx and this opened a new world for me. My friend Yolanda had created an artistic nonprofit organization based in the Bronx and it became a new world of creative pursuits. Together on our motorcycles, my boyfriend and I got to explore everything that the Boogie Down Bronx and the upper west side of Manhattan had to offer. One of the great places was a writing workshop with the Bronx Memoir Project. I wanted to focus on my creative writing, and he was more than excited about me pursuing this creative side of me. He even came with me to my first writing workshop and I was thrilled. In June 2017, I published a writing piece with the Bronx Memoir Project anthology. This newfound literary fire was burning and publishing my first creative writing project was the spark.

My live-in boyfriend wanted to come with me to Puerto Rico, but he had started a new construction job (this was the second one since I had met him) and he didn't have any vacation time yet. He encouraged me to follow my dreams and work on my mother's house. It was the best feeling to finally have the support of my partner as I pursued the things that brought me joy.

With his blessing, in July 2017, I went back to Puerto Rico with the original documentary crew and we continued with the last leg of the filming on the island. We went back with a specific purpose to show the transformation that took place with the restoration of the house. With the extra time of saving money for those two years, I was able to pull together enough funds to house the documentary team in a nice penthouse duplex in Dorado where we conducted many interviews with community activists and guest speakers. Having that place to strategize, coordinate, and decompress after long days of filming around the island was a gift to our spirits. For my 48th birthday celebration, we took a trip to the Yunque tropical forest, and the beautiful caves of Puerto Rico called *La Ventanilla*. From inside the caves, we witnessed the beauty of the cave openings. They looked like windows into the heart of Puerto Rico's lush landscape. We spotted several Taíno indigenous cave paintings, always being mindful that looming nearby and clinging upside down to the cave ceilings was a huge colony of bats.

The second trip to visit my mother's house was a significantly different trip than the first one. The last time I was there, I walked into a disheveled and messy space. This time we filmed ourselves painting the inside walls of La Casa de María. Filming the electrical work that was done inside the house. Electrical outlets were all installed and the next step was to focus on the plumbing of the house. We filmed moments of Chino mixing cement as he patched up walls inside and outside of the house. There wasn't a hint of graffiti anywhere in that house. We were able to capture moments within the installation of electricity wiring throughout the house as well as the improvements to the room and the interior walls of the house. As Joe filmed the work, I was able to have some wonderful conversations with my Tio Nolin and with Titi Teresa who looked truly excited about the prospect of me fixing my mother's home so that I could visit her more. She would enter the house and take stock of all the work that was accomplished. Titi Teresa looked proud. Tio Nolin looked happy. Their niece was working hard on fulfilling her promise to their sister. All of this construction activity was like a healing balm to my spirit.

Then I learned that Yaya was suffering from cancer and she was a shell of a woman compared to the vibrant being that I witnessed two years earlier. I brought her a beautiful framed photo that Joe had taken of her during our documentary filming. It was a picture of her with a red flower in her hair. A classic Puerto Rican beauty. A classic Taína indigenous woman. It broke my heart to see her like that. Yaya told me that she was very happy I was fixing Conchita's house. *La hija de Conchita* was coming through with her promise. I felt in my heart that this was going to be the last time I saw her. I smiled, hugged her, and tried to make her laugh with my *Nuyorican gringa* Spanish accent. She loved every moment we spent together chatting. I asked her brothers to please keep in touch with me and keep me posted on her progress.

They had my number and I was grateful that her brother's friend was the one doing the electrical work in La Casa de María.

One of the last filming sessions was a painting party we had with Chino. We were recording our painting antics and my ridiculous attempt to look like a Taína goddess with strips of white paint under my eyes like warrior paint. Perhaps that was a foreshadowing instance that would foretell what the next few years had in store. After filming that moment, I would really need to channel the true warrior spirit that I had in this Taína being.

Two weeks after leaving Puerto Rico, I received a heartbreaking phone call sharing that Yaya had passed away in her sleep. My heart was truly broken. I was grateful for the visits that I shared with this beautiful older woman. The one that took care of my mother in her young days, and the one that was taking care of me and guiding me in my dream to finish my mother's home.

A month later, on September 20, 2017, the deadly Category 5 Hurricane María came to Puerto Rico and devastated the island. It was regarded as the worst natural disaster to have affected the northeastern Caribbean. I remember feeling grateful that Yaya was not alive to witness that horrible storm and the isolation that the Puerto Rican people dealt with. They were not equipped to handle such a bad storm. The island was dealing with so many infrastructural problems with roads, electricity, and clean and fresh water, and there were so many obstacles to getting immediate aid to the island. Then to add insult to injury, President Trump visited the island and thought it is a good idea to throw rolls of paper towels into a crowd of Puerto Ricans caught up in this crisis. I remember feeling such despair.

Joe on the other hand got the support of his church in Florida to be able to deliver some generators to some families in Puerto Rico. I am grateful that there were altruistic hearts coordinating these humanitarian efforts. It was a scary time for so many families in the United States who had loved ones on the island. Thankfully, I was able to communicate with my cousin David, his wife, and Yaya's brothers. All was well and they were slowly getting power to Toa Alta. But as you can imagine this really threw a huge wrench into my plans to continue doing the work.

Communicating with Chino was impossible. He did not return my calls and when I reached out to his daughter, she would tell me he left Puerto Rico to go to Ohio to do some construction work. A huge part of me didn't believe it. But what was more unsettling was that I made the huge mistake of giving him a payment advance of over a thousand dollars to paint the outside of the house. Before leaving Puerto Rico, we had gone to the local hardware store to purchase the paint and we stored it in the kitchen area so that he could work on that when I left. I had reached out to a cousin of my boyfriend's who was a police officer in Vega Alta, which was not too far from Toa Alta. As it turns out, she took pictures of the house and Chino DID NOT paint the house. In fact, she was able to push on the metal aluminum blinds to peek in and there wasn't any paint in the home. It turns out that he sold the paint, took the money I gave him, and left after Hurricane María. That was the end of my support in Puerto Rico for quite some time. I was feeling defeated and heartbroken.

My resignation was not easy to come to at first. I took stock and I knew that I had at least seven more years until I could retire to fully focus on this project. Things on the homefront in New York City with my boyfriend were getting complicated fast. Again he ended up getting a different construction job and all he would say was that he was at odds with the foreman. I felt something was totally off, but I needed to regroup and focus on my writing. If I couldn't at least work on the house in Puerto Rico, I could work on my writing.

All of my time working on my writing brought me closer to the idea of learning more about my Cabán history. I didn't know if my father was dead or alive. I didn't know if I had any siblings. My boyfriend purchased a subscription to Ancestry.com for the holidays and I was on the hunt to connect with my siblings. I set up my profile and simply waited for the best.

As it turned out, one of the research colleagues that I collaborated with and who worked for the Department of Justice was very helpful in connecting me to my long-lost siblings. We met when I was doing research work on *los niños de la frontera* that were being used by drug smugglers to bring drugs into the United States coming from Guatemala. Elias and I had the same last name. I had asked him if by chance he had family in Ponce or near Bayamón. Of course, he looked into it and we even checked if we were family on Ancestry. However, it was confirmed we weren't family. So Elias pulled some favors and with his resources as an intelligence research specialist for the Drug Enforcement Agency I was able to get some answers.

In February 2019, I learned that I had family in Puerto Rico in La Playa de Ponce, Florida, and New York City. I was shocked to learn from this source, that my father had died in 1989 from liver failure and he was an alcoholic. Turned out that he witnessed the tragic death of my older half-brother in Brooklyn and after that, his drinking was out of control. The final piece of the puzzle was to reach out to my older sisters from La Playa de Ponce that were living in Florida. Through social media, I reached out to the eldest sister Lizzie and she was so open to learning more about me and helping me fill in the gaps about the paternal side of my family.

My boyfriend's behavior had become very erratic, jealous, and downright mean. He had always been quite moody, but as a smoker, I just chalked it up to him needing a cigarette. But as my truth was revealed, he was worried that somehow his truth would leak out...especially after he learned that it was a DEA agent who helped me find the truth about my father.

I was horrified to discover that he had an addiction to cocaine. I unearthed his truth when I found his stash in a dresser drawer. After that, things truly hit the fan. For three months, I did my best to stand by his side, but once the cat was out of the bag, he just became more belligerent and mean. Refusing to get any help or counseling, I had no other recourse but to step away from this very unhealthy and toxic relationship. I ran to my dear friend's house and lay low until I could figure out a plan.

As painstaking as it was, after four years together, I had to break up with him. He wanted to break the lease but I didn't want to compromise my credit. So he moved out and I remained in that home. My son was thinking of a career change leaving his environmental scientist position to pursue nursing just like his fiance Vanessa. So they moved in with me so that I wouldn't be alone in that haunted Bronx home.

What I didn't realize after a few weeks of staying in the place was that the idiot moved next door with his sons and one of his son's girlfriends. He was such a deadbeat that he couldn't survive on his own. He must have spiraled out of control and now he was using his sons to survive. Oh my goodness, how could this happen?! I was going to be stronger than ever. If my mother lived with an abuser for 27 years, this chick could handle seeing this moron next to me for another 12 months until I was free from that lease.

I am sure the moment he realized that I didn't break the lease was quite a shock for him. It was more of a shock for me to see him every freaking day turning on his motorcycle to go to work and hearing him arrive in the evening. Every time I heard the roar of the Harley engine it was like receiving a jolt to my nervous system. After a while, I would jump on my Harley to get away and superimpose the sound of his engine with mine. I learned how to ride before him. I wasn't going to stop now! Soon after this lease was over, I would be able to leave behind my dreams of being a Bronx writer. I would choose to leave this God-forsaken place to be closer to my family in Connecticut. I just had to hang in there.

Living with my son got me through that horrible traumatic season. Being in the city was simply too triggering. I was happy to see a U-Haul moving truck arrive next door in February 2020, and I thanked God for breaking this curse next door. Finally, he would be gone. At last, I would be completely free. Without him, I could still make it. Without him, I could still pursue my dream to fix my mother's house. It just would take longer.

A month after seeing him move out, the world came to an abrupt halt as we dealt with the global pandemic of COVID-19. I was safely away from the man who broke my heart with his lies and deceptions. I was putting the pieces of my heart back together with the virtual but ever-present love and support of family and friends.

My writing was the healing source that reinvigorated me. It helped me get stronger. The Covid-19 pandemic had pretty much frozen travel to Puerto Rico. So I chose to do the things that brought me joy. I purchased a 20-foot boat, and I traded in my Sportster Harley for a huge Road King Harley motorcycle. I taught during the most grueling three years of my teaching career using remote instruction, hybrid instruction, full classes with plexiglass, vaccinations, no vaccinations, K95 masks, social distancing, Zoom calls, double masks, and voice amplifiers.

Through it all I didn't forget about my dream to go back and continue fixing La Casa de María. My friend Joe was still living in Florida and he was working hard on his ministry work becoming a pastor! I was so proud of all that he had accomplished. Joe suggested that we finish the last interview and wrap up the documentary with a Zoom call which would really be a signature time stamp of the times during this pandemic. That is exactly what we did. The final documentary interview was in July of 2021 and it recapped everything I had experienced since Hurricane María and how my dream shifted from opening up a seasonal cultural center to actually opening up my own publishing house in Puerto Rico called Casa de María Press. My goal was to offer a platform for women to share their stories of struggle, triumph, pain, and passion. I am happy to share that *La Casa de María Documentary* would premiere at the Bregamos Community Theater in New Haven, Connecticut as well as in other community theaters and cultural centers in the tri-state area. This memoir will serve as the backstory describing the events that led up to me fixing my mother's home in Puerto Rico.

In the summer of 2022, after five years of not traveling to Puerto Rico, I put on a K-94 mask to board the plane to Puerto Rico. I decided to go and check up on things in Toa Alta. I went with a dear friend and colleague JB. I was so blessed to have her moral support on that trip. My teaching partner of eight years was willing to leave behind her two children and her husband to accompany me on this odyssey. She convinced her father-in-law to have us stay in his home 40 minutes away from Toa Alta. I am grateful that he even flew out to make sure we were safe in his isolated home in the mountains. My dearest JB went with me to my biological father's hometown of Playa de Ponce. The Cabán mystery was solved in 2019, but I wanted to walk in the footsteps of my biological father in his hometown. I sat on the bench at the plaza which more than likely was the same place he romanced his victims. I strolled along the rocky shore of the beach, where he probably gazed at the sunset with his sweethearts. I was able to visit and bear witness to the living spirit of my destiny along the different parts of the island. This would heal my spirit and help me put the pieces back together.

JB encouraged me to handle the logistics of looking into the transfer of my mother's property. She offered to go with me to the Bayamón property registry to begin inquiring about the probate process of placing the house under my name. How would I go about doing that? Every time I saw Tio Nolin, he was encouraging me to fix my mom's house. I didn't want to have a direct conversation about how I would transfer the home into her children's name. In the past, my mother had mentioned how there were other cousins who would demand their heir rights from Tio Nolin and the conversations were not positive. Many times, he would come out with a machete yelling profanities and sending everybody to hell. I was terrified. Every time I brought up this topic with other first or second-generation friends who also had family in Puerto Rico, the majority of the people would joke and say that everyone in Puerto Rico was always fighting with a family member about their heir rights to a property. I wanted to have peace in my family, so I chose not to have those awkward conversations.

My Tio Nolin was the patriarch of the family, and I trusted that he would take care of me. In that brief visit, I learned from a Puerto Rican lawyer in the town of Bayamón that according to Puerto Rican law, my mother's children still inherited the structure and that no one can lay claim to that structure as long as I had my mother's death certificate and birth certificate, as well as my birth certificate. It would be best to have an affidavit statement from the surviving children of my grandfather and grandmother. The three surviving children were Tio Nolin, Titi Teresa (who had moved to New Jersey), and my Titi

Lola (who lived in Connecticut). The affidavit must declare that the structure belonged to my mother and it was built by my uncle. I was scared to ask Tio Nolin for a letter. Perhaps with time, I would try to sit down with Tio and make that transfer of the land, but I still had two years to officially move over to Puerto Rico to fix the house full-time. I realized that he was getting older as he was 94. He was slowing down a bit, but still sharpening his machete and getting up early. I believed that I had time.

In April 2023, my beloved Tio Nolin passed away in his home. I received the news from my Titi Lola and it was heartbreaking. She had received the news from one of her nieces that lived in Puerto Rico. I reached out to my cousin David who was handling all of the funeral arrangements. At that time, my poor cousin David was struggling with serious health issues and he was going to make the arrangements as soon as he was out of the intensive care unit.

I am grateful to share that my dear cousin got stronger and was able to do such a beautiful service for my uncle. The images and videos captured shared the story of a strong man who loved his family. At the same time when David was able to hold the funeral, I was running my half marathon in Washington D.C. In the same moments when there was an eulogy for Tio Nolin, I played worship music to get me through that tough race. I wanted to go to the service, but not having a set plan to take personal days off for this funeral was going to be very taxing during the busiest season at work. I had already put in for the personal days almost a year in advance for my half-marathon race. In addition, I didn't want to put any pressure on my cousin to give me an exact date while he was literally fighting for his life in the ICU. So I left it in God's hands and asked God to reveal the best time to go back to Puerto Rico.

The time to go back to Puerto Rico was when my cousin David was stronger. It was in the summer of 2023 that I made a trip to go with Titi Lola and my cousin Yolanda. Together we had a beautiful trip visiting family in Puerto Rico. We had the great moment of breaking bread with my cousin David in his home. He shared such loving memories with our Tio Nolin. We poured over photos of the house and he explained so much to me about our family history. Now David was our family patriarch and I looked at him with such hope and compassion and he was working to get stronger.

I shared with David and his beautiful wife that after I retired from teaching for 32 years, I was moving to Puerto Rico in July 2024. David and his wife were so happy for me. Even though he was still recovering from his pulmonary illness, he was going to help me coordinate the next crucial steps in fixing my beloved mother's home. We walked over to La Casa de María to survey what had to be done. We walked around the property. My cousin shared ideas on how I could create a project timeline to complete the next steps in finishing the interior construction of the plumbing, tiling, bathroom, and kitchen renovation. He gave me suggestions on where I could place the septic tank. David would help me connect with local tradesmen that could do the work for me at a fair price and he would make sure they were going to complete the work. *Yo tengo familia en Toa Alta que me pueden representar.*

I was excited to learn that he had a large digger. With great boldness, I jumped onto that giant machine like a giddy little girl exploring her brother's Tonka trucks. What a memory! In those moments, my cousin took pictures of me sitting on it envisioning how God was going to break ground on this next leg in my construction journey. David shared how I could create a small terrace space on the side of the house and enjoy the beauty under the large mango tree. He shared such beautiful memories of how during the holidays they roasted the Christmas *lechon* and collected ripe mangoes and coconuts from the large palm trees in the back of the property. He was genuinely happy and excited to help me prepare for this next leg in my journey. He encouraged me and prayed with me to have God release all of His great promises in my life.

Later that day, he took us to the cemetery where our Tio Nolin was laid to rest in eternal peace. It was one of the most peaceful moments I experienced on the island. Even though my dear cousin was not feeling a hundred percent, he came with his portable oxygen pack and took us to the family gravesite. Together we prayed, shared memories, smiled, and took pictures rejoicing about Tio Nolin's legacy and how much he meant to us. The next day he came to visit us in our Air BNB and we enjoyed more family time together. It was like years were compressed into seconds. We had so much joy around us as we talked about our dreams and how God was going to heal David. I am so grateful for that family moment together.

Ultimately in July 2024, I will retire from teaching in New York. My dream to open up a publishing house there and begin making Toa Alta my retirement home will be waiting for me in the tropical island breeze. *La Casa de María Press* will be a future site to invite other writers for their writing retreats. They will be greeted by Bomba dancers from Loiza, Puerto Rico to spiritually cleanse the ground and space for their future writing. Dancing to the rhythm of the drums and the writers' hearts, stories will come forth and leap onto the page. They will be able to #pentheirpain. They will be excited to #pentheirpassion, and they will be brave to #pentheirpersonalpromises. This humble servant will cook some of the recipes my beloved mother Maria showed me how to cook. The recipes of love, perseverance, grace, and compassion. With the vegetables and organic food grown in the backyard, La Casa de Maria Press writers will be nurtured and fed nutritious soul food. Stirring hearts and stirring souls.

Instagram will be flooded with these hashtags as well as with images of women finding their voice in so many different places on the island. My goal is to coordinate special writing excursions on my boat (that I will ship to Puerto Rico in the summer of 2024). S.S. Luz with Captain Vilma Luz will dock and leave port from the Puerto Chico Marina in Fajardo, Puerto Rico. Recently, I learned that my name means determined light. Shining bright and bold, the S.S. Luz will lead the way for our future writers.

Future writers of La Casa de María Press Anthology will be able to publish their pieces from the writing they harvested in my writing retreats. They will be able to go to the tropical rainforest of El Yunque and write about their dreams. Writers will be able to visit the San Juan Fort *El Morro* and fortify their spirits writing about their futures. My future published writers will write about their setbacks and learn more about themselves as human beings breaking through to the other side of fulfillment and peace. La Casa de María will be the place where I will live the dream that my beloved mother was not able to live. Every mother's dream is for their daughter to feel freer than she did at her age. At the age of 55, my mother's dream was to go to her retreat in her ancestral home. This did not happen, so I will go in her stead.

–La hija, Vilma Luz, estará soñando en la casa de María.–

Rooftop picture of Maria
and her twin sister Lola
1967.

Maria and Julio Summer 1968.
The only picture Vilma has of
her parents together.

8-year-old Vilma with her
mother Maria.

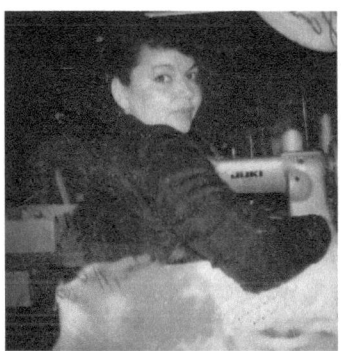

Vilma's mother sitting at her sewing machine inside a garment factory. (Fall 1981.)

Vilma in her senior year of high school in 1986.

Math research in Siem Reap,
Cambodia.

Interview with a Maasai
woman who would perform the
FGM practice.

Watching the sunset on top of a
sand dune in the Sahara Desert.

*Painting the graffiti left by
squatters.*

*Installing the electrical system
inside La Casa de María.*

A tender moment with Yaya.

Director Joe Negron taking pic-
tures of the construction work.
(July 2017 - Before Hurricane
Maria.)

2023 Puerto Rico visit with
family and making plans.

*Vilma enjoys time with all of
her nieces and nephews.*

Visiting Puerto Rico in 2022.

*Documentary editorial work
with director Joe Negron.
(Naples, Florida.)*

*Boating with her son Christo-
pher in Milford, Connecticut.*

*Sitting on her Harley "La
Reina" as she gets ready to rock
and roll!*

*She is the captain of her own
ship.*

Christopher is Vilma's rock!

*Christopher's Godmother
Rachel with her beloved father
Dr. Andrés Torres.*

Vilma is excited about break-
ing ground for her Summer
2024 construction project finish-
ing her mother's home. La Casa
de María!

EPILOGUE:
POETIC PROSE

P art of my healing occurred by writing poetry during the pandemic. I had the great fortune of performing these two poems for the Nuyorican Poets Cafe which is ironically three blocks away from where I lived as an infant in Alphabet City. It came full circle for me. A poet sharing her pain, her journey, and her healing.

BLOW IT AWAY

NUYORICAN POETS CAFE: THURSDAY NIGHT OPEN MIC 2/24/22

I tried to cry it away,
but it only made you meaner.
I tried to talk it away,
but it only made you a stone-cold retreater.
Every time I told you to stop,
you justified it as recreational pass time.

I tried to count the days away,
A faithful calendar keeper.
To show you a pattern of wrongs,
and how we can mend your soul to be a feeler.
You told me that you were not strong,
and that you needed ME–to see YOU.

But I pushed it away.
I counted away.
Marking each day you came home drunk,
trying to come down from that

HIGH blow feeling.

One day I took a big stand.
Showing you those calendar sheets
as I flung them towards the ceiling.
Your eyes looked like daggers,
when I showed you what I had been seeing.

This was not recreational "joy".
Tracking your lost days of not feeling.
This was you running from your past,
and you needed deep healing.

After you got off your high ivory tower,
full of distorted perceptions of my high and mighty intentions.
You got in my face and YOU took your stand.
PULLED UP IN MY FACE.
Toe to toe with this fighter.
My only words were... "If you hit me, you better make sure...
I don't get the fuck back up."
You quietly stepped away. I quietly let go of my breath.
Grateful that you didn't hit me.

It's like herding feral cats.
Cornered and fierce.
You hissed me away.
You scratched me away.
You charged me away.

Little did I know that the path to your healing
was for ME to step away.
Quickly I packed my bags and left.

But it's not until I truly moved myself away.
To another state of conscientiousness away.

Where I discovered that I couldn't help heal someone
THEY needed to want healing for THEMSELVES.
This is when I discovered that I wanted my OWN healing.

I tried to dance it away.
I tried to drink it away.
I tried to smoke it away.
They say a smooth cigar can really do wonders.
I tried to run it away.
I tried to write it away.
I tried to ride it away.
They say a Harley can really do wonders.

My pendulum shifted.
Taking stock of how far I had gotten away.
A universe away–
Stepped into a new world away into greater possibilities.

Family and friends helped me get away–
to a little cape of hope away.
To a new sanctuary away.
On the water away.

As I cried it away...
Away...
Away...
Blow it away.

ROARRRRRRRRR

Nuyorican Poets Cafe : Monday Night Open Mic 6/27/22

Such a distinctive sound
Low vibration...Deep throated
Oh....the syncopated roar of the Harley engine

The first time I heard it was when he rolled up to my place
A little cottage in the backroads of a sleepy Connecticut hamlet

I heard him less than a mile away
It was like a TAP to my soul

P - o - ta - to - po - ta - to -
VROOOOOOOOOMMMM–VROOOOOOOOOOMMMM

Such a different sound than the beefy Yamaha YZF
The one I was riding for about 2 years
Right after my upgrade from my black Ninja

Crotch rockets...

His Harley Deluxe excited me
It shifted a slacked gear in my soul from neutral to 5th gear
Revving me up
Here I was thinking we were riding our own
But his intention was to pick me up
Tell me to *ride bitch*

I resisted proudly declaring that "I ride my own"
But he insisted...
Said that there would be no turning back after this ride
Enticed...
Exhilarated...
Teased, I straddled my passenger seat and I snug close
I submitted and held on for dear life

Down those winding scenic roads
that make you feel
like you never want to get off

Enjoying the moment you are breathing in the same wind
Filling the space in your being
where your soul seeks another
That is when I realized
I wanted him and I was coveting his Harley

After a year of dating
I bought my first Harley Sportster
I never looked back

The thought of his and her Harleys was thrilling
Pretty badass
Little did I know that I was with a badass
That rode H-I-G-H

Placing my life in danger
My guardian angels were working triple time
every time I was his passenger

4 years later after sharing the same home
I discovered His truth
And begged him to get help
He clung to his lifestyle
Rode like a bat out of hell!

So I did what I needed to do
Biding my time
Until he decided to leave the place we called home
I came back to fulfill my legal obligation
One more year in the space where the ugly truth was revealed
Walking into rooms with flashbacks
Walking down stairs with echoing memories
of angry words exchanged

Outside on the driveway
My Harley remained
Covered under the blanket of flashbacks, pain, and loss
I lost interest and just didn't want to look at her
One day I shook off the Post Traumatic stress
Dusted her off and named her "Raven"
Turned on the ignition and there HE was...
The plug firing sequencing...
The Harley heartbeat echoing in my brain's trauma cells
How do I release it?
I became nauseous before mounting Raven
Self-talk was my gas
"Push through the headache"...and I pulled back on the throttle
"Push through the heart palpitations"...and I sped off
Damn it!
I am not giving up my Sportster

I have to ride free
Enjoyed some wind therapy
to heal from the deception and disappointment
That is when I decided that I was going to
SUPERIMPOSE MY riding memories Over HIS memories
Created with a heartless Harley rider

One morning I heard his bike
Thought I was losing my mind
What do I need to do to erase this sound
from my trauma memory cells?!

One night I heard his bike
I looked out the window
He was driving onto the driveway right next door to me
What was he doing there?!

Here I was now living alone walking through this haunted house
NOW I have to contend with this sight and sound
What the hell is he doing there?!
Oh HELL to the NOOOOO!

My fight...and Flight instinct vacillated within my shaky breathes
Which one would take over.
I kicked into high gear
Put on my riding chaps
Riding boots
Riding jacket
Slapping on my red lipstick
Because this mofo was not going to see me busted!!!

I turned on Raven
Warmed her up
Revved her up
Used my heel to kick up the kickstand

As I sped off
Showing him that I still ride
He didn't take that away from me

When I got back
I saw that the bike was gone
Thought perhaps he was visiting the old neighbor

However, 2 weeks later
I figured out that the mofo moved next door
Renting the house from the neighbor who was living abroad.
Now I had to hear that damn sound
Every time he took off and came home

It was a living hell.
Really?!?!
How the hell did he decide to move next door to me?!

With a persistent spirit,
I was digging my riding boots in the ground
I was not leaving. Hell no YOU must go!
Thankfully, the pandemic came
A moving truck came
I saw him roll away on his bike
That is when my true healing started!

Next my moving truck came.
I moved...I overcame!
Now I upgraded to a Road King
I call her "La Reina"

And this chick will never *ride bitch* again
Cuz "I ride my own!"
I ride freeeeee.
Writing about my Harley trauma

How I am in my own zone!

GRATITUDE

T hroughout this memoir writing process, I received love and support from my beloved son Christopher William. *Mi hijo* Chris was curious about my experiences as a child growing up in the Bronx as well as my hopes and dreams. Chris was very pleased about his mother serving as an educator. He witnessed my profound joy working with young minds. Moreover, Chris was proud of my capabilities both as a researcher and humanitarian. Every time I traveled, he wanted to learn about my globe trekking adventures. He reminded me to be safe. My dear son appreciated my free-spirit and my passion for living life and taking risks. With his series of reflective questions and our mother-son talks, he fostered my writer's voice as I searched for the key moments that I wanted to share in this memoir. I am blessed to have such a beautiful relationship with my son and my gorgeous daughter-in-love Vanessa. This beautiful soul is the daughter that God gave to me much later in life.

For several years, I followed Charlie Vazquez on Twitter. He was the Executive Director of the Bronx Council on the Arts, and the lead organizer for The Bronx Writers Center. I joined the Bronx Memoir Project in 2017, which seasonally published an anthology of short memoir stories written by native Bronx writers. The Bronx Council on the Arts sponsored the project with a grant from the National Endowment of the Arts. When I chose to join this writing community support group at the Edgar Allan Poe center, I declared my creative intention to discover my writer's voice. Thank you Charlie for supporting my early writing endeavors.

Published authors like Orlando Ferrand, John Roche, and Caroline Rothstein led these writing sessions to help aspiring Bronx authors. I identified with so many of the New York City writers in this group. They encouraged me to continue nurturing my writer's voice. These authors urged me to seek resources and networks to elevate my writing craft. Moreover, they fostered my desire to write by sharing technical memoir writing strategies, key insights into publishing industry standards, and numerous reflective writing prompts. I am grateful for their guidance. I am especially grateful to Ron Marc Thomson (fellow Bronx writer) for his friendship and encouragement as founder of the Bx Arts Hub nonprofit organization that supports the Arts. Ron always kept me in the loop about the latest events and opportunities to share my writing. In addition, I am grateful that he connected me to his network with The Nuyorican Poets Cafe where I have shared poetry that stemmed from my memoir project. A huge thank you to the amazing and talented Caridad de la Luz who is the Executive Director of the Nuyorican Poets Cafe and the talented Emmy Award-winning poet! Your encouragement to perform and share my poetic voice means so much. Furthermore, I am deeply grateful to Crystal Valentine who became the next editor of the Bronx Memoir Project. Crystal continued to lead the way as I published within two more anthologies with the Bronx Council on the Arts. I am grateful for her guidance and continued encouragement.

This initial work ignited a desire to write my memoir. I am grateful for the support I received from Orlando Ferrand who became my developmental editor. As a Columbia University and Princeton University-trained scholar, Orlando understood the intricacies of working within the broad aperture of the memoir genre. With his expertise, I was able to develop the trajectory of this memoir focusing on the different phases that brought me where I am today. Orlando helped me realize that this memoir is not about the reader, meta-data, or marketing book trends. It is not about selling a million copies and converting a writer's dollar bill into a massive sum. It is about releasing the gift to myself that dwelled in my spirit. His passion for life and the literary arts is a gift to witness!

Afterwards, I had the great fortune of meeting Michael J. Wilson at a cultural arts event in the Bronx (not too far from the center where my writing dream began). He was the editor of the Sojourner Truth Newsletter for the Center of African Studies at Central Connecticut Central Connecticut State University. After writing several articles for his newsletter, I was led to ask Michael to become my line editor. Thankfully, he accepted the invitation and I was deeply grateful for his candor, literary insight, and solid suggestions for reiterations. Michael is a colleague, an inspirational artist, and a dear friend!

In the early stages of shaping my memoir, I reached out to a dear long-time friend Yarina and her husband Max. I was able to break bread in their home as Max shared more insight about publishing industry standards. Max was the editor for QBR: The Black Book Review, and the founder of the Harlem Book Fair. It was the busiest season for him as they were gearing up to prepare for the 20th Anniversary of the Harlem Book Fair event. This is a three-day literary event, which is broadcast on CSPAN *BookTV* in collaboration with The Schomburg Center for Research in Black Culture and Columbia University. The fact that Max was willing to carve out time to meet with me, an aspiring writer, was a tremendous sign of support. I will forever be grateful for their guidance.

We all have divine appointments. Mine happened eight years ago when I met the remarkable socio-political artist Hiram Melendez. We met at a cultural event hosted by Yolanda Rodriguez, the director of Visiones Culturales and one of the founders of the Bx Arts Factory. (Thank you Yoli for your amazing contribution to the Bronx!) When I met Hiram, he was discussing his art at an installation in the Andrew Freedman Mansion located in the Bronx. I was intrigued by his artistic style and political messages. A few weeks after meeting, I approached him about commissioning an art piece that I would use as a cover for my book. At the time I believed it was for my research in Morocco, but my Heavenly Father had bigger plans. Today it is the cover of this memoir. Thank you Hiram for your artistic talents and for sharing your gifts with us. Another visual artist that I am deeply grateful to is Nelson Host Santiago for helping me learn more about Puerto Rican Art. His work inspires me to continue learning more about the Puerto Rican Diaspora. Thank you Nelson for offering a space to learn about your craft. I pray that La Casa de Maria can publish your work narrating the stories behind your Puerto Rican artwork.

Without vision, we will perish. Thank you Joe Negron for the vision and for becoming the director of *La Casa de Maria Documentary*. Your friendship means the universe to me! I am so grateful for the way we met and for your willingness to support me in my vision in chronicling my mother's story. Our laughs, travels, hours of editing film, and talking about our dreams kept me going! You are my brother in faith and for this I am eternally grateful! I can't wait to see where you continue to grow in your faith leadership. You make me a proud sister in faith!

When one thinks of a writer fully committed and submersed in a writing project, it conjures mental images of an obsessed and self-absorbed writing hermit confined to a life of solitude and deep reflection. I consider myself to be a strongly social being, and I struggled with this vision. As I mentally geared up to undertake this new writing path, I was petrified. I leaned on my faith, my family, and my devoted circle of friends and professional supporters to help me move along. I strongly believe that we can lean on our tribe to be successful. It is a shared success. I couldn't have done this without my beautiful team of encouragers. I am grateful to my beloved brothers Nelson, Freddy, and Rafy and their beautiful wives Saadia and Olga for their unconditional love. My time with family centered me and grounded me as I played with my nieces and nephews Carolyn, Gio, Lola, Ale, Sergio, and Godson Rafael. I am also grateful to my paternal sister Joanne who found me in October 2019. We have remained beautifully connected ever since. Our chance encounter on Ancestry.com and then at Mon Amour Cafe will always be a shining moment in my life. Between the many moments of uncertainty, I would reach out to family and their close circle of friends. They offered healthy distractions and different ways to recharge my creative spirit.

I am grateful for those times with my beloved cousin Yolanda chatting it up over martinis or going for a boat ride to unplug from the laptop. I love you Prima! I would not be where I am without your love, steady encouragement, and a place to call home when I needed to get away. Thank you for bringing into the fold with your circle of *comadres* that became my new friends. Our book clubs, our time making pasteles, and our time partying have been such a gift to my soul. I love these women! Nancy JR, Carmen, Adelita, Norma, Alma, Aida, Ada, Tammy, Brenda, Johanna, Nancy P, Jessica, Raquel, and Lissette. They made my new homespace in Connecticut feel like home. I can't wait for our next book club (or as they framed it –"a focus group"!)

Riding on the wave of gratitude, I am eternally grateful to my dear friends Loida, Sandy, Rachel, Yvette, Lisa, Johaira, and Jacquie who always checked in to see how I was doing. These women literally gave me shelter in times of crisis. They picked me up when I fell hard. Where would I be without them? After our mini-therapy sessions, social time, and/or shared workouts at the gym or yoga, I would mentally flesh out countless hours of writing details. Afterwards, I would feel brave to move forward. Their empathetic hugs, encouraging calls, laughs, text messages, and giddy girl talks would help me summon the strength to continue writing. After those moments of sisterly respite, I would get back into the ring and go round after round lost in my cathartic writing sessions.

Thank you Loida and Albert for always offering a refugee to rest and recharge in your home. Riding horses in the Dominican Republic and staying in your beautiful getaway in my sister island truly saved me in so many ways. Loida, you are my sister from a Dominican mister! I am grateful for all of the love and support you and your husband gave me in my early years of domestic violence research. You planted seeds of change in that work.

I believe that a close circle of friends can be the gift that gives that final, but loving, push off the diving board called self-doubt. At times, my dear friends even joined me on some of my writing retreats. They mostly consisted of day trips to different places to activate memories. We had international travels to unwind and many girls nights out dancing to inspire this kindred spirit and stir the soul. I am eternally grateful for their seeds of hope and encouragement. This group of women all helped to lay the creative foundation to unapologetically write. It was time to delve deeper into the abyss...my past. Every time I had a small publishing victory with a college newsletter or my work with the Bronx Memoir Project, my sister-friends did all they could to support me. This steady level of love and encouragement got me through dry writing spells. Knowing that they were bound to ask me how things were going, they kept me accountable and focused on my writing goals. Johaira thank you for being my rock at work day in and day out. Our trip to Puerto Rico together was magical and I am so thankful that your dear family supported this journey. Thank you to both Sr. Buxo's for their love and support!

While writing this memoir, I was teaching full-time, managing different personal ventures with my documentary project, and serving on different staff development initiatives as well as leadership committees within my school district and Manhattanville College. It was professionally demanding having to teach full-time, juggle meetings, attend mandatory events, and present at professional conferences. Doing all this and teaching in the midst of a global pandemic was paralyzing at times. But I pressed through. They encouraged me to take chances and reach for the stars. It was the loving messages from my colleagues that kept me going. They were my devoted friends and loving cheerleaders at work. Kayleen, Guerlande, and Kelly who were always checking in on how I was doing emotionally. Prayer groups, work parties, group text messages, and dinners at Abatinos over a glass of wine kept me sane. I love my grade level team at work! As tired as they saw me everyday dragging myself in, I always received smiles, laughter, jokes, and much love and encouragement. I work with an incredible and talented team of teachers, teaching assistants, and rock stars!

In the summer of 2022, joining the One Circle Foundation as an Executive Board Member was a huge accomplishment for me. I am grateful for the opportunity to serve and learn with this organization. A special thank you to Beth Hossfeld and Nancy Roldan Johnson who are the co-presidents of this foundation seeking to cultivate life-changing circles of change. Thank you for believing in me as you recommended me to the executive board. It has been a joy being a part of the team and witnessing the great leadership of our Executive Director Jana Hiraga. Everyone on that executive board has been such a source of inspiration and personal growth. The One Circle Foundation has a small but mighty staff. Together they are making it happen!

I am deeply grateful to Teodoro Anderson-Diaz. Your unconditional love and unrelenting support throughout my final writing process was the push I needed to get to the other side. Your invitation to a leadership fundraiser in Hartford, Connecticut truly changed my writing life. There I met the author Doe Hentschel who had just released her memoir *Look Ma! No Hands!* At the event, I saw a flier for her book launch at a local venue. I recognized that the lady that greeted us at the door was none other than Doe herself. I approached her and shared that I was interested in publishing my memoir.

Doe encouraged me to come to the event to learn more about the process and to meet the CEO Elizabeth Hill of Green Heart Living Press. I was feeling nervous about asking questions, but I would certainly go to support this author who had such a compelling and heartwarming story. When I saw her at her book reading, she autographed my book with the words "I look forward to your book!!" The rest as they say is her-story. I am grateful for that divine encounter wherein the constellations of hope and encouragement led the way.

Last but certainly not least, thank you Elizabeth Hill and the talented team of editors and publication professionals at Green Heart Living Press. Your support in making this dream come true is a gift that will never stop giving! I persisted. I persevered. I published.

ABOUT THE AUTHOR

D r. Vilma Luz Cabán is a dedicated educator for over 30 years in Westchester County, New York. She serves as an Executive Board member for the One Circle Foundation. Her personal passion lies in addressing social and economic inequities. Vilma produced a documentary project titled *La Casa de Maria*. Her creative goal is to channel her personal writing experiences to support marginalized writers. Her adventurous spirit enables her to paddle her kayak, ride her Harley, steer her boat, and run half marathons to beat her personal record.

www.vilmaluzcaban.com